ENCYCLOPAEDIA OF
COMPUTER SOFTWARE TECHNOLOGY

ENCYCLOPAEDIA OF COMPUTER SOFTWARE TECHNOLOGY

[Volume – One]

Editor-in-Chief

Ajay Kumar

INSTITUTE FOR SUSTAINABLE DEVELOPMENT
LUCKNOW
&
ANMOL PUBLICATIONS PVT. LTD.
NEW DELHI - 110 002 (INDIA)

ANMOL PUBLICATIONS PVT. LTD.
4374/4B, Ansari Road, Daryaganj
New Delhi - 110 002
Ph.: 3261597, 3278000
Visit us at: www.anmolbooks.com

Encyclopaedia of Computer Software Technology

First Edition, 2003

ISBN 81-261-1385-5 (Set)

PRINTED IN INDIA

Published by J.L. Kumar for Anmol Publications Pvt. Ltd., New Delhi and Printed at Mehra Offset Press, Delhi.

Contents

Vol. 3

Preface

Today, the term 'computer' is synonymous with digital computer, but until the 1960s, analog computers were popular. An analog computer relies on analogies between physical effects to make calculations. For example, the voltages in an analog computer may represent temperatures in a heat exchanger, capacitors may represent heat storage capacity, electrical currents may represent heat flow, and so forth. A digital computer, in contrast, deals with values as numerical digits. Because of their versatility, speed, and relatively low cost, digital computers have almost entirely replaced the analog variety.

Computer programs, the software that is becoming an ever-larger part of the computer system, are growing more and more complicated, requiring teams of programmes and years of effort to develop. As a consequence, a new subdiscipline, software engineering, has arisen. As the size and complexity of software has grown, the concept of reuse has become increasingly important in software engineering, since it is clear that extensive new software cannot be created cheaply and rapidly without incorporating existing program modules (subroutines, or pieces of computer code). Sophisticated techniques for testing software have therefore been designed. The need for better trained software engineers has led to the development of educational programs in separate program. The recommendation that software engineers, like other engineers, be licensed or certified is gaining increasing support, as is the momentum toward the accreditation of software engineering degree programs.

The lack of standardization and smooth interoperability in UNIX led Microsoft to develop Windows NT, an operating system that overcome these problems and also provided an integral GUI. From the outside, the system appears much the same as Windows 95 or a Macintosh system, with icons and a mouse. Internally it is quite different, structured so that it can serve in a hand-alone workstation or in a file server on a network, depending on the version of the product. The system also provides easy networking in a commercial environment; adding file servers or shared peripherals is a simple setup task that requires little more than physically interconnecting equipment and setting parameters in a menu.

Windows 95, MS-DOS, OS/2, and other common operating systems are then run as client processes under Windows NT, much in the same way CMS and MVS run under VM on IBM mainframes. A so-called hardware abstraction layer isolates the software from the details of the underlying hardware, giving Windows NT platform-independence. The operating system is therefore portable from one platform to another. Windows NT is used with the upper-end Intel microprocessors and DEC's Alpha chip, a microprocessor for the VAX computer, and will undoubtedly be transport to other platforms.

The present book in three volumes is welcome addition to the existing literature which is really encyclopaedic in nature. The entire information is gathered under twenty nine chapters followed by an exhaustive glossary and Index.

Finally, we will be failing in our duty if we do not acknowledge the kind of assistance we received from our colleagues at the Institute in completion of this volume. We are equally indebted to Shri J.L. Kumar, Managing Director, Anmol Publications Pvt. Ltd., New Delhi for publishing this manuscript in a very limited time.

—Editor-in-Chief

1

Computer Science: An Electronic Revolution

Computer, electronic device that can receive a set of instructions, or program, and then carry out these instructions by performing calculations on numerical data or by compiling and correlating other forms of information. The modern world of high technology could not have come about without the invention of the computer. Computers are used throughout society for the storage and handling of data—from secret governmental files to banking transactions to private household accounts. Computers have opened up a new era in manufacturing through the techniques of *automation*, and they have enhanced modern communication systems. They are essential tools in almost every field of research and applied technology, from the construction of models of the universe to the production of tomorrow's weather reports, and their use has in itself opened up new areas of conjecture. *Database* services and computer networks make available a great variety of information sources.

Computers come in a wide range of sizes. Supercomputers analyze massive, complexly interrelated sets of data. For example, they solve problems in aerodynamic design of supersonic aircraft, predict the weather, and come up with new designs for disease-specific drugs. Mainframe computers and their smaller cousins, minicomputers, are the workhorses of commerce and industry. These centralized machines maintain records, calculate payrolls, and analyze statistics, among many other jobs.

The familiar *personal computer*, also known as a PC, desktop computer, or microcomputer, is used for word processing, accounting, and record keeping in businesses and homes. In business and industry, employees use PCs for their everyday work and to access other computers, larger or more specialized, for work of greater complexity. Increasingly, PCs are also an instrument of *communication* and information gathering through the *Internet* and the *World Wide Web.*

Slightly larger than PCs, but considerably more powerful, workstations are used in such diverse tasks as designing machines, electronic circuits and structures; creating advertisements, brochures, and magazines using desktop publishing software; and training doctors in surgical techniques.

Now rivaling desktop computers in computer power, but considerably smaller in size, laptop and notebook computers have become a favorite tool of business people. Travelers carry these light, battery-powered computers into trains, planes, and hotel rooms to do their work much as if they were in the office. Through small modules called docking stations, these users can link their laptops to a variety of external services such as printers and communication networks.

"Embedded" computers are hidden in equipment. They perform such simple tasks as preventing a car's brakes from locking or such complex ones as instructing a machine tool to perform a task or stabilizing a jumbo jet.

Today, the term *computer* is synonymous with digital computer, but until the 1960s, analog computers were popular. An analog computer relies on analogies between physical effects to make calculations. For example, the voltages in an analog computer may represent temperatures in a heat exchanger, capacitors may represent heat storage capacity, electrical currents may represent heat flow, and so forth. A digital computer, in contrast, deals with values as numerical digits. Because of their versatility, speed, and relatively low cost, digital computers have almost entirely replaced the analog variety.

Conversion between analog (continuously variable) signals and digital (discrete numerical value) signals is often necessary, however. In digital computer control of a chemical process such as pharmaceutical production, for example, the process variables are measured as analog signals representing pressure, temperature, and flow. They must be changed into digital signals by an *analog-to-digital converter* so that the computer can operate on them. Similarly, the digital signals mat result from the computer operations must be changed into analog signals by a *digital-to-analog converter* to regulate pump speeds, heaters, coolers, and other control devices.

History

Computer Speed

The first adding machine, a precursor of the digital computer, was devised in 1642 by the French philosopher Blaise Pascal. This device employed a series of ten-toothed wheels, each tooth representing a digit from 0 to 9. The wheels were connected so that numbers could be added to each other by advancing the wheels by a correct number of teeth. In the 1670s the German philosopher and mathematician Gottfried Wilhelm von Leibniz improved on this machine by devising one that could also multiply.

The French inventor Joseph Marie Jacquard (1752-1834), in designing an automatic loom, used thin, perforated wooden boards to control the weaving of complicated designs. During the 1880s the American statistician Herman Hollerith (1860-1929) conceived the idea of using perforated cards, similar to Jacquard's boards, for processing data. Employing a system that passed punched cards over electrical contacts, he was able to compile statistical information for the 1890 U.S. census.

The Analytical Engine

Computer: Valves

Also in the 19th century, the British mathematician and inventor Charles Babbage worked out the principles of the modern digital computer. He conceived a number of machines, such as the Difference Engine, that were designed to handle complicated mathematical problems. Many historians consider Babbage and his associate, the British mathematician Augusta Ada Byron (Lady Lovelace, 1815-52), the daughter of the English poet Lord Byron, the true inventors of the modern digital computer. The technology of their time was not capable of translating their sound concepts into practice; but one of their inventions, the Analytical Engine, had many features of a modern computer. It had an input stream in the form of a deck of punched cards, a "store" for saving data, a "mill" for arithmetic operations, and a printer that made a permanent record.

Early Computers

Aiken, Howard

The building of analog computers began at the start of the 20th century. Early models calculated by means of rotating shafts and gears. Numerical approximations of equations too difficult to solve in any other way were evaluated with such machines. During both world wars, mechanical and, later, electrical analog computing systems were used as torpedo course predictors in submarines and as bombsight controllers in aircraft. Another system was designed to predict spring floods in the Mississippi River Basin.

In the 1940s, Howard Aiken (1900-73), a Harvard University mathematician, created the Mark I, usually considered the first digital computer. This machine was constructed from mechanical adding machine parts. The instruction sequence to be used to solve a problem was fed into the machine on a roll of punched paper tape, rather than being stored in the computer. In 1945, however, a computer with program storage was built, based on the concepts of the Hungarian-American mathematician John von Neumann. The instructions were stored within a so-called memory, freeing the computer from the speed limitations of the paper tape reader during execution and permitting problems to be solved without rewiring the computer.

Electronic Computers

The rapidly advancing field of *electronics* led to construction of the first all-electronic computer in 1946 at the University of Pennsylvania by the American engineer John Presper Eckert, Jr. (1919-95) and the American physicist John William Mauchly (1907-80). (Another American physicist, John Vincent Atanasoff, later successfully claimed that certain basic techniques he had developed were used in this computer.) Called ENIAC, for Electronic Numerical Integrator And Computer, the device contained 18,000 vacuum tubes and had a speed of several hundred multiplications per minute. Its program was wired into the processor and had to be manually altered. The use of the *transistor* in computers in the late 1950s marked the advent of smaller, faster, and more versatile logical elements than were possible with vacuum-tube machines. The first commercial computer to use transistors was developed in 1957 by Seymour R. Cray, a pioneer in the design of supercomputers. Because transistors use much less power and have a much longer life, this development alone was responsible for the improved machines called second-generation computers. Components became smaller, as did intercomponent spacings, and the system became much less expensive to build.

Integrated Circuits

In the late 1950s, the *integrated circuit*, or IC, was introduced, making it possible for many transistors to be fabricated on one silicon substrate, or "chip," with interconnecting wires plated in place. The IC resulted in a further reduction in price, size, and failure rate. The *microprocessor* became a reality in the mid-1970s with the introduction of the large scale IC (LSI) and, later, the very large scale IC (VLSI), with many thousands of interconnected transistors etched into a single silicon chip. Today, a single microprocessor chip may contain millions of transistors.

Computer Speed

Everything that a digital computer does is based on one operation: the ability to determine if a switch, or "gate," is open or closed. That is, the computer can recognize only two states in any of its microscopic circuits: on or off, high voltage or low voltage, or-in the case of numbers-0 or 1. The speed at which the computer performs this simple act, however, is what makes it a marvel of modern technology.

A key factor in a computer's speed is its clock—a timing device that sends rapid pulses to the components to synchronize and pace them. The faster the clock, the more operations per second the computer will perform, all other things being equal.

Modern personal computers readily perform 150 million switching operations per second; such machines are said to have a speed of 150 megahertz (MHz), and the speed goes up with each new product introduction. At the other extreme, supercomputers, which handle vastly larger and more complex instructions, perform 10 billion or more operations per second (10 gigahertz, or GHz).

Digital computer speed and calculating power are further enhanced by the amount of data handled during each cycle. If a computer checks only one switch at a time, that switch can represent only two commands or numbers; thus ON would symbolize one operation or number, and OFF would symbolize another. By checking groups of switches linked as a unit, however,the computer increases the number of operations it can recognize at each cycle. For example, a computer that checks two switches at one time can represent four numbers (0 to 3) or can execute one of four instructions at each cycle, one for each of the following switch patterns: OFF-OFF (0); OFF-ON (1); ON-OFF (2); or ON-ON (3).

A variety of schemes are used to further boost computer speed. A cache memory is a small memory close to (or on) a microprocessor that stores recently used data on the valid premise that if the microprocessor has needed certain data recently, it is likely to need it again in the immediate future. Having the data nearby or actually on the microprocessor greatly reduces the time to access it.

Multiprocessing, or parallel processing, boosts speed by performing many operations simultaneously on two or more chips. As many as a thousand microprocessor chips work together in massively parallel processing. The software instructions that regulate the flow of data among the chips are complex indeed.

RISC (reduced instruction set computing) boosts speed by cutting the number of instructions for a computer to the bare minimum. With fewer instructions, the computer completes calculations faster. RISC machines tailor the instructions to the specific computational case, unlike conventional computers (called CISC for complex instruction set computers), which provide only general-purpose instructions, many of which may not be needed in the specific case. Computers in the 1970s generally were able to check eight switches at a time. That is, they could check eight *binary digits*, or bits, of data, at every cycle. A group of 8 bits is called a byte, each byte containing 256 possible patterns of ONs and OFFs (or 1's and O's). Each pattern is the equivalent of an instruction, a part of an instruction, or a particular type of datum, such as a number or a character or a graphics symbol. The pattern 11010010, for example, might be binary data-in this case, the decimal number 210 or it might tell the computer to compare data stored in its switches to data stored in a certain memory-chip location.

The development of processors that can handle 16, 32, and 64 bits of data at a time has increased the speed of computers. The complete collection of recognizable patterns-the total list of operations-of which a computer is capable is called its instruction set. Both factors-number of bits at a time, and size of instruction sets-continue to increase with the ongoing development of modern digital computers.

Hardware

Operating Systems

A digital computer is not actually a single machine, in the sense that most people think of computers. Instead it is a system composed of five distinct elements: (1) a central processing unit; (2) input devices; (3) memory storage devices; (4) output devices; and (5) a communications network, called a "bus," that links all the elements of the system and connects the system to the external world.

Central Processing Unit (CPU)

Computer: Central Processing Unit

The CPU may be a single chip (a microprocessor) or a series of chips that performs arithmetic and logical calculations and that times and controls the operations of the other elements of the system. Most CPU chips and microprocessors are composed of four functional sections: (1) an arithmetic/logic unit; (2) registers; (3) a control section; and (4) an internal bus. The arithmetic/logic unit gives the chip its calculating ability and permits arithmetical and logical operations. The registers are temporary storage areas that hold data, keep track of instructions, and hold the location and results of these operations. The control section has three principal duties. It times and regulates the operations of the entire computer system; its instruction decoder reads the patterns of data in a designated register and translates the pattern into an activity, such as adding or comparing; and its interrupt unit indicates the order in which individual operations use the CPU, and regulates the amount of CPU time that each operation may consume.

The CPU's internal bus is a network of communication lines that connects the internal elements of the processor and also leads to external connectors that link the processor to the other elements of the computer system. The three types of CPU buses are: (1) a control bus consisting of a line that senses input signals and another line that generates control signals from within the CPU; (2) the address bus, a one-way line from the processor that handles the location of data in memory addresses; and (3) the data bus, a two-way transfer line that both reads data from memory and writes new data into memory.

Input Devices

Computer: Disks

These devices enable a computer user to enter data, commands, and programs into the CPU. The most common input device is the *keyboard*. Information typed at the typewriter-like keyboard is translated by the computer into recognizable patterns. Almost as common is the "mouse," a hand-guided pointing device that moves a pointer on a screen. Other input devices include light pens, which transfer graphics information from electronic pads into the computer; joysticks, which translate physical motion into motion on a computer video display screen; light scanners, which "read" words or symbols on a printed page and "translate" them into electronic patterns that the computer can manipulate and store; and voice recognition modules, which take spoken words and translate them into digital signals for the computer. Storage devices can also be used to input data into the processing unit.

Storage Devices

Computer: Floppy Discs

Computer systems can store data internally (in memory) and externally (on storage devices). Internally, temporary instructions or data can be stored in silicon RAM (Random Access Memory) chips that are mounted directly on the computer's main circuit board, or in chips mounted on peripheral cards that plug into the computer's main circuit board. A RAM chip consists of switches that are sensitive to changes in electric current. So-called static RAM (SRAM) chips hold their bits of data as long as current flows through the circuit, whereas dynamic RAM (DRAM) chips need high or low voltages applied at regular intervals-every two milliseconds or so-if they are not to lose their information. SRAMs also access their data faster than DRAMs, although DRAM chips store more data.

Another type of internal memory consists of silicon chips on which all switches are already set. The patterns on these ROM (Read-Only Memory) chips form "firmware"-permanent commands, data, or programs that the computer needs to function correctly. RAM chips are like pieces of paper that can be written on, erased, and used again; ROM chips are like a book, with its words already set on each page. Both RAM and ROM chips are linked by circuitry to the CPU.

External storage devices, which may physically reside within the computer's main processing unit, are external to the main circuit board. These devices store data as charges on a magnetically sensitive medium such as an audio tape or, more commonly, on a disk coated with a fine layer of metallic particles. The most common external storage devices are so-called floppy and hard disks, although most large computer systems use banks of magnetic tape storage units as well as hard disks. Floppy disks can easily be inserted and removed; they can contain from several hundred thousand bytes of data to well more than a million bytes, depending on the system. Hard disks are permanently mounted in their cabinets, which contain the electronics to read data from and write data onto the magnetic disk surfaces. Hard disks can store from several million bytes to a few billion bytes. Using the same laser techniques that are used to create audio compact disks (CDs), CD-ROM technology offers storage capacities in the range of several gigabytes (billion bytes) of data. The entire text of this encyclopedia fills only about one fourth of a single standard-size CD-ROM; the disk can therefore accommodate extensive digital graphics, video clips, and sound clips.

Output Devices

These devices enable the user to see the results of the computer's calculations or data manipulations. The most common output device is the video display terminal, a monitor that displays characters and graphics on a television-like screen. A video display terminal usually has a cathode-ray tube (CRT) like an ordinary television set, but small, portable computers use flat panel displays containing small cells that transmit or block light. Other standard output devices include printers and modems. A *modem* links two or more computers by translating data signals for transmission over *telecommunications* links.

Operating Systems

Different types of peripheral devices-disk drives, printers, communications networks, and so on-handle and store data differently from the way the computer handles and stores it. Internal operating systems, usually stored in ROM, were developed primarily to coordinate and translate data flows from dissimilar sources, such as disk drives or co-processors (processing chips that perform simultaneous but different operations from the central processing unit). An operating system, often described as a "traffic cop," is a master control program, permanently stored in memory, that interprets user commands requesting various kinds of services, such as display, print, or copy a data file; list all files in a directory; or execute a particular program. The operating system then ensures that the commands are executed and regulates the flow of data and instructions.

Operating systems range in size from tens of millions of bytes for mainframes to tens of thousands of bytes for PCs. Some operating systems were developed for specific products-VM/CMS for International Business Machines (IBM) mainframes, for example. Others were developed to meet specific needs, rather than for specific products, and have gained wide acceptance for that reason. American Telephone and Telegraph (AT&T) developed the UNIX operating system to help computers work together in a network and to establish "platform independence" (compatibility with all computer architectures); many other computer manufacturers have since adopted UNIX and workstations use it almost exclusively.

Microsoft Corp. developed the Microsoft Disk Operating System (MS-DOS) for IBM PCs. As businesses and households enthusiastically adopted PCs, countless manufacturers of IBM "clones" adopted MS-DOS.

Software for windows is widely popular; such software treats the various programs in a computer as sheets of paper, or windows, that a user can overlap or overlay on the screen so that they can be worked on together. A windows environment also lets the user exchange information easily between programs-from a spreadsheet or graphics program to a word processing program, fore xample. Apple Computer, Inc., was the first to introduce windows in PCs in 1984. This feature, together with a graphical user interface containing icons (screen images that the user clicks to open programs and execute commands), accounts for the famous "user-friendliness" of Apple's Macintosh computers. In 1985, Microsoft introduced Microsoft Windows to enhance MS-DOS with the same intuitive graphical conveniences. Ten years later, Microsoft introduced a new operating system, Windows 95, which is even more convenient for users.

Programming

Languages

A program is a sequence of instructions that tells the hardware of a computer what operations to perform on data. Programs can be built into the hardware itself, or they may exist independently in a form known as software. In some specialized, or embedded, computers the operating instructions are contained in their circuitry; common examples are the microcomputers found in calculators, wristwatches, automobile engines, and microwave ovens. A general-purpose computer, on the other hand, contains some built-in programs (in ROM) or instructions (in the processor chip), but it depends on external programs to perform useful tasks. Once a computer has been programmed, it can do only as much or as little as the software controlling it at any given moment enables it to do. Software in widespread use includes a wide range of applications programs (instructions to the computer on how to perform various tasks).

Languages

High-level Languages

A computer must be given instructions in a "language" that it understands-that is, a particular pattern of binary digital information. On the earliest computers, programming was a difficult, laborious task, because vacuum-tube ON-OFF switches had to be set by hand. Teams of programmers often took days to program simple tasks such as sorting a list of names. Since that time a number of computer languages have been devised, some with particular kinds of functioning in mind and others aimed more at ease of use-the "user-friendly" approach.

Machine Language

Unfortunately, the computer's own binary-based language, or machine language, is difficult for humans to use. The programmer must input every command and all data in binary form, and a basic operation such as comparing the contents of a register to the data in a memory-chip location might look like this: 11001010 00010111 11110101 00101011. Machine-language programming is such a tedious, time-consuming task that the time saved in running the program rarely justifies the days or weeks needed to write the program.

Assembly Language

One method programmers devised to shorten and simplify the process is called "assembly-language" programming. By assigning a short (usually three-letter) mnemonic code to each machine-language command, assembly-language programs could be written and "debugged"-cleaned of logic and data errors-in a fraction of the time needed by machine-language programmers. In assembly language, each mnemonic command and its symbolic operands equals one machine instruction. An "assembler" program translates the mnemonic "op-codes" (operation codes) and symbolic operands into binary language and executes the program.

An assembly language, however, can be used only with one type of CPU chip or microprocessor. Programmers who expended much time and effort to learn how to program one computer had to learn a new programming style each time they worked on another machine. What was needed was a shorthand method by which one symbolic statement could represent a sequence of many machine-language instructions, and a method that would allow the same program to run on several types of machines. These needs led to the development of so-called high-level languages.

High-level Languages

High-level languages often use English-like words-for example, LIST, PRINT, OPEN, and soon-as commands that might stand for a sequence of tens or hundreds of machine-language instructions. The commands are entered from the keyboard or from a program in memory or in a storage device, and they are intercepted by a program mat translates them into machine-language instructions.

Translator programs are of two kinds: interpreters and compilers. With an interpreter, programs that "loop" back to re-execute part of their instructions reinterpret the same instruction each time it appears, so interpreted programs run much more slowly than machine-language programs. Compilers, by contrast, translate an entire program into machine language prior to execution, so such programs run as rapidly as though they were written directly in machine language.

The first commercial programmer was probably Grace Hopper, an American. After programming the Mark I, the experimental computer created by Aiken at Harvard, she worked on the UNIVAC I and II computers and developed a commercially usable high-level programming language called FLOWMATIC. To facilitate computer use in scientific applications, IBM then developed a language that would simplify work involving complicated mathematical formulas: Begun in 1954 and completed in 1957, FORTRAN (FORmula TRANslator) was the first comprehensive high-level programming language that was widely used.

In 1957, the Association for Computing Machinery set out to develop a universal language that would correct some of FORTRAN'S perceived faults. A year later they released ALGOL (ALGOrithmic Language), another scientifically oriented language; widely used in Europe in the 1960s and 1970s, it has since been superseded by newer languages, while FORTRAN continues to be used because of the huge investment in existing programs. COBOL (Common Business Oriented Language), a commercial and business programming language, concentrated on data organization and file handling and is widely used today in business.

BASIC (Beginner's All-purpose Symbolic Instruction Code) was developed at Dartmouth College in the early 1960s for use by nonprofessional computer users. The language came into almost universal use with the microcomputer explosion of the 1970s and 1980s. Condemned as slow, inefficient, and inelegant by its detractors, BASIC is nevertheless simple to learn and easy to use. Because many early microcomputers were sold with BASIC built into the hardware (in ROM memory) the language rapidly came into widespread use. As a very simple example of a BASIC program, consider the addition of the numbers 1 and 2, and the display of the result. This is written as follows (the numerals 10-40 are line numbers):

```
10 A □ 1
20 B □ 2
30 C □ A □ B
40 PRINT C
```

Although hundreds of different computer languages and variants exist, several others deserve mention. PASCAL, originally designed as a teaching tool, is now one of the most popular microcomputer languages. LOGO was developed to introduce children to computers. C, a language Bell Laboratories designed in the 1970s, is widely used in developing systems programs, such as language translators. LISP and PROLOG are widely used in *artificial intelligence.*

A descendant of PASCAL, Ada language (named for Lady Lovelace; see History, above) was designed for military applications such as the Strategic Defense Initiative ("Star Wars") missile program. Since then it has been adopted for such diverse uses as operating dialysis machines and controlling aircraft because of its real-time capability; that is, it responds almost instantaneously. Its military originators also insisted on absolute standardization in Ada programs—no dialects whatsoever-so that a program written in Ada language can run without modification on virtually any computer.

C++ is a popular descendant of C that shares that language's ability to adapt to a wide range of machines, from microprocessors to mainframes. In addition, it is object-oriented, that is, it consists of modules, called objects, of data and instructions. Object-oriented languages are easy for programmers to use; instead of writing instructions for a task line by line, a programmer simply calls on an object to do the job.

Future Developments

Computer: CD-ROM

Engineers continue to compress more circuit elements into smaller chip space. This not only makes computers more compact and less expensive, but it also allows them to operate faster, since signals are subjected to less delay in traveling between elements.

In the quest for speed, engineers are also chilling chips with liquid nitrogen. At the low temperature of liquid nitrogen (77K), chips run much faster; a microprocessor that runs at 100 MHz at room temperature can run at 250 MHz at 77K.

Engineers are also enthusiastic about experimental chips with switching devices made from superconducting materials. Such materials lose all their resistance when chilled, and can switch billions of times a second. New "high-temperature" superconductors, usually thin, copper-bearing ceramic films, need be chilled only to liquid nitrogen temperature-easier to attain than the 4.2K liquid-helium temperature previously required.

Meanwhile, multimedia desktop computers are on the verge of developing their full potential. Already equipped with CD-ROM players, multimedia PCs can tap a vast library of information, presented in both sound and video, on science, music, history, and art, for example. No longer limited to still or slow-moving displays, the newer machines can show action on the screen.

The growth of networking and the Internet will continue apace as computer users subscribe to services that provide information, "bulletin boards," and *electronic mail.* Users can now set up voice conversations over the Internet. A limited form of video phone service is also available, and development is ongoing. Information "superhighways" are being built with optical fibers that transfer vast amounts of data between computers at breathtaking speeds. With this information transfer capacity, PC-based video phone service will become commonplace; people will confer with colleagues, viewing their live images on a screen shared with whatever text and graphics are needed for the discussion.

Further into the future, the elusive goal of artificial intelligence (AI) looms. AI means computers mat learn, understand, recognize, and reason much as humans do. Although research on AI abounds, little in the way of solid results has been achieved except for expert systems, which are computers that have been provided with the knowledge and intuition of human experts in a given field. Expert systems advise technologists on such diverse tasks as troubleshooting communications networks, analyzing spectrograms, and diagnosing illness.

COMPUTER SECURITY, the techniques developed to protect single computers and network-linked computer systems from accidental or intentional harm. Such harm includes destruction of computer hardware and software, physical loss of data, and the deliberate invasion of databases by unauthorized individuals. Data may be protected by such basic methods as locking up terminals and replicating data in other storage facilities. More sophisticated methods include limiting data access by requiring the user to have an encoded card or to supply an identification number or password. Such procedures can apply to the computer-data system as a whole or may be pinpointed for particular information banks or programs.

Operating systems and programs may also incorporate built-in safeguards, and data may be encoded in various ways to prevent unauthorized persons from interpreting or even copying the material. The encoding system most widely used in the United States is the Data Encryption Standard (DES) designed by IBM and approved for use by the National Bureau of Standards in 1976. DES involves a number of basic encrypting procedures that are men repeated several times. Very-large-scale computer systems, for example, the U.S. military's Advanced Research Project Agency Network (ARPANET), may be broken up into subsystems for security purposes, but smaller systems are more prone to invasion.

Most invasions of computer systems are for international or corporate spying or sabotage, but some computer "hackers" may have no object in mind other than accomplishing a technological feat. Of growing concern is the deliberate implantation in computer programs of "worms" or "viruses" that, if undetected, may progressively destroy databases and other software. Such infected programs have appeared in the electronic bulletin boards available to computer users. Other viruses have been incorporated into computer software sold commercially.

COMPUTER OPERATING SYSTEM, the master control program that coordinates the operations of the hardware and software elements of a computer so that they perform quickly and efficiently. An operating system is generally embodied in both software and "firmware" (integrated circuits programmed with the operating system instructions). The software resides on the computer's hard disk, from which it is sent to the computer's random-access memory (RAM) as needed; the firmware is the computer's read-only memory. Early computer operating systems (those in service about 1955-65), usually known as executives or monitors, which ran only one program at a time were inefficient because most of the hardware was idle much of the time. For example, no computation could take place during printing. Further, earlier operating systems required that the user learn a difficult special language, known as a Job Control Language (JCL) to run each program. Modern operating systems automatically allocate resources according to complex rules and let users run programs using icons, easy-to-understand or "user-friendly" words and pictures. Even a computer game has a primitive operating system, hidden from the player, that provides the necessary control of the computer's processor, memory, and peripheral devices.

The Operating System's Role

An operating system provides the user interface (the display on the computer monitor) with text or graphics; shares the hardware among processes such as user programs; allows processes to share data and controls their sharing; enables the computer to access input and output devices such as keyboards, joysticks, monitors, printers, and modems; and, in multiuser systems, schedules resources among users as well as processes.

Word processing offers a representative example of the role of an operating system: (1) The user requests word processing software; the operating system accesses hard-disk storage and loads the word processor program into the computer's RAM. (2) The user requests a file to edit; the operating system locates the desired file and places it in a buffer area for processing. (3) After editing the file, the user executes the command to save the file; the operating system stores the revised file on the hard disk, perhaps automatically saving the old version into a "backup" copy in case the user has a change of mind. (4) The user requests a printed copy of the file; the operating system loads the printer driver software into RAM and initiates the print job. If the printer is slow, or the document is large, the print job may be temporarily placed on the hard disk and sent to the printer as it requests more output from the word processing program. (5) The user exits the word processing software; the operating system removes the word processor from RAM, freeing it for the next task. Through all of this, the operating system allocates and manages all the computer's resources-keyboard, mouse, screen, printer, disks, central processing unit, and memory.

The operating system relies on special instructions within the computer's instruction set (basic commands). These instructions allow only the operating system to access peripheral (input/output or I/O) devices and memory resources. It is also subject to interrupts (requests from programs or peripheral devices that force it to perform a specific task, such as sending or receiving data).

Major Operating Systems

Network Operating Systems

Operating systems may be preloaded into the computer by the manufacturer or purchased from a vendor and then loaded onto the computer. Some are intended for large, mainframe computers, others for smaller minicomputers, and others for small desktop models; some are for groups of computers joined together in a network; some are usable only on specific platforms (computer architectures that employ the same instruction set, memory management, and resource control patterns), while others are platform-independent.

Platform-Dependent Systems

Intel

Most operating systems were developed for specific computer products. They cannot function on architectures other than the one they were designed for, and they generally can use only software that was developed expressly for them.

VMS

The Virtual Memory System (VMS) operating system is used in the Virtual Address eXtension (VAX) series of medium-size computers manufactured by the Digital Equipment Corp. (DEC), and provides a text-based interface for multiple users. The VMS operating system handles files with a high degree of security (privacy) and accommodates a wide variety of peripheral devices such as terminals, disks, tapes, and printers. In addition, it can easily be connected to a network of many other computer systems. VMS functions well with a wide variety of programming languages, such as COBOL, FORTRAN, Pascal, and C. It also supports large databases and many other products, such as accounting systems and computer-aided design/computer-aided manufacture (q.v.; CAD/CAM) systems, provided by outside vendors. DEC'S VAX system is used extensively in businesses, factories, and universities.

VM and Clients

The operating system on the 360/370/390 mainframe computers manufactured by International Business Machines (IBM) is remarkable in that it is actually a series of operating systems. The "host" operating system, known as VM for Virtual Machine, supplies the basic functions on which other operating systems ("clients") can run. A typical client system is the Conversational Monitor System (CMS), which deals with creating, updating, and managing files, as well as compiling and loading programs. CMS works in tandem with the Control Program (CP), which handles hardware devices required to store files (disks and tapes), work on files (terminals and memory), and output files (printers and terminals). VM/CMS is primarily used in large-scale commercial and scientific computations. Multiple Virtual Storage (MVS) is another common IBM mainframe operating system that runs as a client under VM. MVS controls batch processing and large databases.

IBM and other companies offer a wide variety of applications. Many different languages and support systems are available for those who wish to do their own program and system development. VM and its client operating systems may readily be integrated in networks that provide worldwide data communication for multinational companies, as well as smaller networks.

Macintosh

The operating system for the Apple Computer Co.'s Macintosh desktop computer provided the first generally available graphical user interface (GUI, pronounced *gooey*) system with a mouse, a hand-guided pointing device with which a user positions a cursor on the monitor screen. The Macintosh operating system grew out of research done" at Xerox Corp.'s Palo

Alto Research Center in the early 1970s. It was a radical departure from the text-oriented operating systems that preceded it. Instead of entering commands in arcane and cryptic words and phrases, a user issues commands primarily by positioning the cursor on icons, and clicking the buttons on the mouse. Clicking on an icon sends a message to the operating system to execute an application or access a file. Commands within an application are initiated through further sets of icons or menus. Apple Macintosh computers use a microprocessor produced by Motorola Corp., or a newer one produced jointly by Motorola and IBM.

Intel

The Intel series of microprocessors (8086/88, 80286, 80386, 80486, Pentium, Pentium Pro) has become dominant in the personal computer (PC) market. A variety of operating systems have been developed for this type of microprocessor in its various models. The first Intel-based operating system. Disk Operating System (DOS), which Microsoft Corp. developed for the IBM PC (PC-DOS) and later adapted for general use (MS-DOS) is a simple text-interface operating system designed for a single user. As more advanced hardware and larger memories became available, newer versions of MS-DOS appeared, but they always maintained "upward compatibility" so that old programs generally can run on the newer systems.

MS-DOS is used in a GUI system known as Windows 95. Like the Macintosh system, Windows 95 supports a mouse and an icon-and-menu display where actions are initiated through mouse clicks and a minimal number of keyboard entries. The underlying MS-DOS remains on the computer to run older MS-DOS-based applications.

Another operating system for the Intel processors is IBM's Operating System 2 (OS/2), which is comparable in functions to Windows 95, but is designed to work well in a multiuser server in a network, not just in a single-user computer.

Platform-Independent Systems

UNIX

Windows NT

Platform-independent operating systems run on diverse computers with various architectures. Two such systems, UNIX and Windows NT (for New Technology) are used on a variety of platforms, from Intel-architecture PCs to, in the case of UNIX, large mainframes. They were developed to provide a single operating system that can run on many computer architectures, thereby eliminating the difficulty and expense of maintaining and supporting a variety of incompatible operating systems and training people to use them.

UNIX

UNIX, the older of the two, was developed at Bell Laboratories, then the research arm of American Telephone & Telegraph (AT&T), in the early 1970s. Because of legal constraints at the time, AT&T was not able to market UNIX as a commercial product. As a consequence, the company distributed UNIX to many organizations under license. Since many of these organizations made extensive modifications in UNIX, adapting it for a variety of computer platforms, there is no standard UNIX, and some versions are quite incompatible. Therefore the goal of full compatibility and software interoperability has not been achieved to the degree originally intended. Nevertheless UNIX has a large following; versions are in use for such wide-ranging platforms as Intel microprocessors (a version called LINUX), Motorola microprocessors, and larger systems such as DEC's VAX (a variant known as ULTRIX). A set of programs, X-Windows, even turns a UNIX system into a GUI.

Windows NT

The lack of standardization and smooth interoperability in UNIX led Microsoft to develop Windows NT, an operating system that overcame these problems and also provided an integral GUI. From the outside, the system appears much the same as Windows 95 or a Macintosh system, with icons and a mouse. Internally it is quite different, structured so that it can serve in a stand-alone workstation or in a file server on a network, depending on the version of the product. The system also provides easy networking in a commercial environment; adding file servers or shared peripherals is a simple setup task that requires little more than physically interconnecting equipment and setting parameters in a menu.

Windows 95, MS-DOS, OS/2, and other common operating systems are then run as client processes under Windows NT, much in the same way CMS and MVS run under VM on IBM mainframes. A so-called hardware abstraction layer isolates the software from the details of the underlying hardware, giving Windows NT platform-independence. The operating system is therefore portable from one platform to another. Windows NT is used with the upper-end Intel microprocessors and DEC's Alpha chip, a microprocessor for the VAX computer, and will undoubtedly be transported to other platforms.

Network Operating Systems

Increasingly, computers of various sizes are being interconnected in networks for ease of file and software sharing. Such networks may be controlled by an auxiliary operating system, such as Novell Netware, or by a computer operating system that contains special provisions for networking, such as UNIX or Windows NT.

As computer networking grows, new operating system extensions such as Java will allow users to download the latest and most reliable versions of applications programs, called "applets," from a central server as needed and simply discard them after use. A relatively simple operating system, with the aid of Java or another interpreter, will be able to handle virtually any applet. Users will no longer have to buy and keep their own copies of applications, but can acquire them inexpensively from the network.

Outlook

Current research is moving along with modest success for recognition of human speech. Recognition of cursive writing (hand-drawn letters or fairly stylized script) is also progressing well. Ideally, the software for these recognition features will be intrinsic to the operating system itself rather than run as separate programs that add to the complexity and inefficiency of the system.

History

Electronics: Integrated Circuit

The basic building block of the 1C is the transistor, which was invented in 1947 at Bell Laboratories, then part of American Telephone and Telegraph (AT&T). At first, transistor circuits were built with discrete packaged transistors and other components soldered onto printed circuit boards. In 1952, British engineer G. W. A. Dummer (1909-) of the Royal Radar Establishment in England, first proposed "electronics equipment in a solid block with no connecting wires." American electrical engineer Jack Kilby (1927-), of Texas Instruments Inc., built the first working IC in 1958-a phase-shift oscillator that operated at about 1.3 megahertz (MHz; 1 MHz = 1 million cycles/second). The oscillator was built from one transistor diffused into a germanium chip, with a semiconductor p-n junction for the capacitor and the germanium itself for the resistance. The elements of the circuit were connected by wires.

The next step came less than a year later. In 1959 a group of scientists at Fairchild Semiconductor, led by American physicist Robert Noyce (1927-90), built the first ICs that used a new planar process (so called because the surface remained flat) developed by Swiss-bom American physicist Jean Hoerni (1924-) of Fairchild, with silicon as the semiconductor. In a process called passivation, the devices were protected by a layer of silicon dioxide. They were connected by patterns of gold or aluminum that were photographically defined and etched during the manufacturing process.

Two of the cofounders of Fairchild, Noyce and American physicist Gordon Moore (1929-), went on to found Intel Corp.; now one of the largest manufacturers of ICs in the world. Moore predicted in 1965 that the number of transistors on an 1C would double every year-a prediction that has come to be known as Moore's law. The law was remarkably accurate for several years; today the growth rate is only slightly slower, doubling every 18 months.

Since the birth of the IC, the dimensions of the electronic components and the interconnects have shrunk steadily and rapidly. The transistors in Kilby's original circuit were cut from a germanium wafer 6.35 mm (0.25 in) in diameter that contained 25 transistors. Today, most wafers are single-crystal silicon and the same area might contain more than 1 million transistors. The number of transistors on an IC has also grown to more man 10 million from the single such device on Kilby's first IC. In research laboratories, some memory ICs with more man 1 billion transistors have been built. ICs are sometimes characterized according to their level of integration. Large-scale integration (LSI) describes ICs having between 1000 and 100,000 transistors. Very large scale integration (VLSI) refers to those ICs with more than 100,000 transistors. Ultra large scale integration is sometimes used to describe ICs that contain more than 1,000,000 transistors. More commonly, the term "deep submicron" is used to describe ICs with several million transistors and line widths of .35 micrometer (um; .000014 inch).

ICs are steadily becoming faster, too. Today, a top-of-the-line *microprocessor*, designed for powerful workstations, operates at speeds greater than 500 MHz. Some ICs, designed for satellite communications, operate faster than 100 gigahertz (GHz; 1 GHz = 1 billion cycles/second). These complex circuits cannot be designed by hand. Elaborate software called computer-aided design (CAD) tools and workstations are required.

Analog ICs

The broadest distinction among ICs is between analog and digital operation. Analog circuits operate over a continuous voltage range. The output of an analog circuit varies as its input changes. Analog ICs are frequently found in consumer products, especially audio and video electronics. Amplitude modulation (AM) and frequency modulation (FM) radio signals and television signals, for example, are analog signals. The analog ICs receive these signals and transform them into signals that we can hear and see. Analog ICs include AM and FM detectors, modulators, demodulators, amplifiers, filters, oscillators, and comparators (circuits that compare voltages).

Digital Operation

Memory Chips

Increasingly, however, signals are being processed or transmitted digitally, requiring converters. Digital circuits operate according to the rules of *Boolean algebra,* which uses such logical functions as AND and OR and such arithmetic functions as add and multiply. The circuits use a binary number system consisting of only two levels: high and low (1s and 0s). If the input to a digital circuit changes from high to low, the output changes from high to low or from low to high. There are many different kinds of digital ICs in use today. One of the most familiar is the microprocessor. These devices manage the operation of computers and run application programs. Other types of logic chips are also needed in electronic systems. Microcontrollers, for example, perform specific control functions such as regulating the temperature of a toaster or the mixture of oxygen and fuel in an automobile engine. The digital signal processor (DSP) is specialized to perform mathematical operations on signals in "real time" (almost instantaneously). They are found in cellular telephones and other communication systems.

Custom ICs

In addition to these standard ICs, electronic products often require custom-designed ICs to perform specific functions. In computers, for example, custom ICs connect the microprocessor to a display or control the transfer of data between the microprocessor and the memory. These ICs come in several varieties. Application-specific ICs (ASICs) comprise blocks of logic, called cells, that are assembled during the design phase from "libraries" of predesigned cells. Gate arrays have preassembled logic blocks that are customized by "hard wiring" (depositing interconnects on the blocks) to perform the desired function. Field-programmable gate arrays (FPGAs) are customized electronically by opening or closing switches on the IC to connect the gates as needed. In some FPGAs the programming is done by applying a voltage between two metals separated by an insulator. The voltage causes a current which shorts the two metals together. This switch is called an antifuse. Other FPGAs use memory cells that are programmed to form the required interconnections.

Memory Chips

Memory ICs (often called memory chips) store the instructions and data used by digital electronic circuits. The most common memory devices are static and dynamic random-access memories (SRAMs and DRAMs). They are called "random access" because data can be written into and read from each memory cell by addressing it individually. DRAMs are very dense because each storage cell consists of one transistor and one capacitor on which the data is stored. Each DRAM cell occupies an area of only a few square micrometers. Modern, commercially available DRAMs have up to 64 million cells. SRAMs store data on special circuits called latches that have either four or six transistors. They are not as compact as DRAMs but they are much faster, so they are used when speed is more important than density.

SRAMs and DRAMs are volatile: they lose their stored data as soon as power is turned off. Other types of memory are nonvolatile; they retain their information in the absence of power. These include read-only memories (ROMs), programmable ROMs (PROMs), electrically programmable ROMs (EPROMs), electrically erasable and programmable ROMs (EEPROMs), and flash EPROMs. The data in ROMs is hard-wired by using photographic masks during the final manufacturing stages. They can be read but never changed (these chips are therefore called "firmware" in contrast to hardware and software). In PROMs a 1 or a 0 is permanently written into a cell by the application of a voltage to a "fuse" or "antifuse." (In ICs, fuses are strips of metal deposited over silicon dioxide that become open when a large current is passed through them. Antifuses are transistors that contain an extra gate, called a floating gate, that has no external connections. The electric charge stored on the floating gate determines whether a 1 or a 0 is stored in the cell. Charge flows to and from the gate through a process called tunneling.)

ICs Today

By far the largest number of ICs are made on silicon wafers out of patterned silicon, silicon dioxide, and metal. The two dominant types of silicon circuits are bipolar and complementary metal-oxide-semiconductor (CMOS). CMOS ICs use less power than bipolar ICs, but bipolar ICs are faster, so they are used when speed is the most important consideration. Some ICs contain both CMOS and bipolar transistors and are called BiCMOS ICs. ICs made with gallium arsenide are used in aircraft navigation, satellite communication, defense, and other applications where speeds of more than 10 GHz are required. These devices are called monolithic microwave ICs (MMICs). Because of their high speed, gallium arsenide digital ICs are sometimes used in supercomputers.

Outlook

The trend toward smaller and smaller transistors and interconnects continues. Experts predict that by 2004 the smallest dimensions of transistors will be 0.13 um. Logic circuits will have more man 25 million transistors per square centimeter and 4-gigabit (GB) memory chips will be commercially available (1 GB = 1 billion bits of information).

IC suppliers look forward to the "system on a chip" in which all the functions of a circuit board are contained on a single IC. Today, ICs are already being built with a combination of circuits. Most microprocessor ICs also contain blocks of SRAM (called cache memory). Some also have DRAMs. ASICs contain embedded microprocessors and microcontrollers surrounded by communications circuits and other logic. Many ICs (called mixed-signal ICs) contain combinations of analog and digital circuits.

Semiconductor manufacturing techniques will be used in unexpected ways. They will be used to make sensors and "micromachines" (tiny motors, sensors, and actuators) directly on silicon alongside the circuits needed to operate them. Already, IC manufacturing techniques are used to make the accelerometers that deploy airbags in automobile crashes.

IC Market

The global market for semiconductors, slightly more than U.S. $100 billion in 1994, is projected to grow to $197 billion by 1999. With 12 per cent of the IC market in 1996, Intel Corp. was the leading producer of ICs. Other major IC manufacturers included Texas Instruments and Motorola in the U.S., NEC, Hitachi, Toshiba, and Fujitsu in Japan, Samsung in Korea, and SGS-Thomson Microelectronics in Europe. In order to reduce costs, have access to technical expertise, and be near their markets, most of these companies are multinational, and maintain manufacturing and development facilities in many countries throughout the world.

The fiercely competitive IC market combined with the mounting expense of developing new processing capabilities and more complex designs is driving many semiconductor and electronics companies to form alliances and consortia mat may even transcend national boundaries. Beginning in 1991, IBM, Motorola, and Apple Computer jointly developed the PowerPC microprocessor architecture and several implementations of it. More general and far-reaching cooperative efforts include Sematech and the Semiconductor Research Corp. in the U.S., the Microelectronics Development for European Applications (Medea) in Europe, and the Association of Super-Advanced Electronics Technologies (ASET) and Semiconductor Leading Edge Technologies, Inc. (Selete), both in Japan. Many of the leading IC manufacturers, recognizing the potential of a huge electronics market in China, are forming partnerships with Chinese firms to produce ICs in that country.

Future Development

Computer: CD-ROM

Engineers continue to compress more circuit elements into smaller chip space. This not only makes computers more compact and less expensive, but it also allows them to operate faster, since signals are subjected to less delay in traveling between elements. In the quest for speed, engineers are also chilling chips with liquid nitrogen. At the low temperature of liquid nitrogen (77K), chips run much faster; a microprocessor that runs at 100 MHz at room temperature can run at 250 MHz at 77K. Engineers are also enthusiastic about experimental chips with switching devices made from superconducting materials. Such materials lose all their resistance when chilled, and can switch billions of times a second. New "high-temperature" superconductors, usually thin, copper-bearing ceramic films, need be chilled only to liquid nitrogen temperature—easier to attain than the 4.2K liquid-helium temperature previously required.

Meanwhile, multimedia desktop computers are on the verge of developing their full potential. Already equipped with CD-ROM players, multimedia PCs can tap a vast library of information, presented in both sound and video, on science, music, history, and art, for example. No longer limited to still or slow-moving displays, the newer machines can show action on the screen.

The growth of networking and the Internet will continue apace as computer users subscribe to services that provide information, "bulletin boards," and *electronic mail.* Users can now set up voice conversations over the Internet. A limited form of video phone service is also available, and development is ongoing. Information "superhighways" are being built with optical fibers that transfer vast amounts of data between computers at breathtaking speeds. With this information transfer capacity, PC-based video phone service will become commonplace; people will confer with colleagues, viewing their live images on a screen shared with whatever text and graphics are needed for the discussion.

2

Software Engineering

Computer programs, the software that is becoming an ever-larger part of the computer system, are growing more and more complicated, requiring teams of programmers and years of effort to develop. As a consequence, a new subdiscipline, software engineering, has arisen. The development of a large piece of software is perceived as an engineering task, to be approached with the same care as the construction of a skyscraper, for example, and with the same attention to cost, reliability, and maintainability of the final product. The software-engineering process is usually described as consisting of several phases, variously defined but in general consisting of: (1) identification and analysis of user requirements, (2) development of system specifications (both hardware and software), (3) software design (perhaps at several successively more detailed levels), (4) implementation (actual coding), (5) testing, and (6) maintenance.

Even with such an engineering discipline in place, the software-development process is expensive and time-consuming. Since the early 1980s, increasingly sophisticated tools have been built to aid the software developer and to automate as much as possible the development process. Such computer-aided software engineering (CASE) tools span a wide range of types, from those that carry out the task of routine coding when given an appropriately detailed design in some specification language to those that incorporate an *expert system* to enforce design rules and eliminate software defects prior to the coding phase.

As the size and complexity of software has grown, the concept of reuse has become increasingly important in software engineering, since it is clear that extensive new software cannot be created cheaply and rapidly without incorporating existing program modules (subroutines, or pieces of computer code). One of the attractive aspects of object-oriented programming (see below Programming languages) is that code written in terms of objects is readily reused. As with other aspects of computer systems, reliability—usually rather vaguely defined as the likelihood of a system to operate correctly over a reasonably long period of time—is a key goal of the finished software product. Sophisticated techniques for *testing* software have therefore been designed. For example, a large software product might be deliberately "seeded" with artificial faults, or *"bugs"*; if they are all discovered through testing, there is a high probability that most actual faults likely to cause computational errors have been discovered as well. The need for better trained software engineers has led to the development of educational programs in which software engineering is either a specialization within computer science or a separate program. The recommendation that software engineers, like other engineers, be licensed or certified is gaining increasing support, as is the momentum toward the accreditation of software engineering degree programs.

Theory

Computational Methods and Numerical Analysis

The mathematical methods needed for computations in engineering and the sciences must be transformed from the continuous to the discrete in order to be carried out on a computer. For example, the computer *integration* of a function over an interval is accomplished not by applying integral calculus to the function expressed as a formula but rather by approximating the area under the function graph by a sum of geometric areas obtained from evaluating the function at discrete points. Similarly, the solution of a differential equation is obtained as a sequence of discrete points determined, in simplistic terms, by approximating the true solution curve by a sequence of tangential line segments. When discretized in this way, many problems can be recast in the form of an equation involving a *matrix* (a rectangular array of numbers) that is solvable with techniques from linear algebra. *Numerical analysis* is the study of such computational methods. Several factors must be considered when applying numerical methods: (1) the conditions under which the method yields a solution, (2) the accuracy of the solution, and, since many methods are iterative, (3) whether the iteration is stable (in the sense of not exhibiting eventual error growth), and (4) how long (in terms of the number of steps) it will generally take to obtain a solution of the desired accuracy.

The need to study ever-larger systems of equations, combined with the development of large and powerful multiprocessors *(supercomputers)* that allow many operations to proceed in parallel by assigning them to separate processing elements, has sparked much interest in the design and analysis of parallel computational methods that may be carried out on such parallel machines.

The Internet

On-line use continued to grow in popularity throughout 1998. An IDC survey predicted that 23% of all U.S. households would be using an on-line service provider by the end of the year. The prediction was based partly on lower prices for PCs; the use of more hybrid PC-TV products, such as WebTV, which allowed TV users to surf some parts of the Internet; and the growing availability of high-speed cable modems. The potential for WebTV-like products was clear. At year's end AOL was said to be seeking a manufacturer of TV set-top boxes so that it could compete with Microsoft's WebTV product. Yet another WebTV-related product emerged from an unlikely source. Sega, known for its computer game consoles, introduced in Japan its new Dreamcast game console, which would also function as a WebTV-like unit. Software to turn the game machine into a Web-browsing device was not expected to be available until mid-1999. In addition, Sony Corp., the leading competitor in home video-game machines, was expected to offer something similar in the future.

Retail sales on the Internet also increased as consumers began to take greater advantage of electronic commerce. On-line sales lived up to expectations during the Christmas holiday season. AOL reported a 350% increase in on-line shopping. Analysts estimated that more than two million households shopped on-line for the first time and that sales in the fourth quarter of 1998 would hit about $3.5 billion, as expected. That was almost three times the 1997 total. The unanswered question was how many of those holiday shoppers would become regular Internet buyers.

The running battle between the computer industry and the federal government over Internet encryption software continued, even though the federal government relaxed its export restrictions. Encryption, or encoding, software was intended to protect the privacy of on-line data transmissions and help safeguard business transactions. The software-encryption industry and some of its key customers had been battling the government for several years, claiming that encryption was important to the development of electronic commerce. In addition, American software companies had complained that export regulations made it difficult for them to compete in the world market for encryption. New rules from the Commerce Department allowed American firms to export products using the 56-bit Data Encryption Standard, the equivalent of an electronic lock with more than 70 quadrillion possible combinations. The government continued to limit exports of more powerful encryption software, although some could be sold in 46 countries to particular industries, such as insurance and health care. Despite relaxing export rules on encryption, the government continued to push for FBI access to computer-industry encryption experts so that potential criminal activity on the Internet would not be protected from government scrutiny. The government promised it would place no limits on the export of encryption products for which the government was provided with codes, or keys, for reading the encrypted messages.

In September the Internet played a role in the White House scandal of 1998. First it was chosen by Congress as the distribution medium for the text of Independent Counsel Kenneth Starr's report on his eight-month investigation into Press. Bill Clinton's relationship with a former White House intern. Only days later it became one of the means of disseminating the video of Clinton's grand-jury testimony in the case. Because the streaming video technique used to deliver Clinton's testimony consumed much more bandwidth than the text-based report, there were concerns of gridlock on the Internet when many people tried to download the video at once. In the end the problem did not arise, because far fewer people downloaded the video man had downloaded Starr's report. The same news story helped boost the fortunes of the Internet's leading gossip columnist, Matt Drudge, who had helped break the White House scandal story in January by posting information on his Web site, the Drudge Report. Drudge, who had no journalistic training, maintained that the Internet opened up new opportunities for people who were not establishment journalists to present news information to a wide audience.

The makeup of that wide Internet audience also became a concern in 1998 when a scientific study suggested that African-Americans were being systematically excluded from the on-line world. In April a study published in the journal *Science* reported that whites in the U.S. with annual household incomes below $40,000 were six times more likely than African-Americans to have used the World Wide Web within the previous week. Among low-income households, whites were found to be twice as likely to own a home computer as blacks. The study contended that because a smaller percentage of black households than white households had incomes of more than $40,000, computer access in the U.S. was being restricted to a smaller portion of the African-American population man the white population. The Internet's role in rearranging American personal habits also was examined in 1998. A study showed that Americans were using the Internet to supplement TV news and newspapers, not to replace them, but it also found that 20% of Americans were going on-line at least once weekly to read the news, compared with 6% two years earlier.

Long-distance telephone service over the Internet, once a technical curiosity, showed signs of becoming a real business in 1998. Several phone companies offered a service in which phone calls were transmitted digitally over the Internet at reduced rates. The Internet was designed to carry data packets, not voice calls, and adapting phone calls to the Net had resulted in some complaints of spotty voice quality. By year's end the service had improved to the point that Internet telephony could compete on the basis of its lower price. Typically the service sold for far less per minute man conventional long-distance service—largely because Internet telephony bypassed much of the conventional telephone switching network but also because Internet telephone service providers were exempt from some fees that conventional long-distance companies had to pay. In a few cases Net phone service was sold for a flat monthly rate that covered unlimited long-distance calling privileges. While relatively few cities were covered by the service, some companies were planning national service introductions by late 1998 or early 1999.

In the U.S. Congress several bills favourable to the computer industry were pending in late 1998. One would expand the ability of American companies to hire skilled foreign workers. Corporations wanted to be able to hire more foreign workers because of a shortage of technology workers in the country. Another bill would benefit firms that sold products over the Internet by giving them a three-year period in which they would not have to charge customers sales tax. During that time the government would devise a tax plan for Internet sales. Legislation also was pending that would create penalties for commercial Web-site operators who offered material considered harmful to minors. This legislation was opposed by the American Civil Liberties Union and some companies with Internet Web sites. Other U.S. government actions affected many public schools and libraries that had hoped for improved Internet access. They were to be beneficiaries of federal telecommunications reforms that allocated money for telecommunications services, Internet access, and some high-tech wiring costs. The subsidy turned out to be less than expected when the Federal Communications Commission (FCC), under pressure from Congress, cut funding for the program by 42% and shifted the emphasis to helping the nation's poorest schools and libraries. The FCC's cuts were made after Congress listened to complaints from long-distance telephone companies, which said they could not provide most of the $2,250,000,000 to fund the program without raising rates paid by their customers.

Computer Crime

Computer security continued to be a major concern as outside electronic attacks by computer "hackers" on government and business computers reached new heights, sparking investigations into who was responsible. Those investigations led to a number of arrests but underscored the vulnerability of many computer systems connected to the Internet. The Computer Security Institute, a nonprofit research group in San Francisco, reported that 24% of corporations participating in its annual survey indicated that they had suffered an outside computer break-in within the previous year. About 44% said they had experienced incidents of unauthorized access to their computer systems by employees. In March a boy was charged in Massachusetts with having caused airport-control-tower computers to be out of service for six hours. The boy accomplished the task by wiping out telephone access to the airport's control tower. The shutdown also affected the airport's fire department and security and weather services and the operations of several private airfreight firms. In April a Canadian man was arrested for having broken into a NASA Web site and caused more than $70,000 worth of damage. That same month the University of Minnesota was hit by a "smurf denial of service" attack on its computer systems, which shut down some computers, caused some data losses, and resulted in network slowdowns. (Such an attack floods the victim's computer network with replies to false tests of remote network computers.) In July two California teenagers pleaded guilty to juvenile delinquency charges after they accessed computers at the Lawrence Livermore National Laboratory and the U.S. Air Force. Although no classified computer systems were breached, the attack raised government fears because it indicated the effectiveness of a well-organized and systematic hacker attack.

That same month flaws were discovered and corrected in two widely used E-mail programs that would potentially allow technically knowledgeable people to sabotage other people's PCs remotely. The unexpected flaws, which turned up in both Microsoft and Netscape E-mail programs, would enable an outsider electronically to crash or steal information from the computer that was using one of the affected programs.

In March more than 60 people were arrested as accused pedophiles who were trying to set up meetings with unsuspecting children over the Internet. New Hampshire police posed as children on the Internet to set up meetings with the accused adults (most of whom lived in northern Europe) and then arranged for them to be arrested. In September police in the U.S. and 11 other countries arrested more than 100 people in an international crackdown on the exchange of child pornography over the Internet.

A puzzling new computer virus struck near the end of the year, but experts were undecided about how big a threat it posed. Called the "Remote Explorer" virus, it was written by clever destruction-oriented programmers and was able to spread itself through corporate computer networks more rapidly than previously known viruses had. The virus attacked only computers using the Windows NT OS and only under certain conditions. Some experts said the virus had the ability to bring entire companies to a halt. It was unclear, however, whether the virus was a widespread phenomenon.

The use of computers to produce pictorial images. The images produced can be printed documents or animated motion pictures, but the term computer graphics refers particularly to images displayed on a video display screen, or display monitor. These screens can display graphic as well as alphanumeric data. A computer-graphics system basically consists of a computer to store and manipulate images, a display screen, various input and output devices, and a graphics software package—*i.e.*, a program that enables a computer to process graphic images by means of mathematical language. These programs enable the computer to draw, colour, shade, and manipulate the images held in its memory.

A computer displays images on the phosphor-coated surface of a graphics display screen by means of an *electron beam* that sweeps the screen many times each second. Those portions of the screen energized by the beam emit light, and changes in the intensity of the beam determine their brightness and hue. The brightness of the resulting image fades quickly, however, and must be continuously "refreshed" by the beam, typically 30 times per second.

Graphics software programs enable a user to draw, colour, shade, and manipulate an image on a display screen with commands input by a keyboard. A picture can be drawn or redrawn onto the screen with the use of a mouse, a pressure-sensitive tablet, or a light pen. Preexisting *images* on paper can be scanned into the computer through the use of scanners, digitizers, pattern-recognition devices, or digital cameras. Frames of images on videotape also can be entered into a computer. Various output devices have been developed as well; special programs send digital data from the computer's memory to an image setter or film recorder, which prints the image on paper or on photographic film. The computer can also generate hard copy by means of plotters and laser or dot-matrix printers.

Pictures are stored and processed in a computer's memory by either of two methods: raster graphics and vector graphics. Raster-type graphics maintain an image as a matrix of independently controlled dots, while vector graphics maintain it as a collection of points, lines, and arcs. Raster graphics are now the dominant computer graphics technology.

In raster graphics, the computer's memory stores an image as a matrix, or grid, of individual dots, or pixels (picture elements). Each pixel is encoded in the computer's memory as one or several bits-*i.e.*, binary digits represented by 0 or 1. A 2-bit pixel can represent either black or white, while a 4-bit pixel can represent any of 16 different colours or shades of gray. The constituent bits that encode a picture in the computer's memory are called a bit map. Computers need large processing and memory capacities to translate the enormous amounts of information contained in a picture into the digital code of a bit map, and graphics software programs use special algorithms (computational processes) to perform these procedures.

In raster graphics, the thousands of tiny pixels that make up an individual image are projected onto a *display* screen as illuminated dots that from a distance appear as a contiguous image. The picture frame consists of hundreds of tiny horizontal rows, each of which contains hundreds of pixels. An electron beam creates the grid of pixels by tracing each horizontal line from left to right, one pixel at a time, from the top line to the bottom line.

Raster graphics create uniform coloured areas and distinct patterns and allow precise manipulation because their constituent images can be altered one dot at a time. Their main disadvantage is that the images are subtly staircase—i.e., diagonal lines and edges appear jagged and less distinct when viewed from a very short distance. A corollary of television technology, raster graphics emerged in the early 1970s and had largely displaced vector systems by the '90s. In vector graphics, images are made up of a series of lines, each of which is stored in the computer's memory as a vector—i.e., as two points on an x-y matrix. On a vector-type display screen, an electron beam sweeps back and forth between the points designated by the computer and the paths so energized emit light, there by creating lines; solid shapes are created by grouping lines closely enough to form a contiguous image. Vector-graphics technology was developed in the mid-1960s and widely used until it was supplanted by raster graphics. Its application is now largely restricted to highly linear work in computer-aided design and architectural drafting, and even this is performed on raster-type screens with the vectors converted into dots.

Computer graphics have found widespread use in printing, product design and manufacturing, scientific research, and entertainment since the 1960s. In the business office, computers routinely create graphs and tables to illustrate text information. Computer-aided design systems have replaced drafting boards in the design of a vast array of products ranging from buildings to automotive bodies and aircraft hulls to electrical and electronic devices. Computers are also often used to test various mechanical, electrical, or thermal properties of the component under design. Scientists use computers to simulate the behaviour of complicated natural systems in animated motion-picture sequences. These pictorial visualizations can afford a clearer understanding of the multiple forces or variables at work in such phenomena as nuclear and chemical reactions, large-scale gravitational interactions, hydraulic flow, load deformation, and physiological systems. Computer graphics are nowhere so visible as in the entertainment industry, which uses mem to create the interactive animations of video games and the special effects in motion pictures. Computers have also come into increasing use in commercial illustration and in the digitalization of images for use in CD-ROM products, online services, and other electronic media.

3

The Fundamentals of DOS

In this and the next chapter, we are going to concentrate on the various services offered by DOS to the user. At one level, the DOS provides a set of user services to do functions that are required by the users of an operating system, i.e. in this case DOS or Disk Operating System. These are, for example, the kind of services that one would find described in the DOS User's Guide, e.g. DIR to see the directory, FORMAT to format a disk, MODE to change the operating mode of some device etc. In a sense, these are utility programs provided by DOS for direct usage. At a lower and deeper level, DOS provides a number of other services which are of use to somebody writing his/her programs to run under DOS. These are provided through various INT n type of instructions or as Function Calls under the INT 21H instruction. As a matter of fact, DOS uses these services to provide the user the first category of DOS utilities. These latter services are the ones of interest to us here.

Before we begin our discussion of the various services provided by DOS, it should be noted that a few of these services are also available at the level of the ROM-BIOS. A distinct difference between the two, however, is the fact that whereas the ROM-BIOS services refer to programs resident in the system's ROM, the DOS services are loaded into the system's RAM when DOS is loaded. The scope and variety of the DOS services is also much greater than what is offered through the ROM-BIOS. The DOS services have also been evolving faster than the BIOS services with constant upgradation from the original DOS 1.0 through to DOS 3.2 (Our discussion here is going to be relevant for DOS version 2.0 and higher.) The evolution of DOS has led to features which have a strong similarity with UNIX at one end while maintaining compatibility, to a large extent, with earlier DOS offerings. The user should also note that if portability of programs is a major concern, then programs should be written using the DOS services rather than the ROM-BIOS services. This is because programs using ROM-BIOS function calls will be able to run only on IBM's family of machines or its close compatibles; whereas programs written using the DOS services can conceivably run on any computer with the DOS operating system.

This chapter is intended to be an introduction for the material presented in the later chapters. It is recommended that, in case of any doubt, the reader should refer to the later chapter which discusses the same topic in more detail.

1. The Loading of DOS and its Basic Structure

When the 8088 CPU is reset, it fetches the next instruction to be executed from location FFFFOH. In the PC, this is an area occupied by the system's ROM, as described in Sec. 4.1.2. The CPU encounters a jump instruction at this location transferring control to system test programs followed by the ROM bootstrap routine. This is where the user sees the memory checking being done. (Some PC models skip the lengthy RAM test in order to provide a faster boot-up.) These programs also check the memory size and the peripheral device configuration which has been set up for the PC. This information is appropriately recorded for later use by the system.

At the end of its bootstrap sequence, the bootstrap program in ROM reads the first sector of the disk in order to load the disk-bootstrap program. In a PC-XT, the machine may be required to boot from the Winchester in drive C rather than from a floppy diskette in drive A. In this case, there should be no diskette in drive A. The ROM program senses the absence of a diskette in drive A and tries to load the disk bootstrap program from drive C.

The disk bootstrap program checks to see if the 'boot' disk contains DOS by checking the first sector of the root directory for the files IO.SYS and DOS.SYS. (These are referred to as IBMBIO.COM and IBMDOS.COM in PCDOS. They may also have other names depending on the brand of the PC or the supplier of the DOS.) If these are not found in the boot-disk, the user is prompted to replace the disk with another one containing the required programs. If the files are found, these files are read into memory by the ROM-bootstrap loader and control is transferred to the program in IO.SYS. The actual location of these programs in memory is not of particular significance to the user at this stage.

The file IO.SYS (or IBMBIO.COM) contains a BIOS which is configured to match DOS with the particular hardware of the PC. It provides the software drivers and the interface for handling the console, printer etc. and also initializes the hardware appropriately. It is followed by a system initialization program which determines the RAM size in the PC and based on this information, moves itself to high memory. Then, it loads the DOS.SYS (or IBMDOS.COM) program to its final memory location or shifts it from its original load location to the final one. The final location of the DOS kernel program, DOS.SYS, may actually over-write the now unnecessary portions of IO.SYS. This sequence finally ends with control being transferred to DOS.SYS; from this point onwards, DOS can be said to have taken control of the system.

The DOS kernel does an extensive amount of work to get DOS up and running. It initializes its tables and sets up its various work areas. It sets up the proper interrupt vectors for the DOS interrupts INT 20H-2FH pointing them to the appropriate service rountines (which are also a part of DOS). It then loads and executes the device drivers that are built into DOS, properly initializing the required hardware and setting-up the appropriate vectors for the hardware interrupts that these devices will use for their operation. It allocates appropriate buffers, e.g. for disks, and finally returns control to the system initialization program. This is the point where the user will usually find the system copyright message on his/her screen.

Based on the fact that both the DOS kernel and the PC's device drivers have been established, the DOS file services are now used to examine the disk to see if the file CONFIG.SYS exists. If it does, it contains a list of additional device drivers that the user wants in his system. Typical examples of such additional drivers are VDISK.SYS to establish a RAM-disk (i.e. an area of memory that behaves exactly like a disk) or ANSI.SYS to load the extended keyboard and screen control programs. This program can also change the default values of the number of files that DOS can simultaneously keep open and the number of buffers allocated for files. An example of CONFIG.SYS is shown below.

```
buffers = 8
files = 20
device = ansi.sys
device = vdisk.sys 256 256 64
```

(Note that lower and upper case are treated as equal in most DOS operations).

Once the device drivers of CONFIG.SYS are loaded and initialized and the file buffers have been appropriately adjusted, the CONFIG.SYS file is searched for the command processor that the user wants executed. (The default processor is COMMAND.COM but the user can substitute a command processor of his own through the CONFIG.SYS file.) This file's name, if any, is stored for later use and control is returned to the system initialization program. In case no CONFIG.SYS file is found in the boot disk, control is retained by the system initialization program skipping the operations mentioned above.

At this point, the system initialization program closes all files (and devices) except the console (CON) as the device for standard input, standard output and standard error, the printer (PRN) as the standard list device, and the auxiliary (AUX) as the standard auxiliary device. (The AUX device is typically initialized as the serial port COMl unless redirected.) The EXEC function of DOS (Function 4BH, INT 21H) is then used to load either the default command processor COMMAND.COM or the user's command processor specified in CONFIG.SYS. Control is then transferred to this command processor which displays an appropriate prompt and waits for further inputs from the user.

DOS can itself be viewed as consisting of three interdependent layers, the BIOS for basic I/O, the DOS kernel containing system functions providing essentially hardware independent services to application programs, and the command processor. This division into layers is convenient to decouple the actual system hardware from the user's perception of the operating system.

The BIOS is the most hardware dependent layer of DOS since it must be configured to run on the particular hardware of the machine. This provides the resident device drivers for the console (CON), the printer' (PRN), the auxiliary device (AUX), the clock device (CLOCK) and the driver for the boot disk. In machines with a ROM-BIOS, the DOS-BIOS may actually use the former for some of its functions. In others, the manufacturer may actually provide a BIOS unique to its hardware which can be used by DOS. Note that there may be another set of device drivers, referred to as installable device drivers, which are installed through the DEVICE command in the CONFIG.SYS file. These may actually be meant for special devices that the user wants to interface to the PC for his particular application. It is also possible for the user to substitute his own device drivers for some devices that are actually installed through the BIOS. The BIOS services are provided by the IO.SYS (or IBMBIO.COM) file loaded into the system's RAM during boot.

The DOS kernel provides system functions as various hardware-independent services. (Note that the hardware dependence gets taken care of by the BIOS which is unique to the machine.) These functions provide the basic INT n (n = 20H-2FH) services discussed in Sec. 7.5. Of these, INT 21H provides a host of different services as Functions 00-63H. The latter represent the services that are recommended for use by user application programs. The set of services offered by these interrupt instructions and function calls allow programs to manage disk files and memory and to do I/O with various devices. They also allow the user to access the system clock for appropriate date and time information. These services provide the approach recommended by DOS for one program to load another 'child' program, execute it, and on its termination, return control to the 'parent' program. The child program may be 'spawned' by the command processor or by a 'parent' program which has in turn been spawned by the former. This kernel is provided by the DOS.SYS (or IBMDOS.COM) file loaded into the system's RAM during boot.

The third component of DOS is the command processor which is also referred to as the operating shell. This is the user's interface to DOS which examines the commands given by the user and gets the appropriate work done by the DOS kernel. The default shell is provided by DOS in the COMMAND.COM file. Unless the user substitutes a command processor of his own (through his CONFIG.SYS file, as mentioned earlier), this command processor is loaded and is finally given control of the system. (If the user has specified his own command processor then that gets control instead.)

The default command processor, COMMAND.COM, may also be viewed us containing a resident portion, an initialization portion and a transient portion. The resident portion, is loaded at boot into the lowest possible memory area above the areas used by the DOS kernel and its buffers and tables. This is never discarded or overwritten as long as the system operates under this shell. It is the responsibility of this resident portion to reload the transient part of COMMAND.COM in case the latter gets overwritten, corrupted or discarded during system operation. It contains the routines necessary to handle Ctrl-C (^C) and Break from the key board and the critical errors that may be encountered during system operation. It also has the responsibility of properly terminating transient child programs and returning control to the respective parent programs.

The initialization section of COMMAND.COM is loaded above the resident portion during boot and is promptly discarded once its work is done. It is primarily intended to process the set of DOS commands that the user may have put in his AUTOEXEC.BAT file. These commands are automatically executed, in the right sequence, once the system is booted; after these commands have been done, the initialization section of COMMAND.COM is discarded, i.e. the area previously occupied by it is released and may be used to load other programs.

The transient portion of COMMAND.COM is loaded in the highest possible area in the system's RAM (recall that the system's memory sue is determined at boot). This puts the DOS prompt on the screen, gets commands from the user either through the keyboard or from a batch file and executes them. These commands may be either internal or external in nature. The internal commands are ones which are implemented by programs which are a part of this transient portion itself, e.g. DIR, COPY etc. Whenever the transient portion is loaded, these get loaded with it. The external commands are stored in the disks as files with either a .COM or EXE extension (eg. CHKDSK program is stored as CHKDSK.COM). In order to execute these commands, COMMAND.COM searches for the corresponding file in the default disk or the user-specified disk, loads the file into memory, and transfers control to that program. Once this program is terminated, control returns to COMMAND.COM and the program for that command is discarded from memory. It is possible that the programs for such commands or the user's application programs may overwrite the transient portion of COMMAND.COM. On termination of these programs, the resident portion of COMMAND.COM checks to see if the transient portion, previously loaded, is still usable (it does this by computing a checksum of its contents). If it is not, it is loaded from the disk once again and control is transferred to it. Note that this reloading of the transient portion of COMMAND.COM will normally be done from the boot disk. This can, however, be changed by changing the COMSPEC variable in the PC's environment list. For example, executing the command.

```
set comspec = d:\command.com
```

will imply that subsequent reloadings of COMMAND.COM will be done from drive D, the Virtual disk or RAM-disk. (Of course, one must ensure that before this set instruction is done, COMMAND.COM is copied from the boot disk to drive D. This modification is useful since it reduces the accesses that have to be done to the floppy or Winchester drives and speeds up the operation of the system.) When a command is given to the COMMAND.COM command processor, it first checks to see if it is an internal command that can then be directly done. If it is not, it checks if the command is external by searching for the corresponding file in the boot disk with either the. COM, EXE or .BAT extension. This is done in the indicated sequence with COMMAND.COM first searching for a file with the .COM extension, then for a file with the .EXE extension and finally for a file with the .BAT (for batch files) extension. If it is found, it is loaded and executed. Otherwise, this search is repeated for each of the directories that the user may have specified in the PC's environment PATH string. If none of these searches are fruitful, the PC declares an error by printing 'Bad command or file name' and returns the system prompt expecting a fresh input. Note that a user program stored in a file with the .COM, .EXE or .BAT extension will get executed in exactly the same way. As far as this processing is concerned, COMMAND.COM makes no distinction between the utilities supplied with DOS and user programs written and stored in files with one of the above extensions.

(Batch commands represent a set of commands written into a file with extension .BAT. This contains a set of internal or external commands and may also have other batch commands. The lines of this batch file are read in sequence and the corresponding commands are executed).

2. Execution of Programs Under DOS

Programs that are executed by the PC, operating under DOS, are of two types- programs that are stored in files with the extension COM and programs that are stored in files with the EXE extension. We will refer to these two types of programs as .COM and .EXE programs, respectively. Functionally, either type may be chosen for the purposes of writing application programs. The significant difference between the two is that .COM programs are stored in their files as a memory image (i.e. exactly as it will look after it is loaded) whereas .EXE programs are stored in a more complicated fashion. The latter format is however more versatile in terms of memory allocation and loading and is probably the preferred format today.

Both .COM and .EXE programs are loaded from disk files through the EXEC function (Function 4BH, INT 21 H) provided by DOS. This loader function of DOS is used by COMMAND.COM or any other (parent) program to load and execute another (child) program. (Note that EXEC may also be used to load overlays of the same program. This usage is, however, somewhat rare.) If the Transient Program Area (TPA) in RAM—the memory remaining for loading new programs- has enough space, then the EXEC function does the following—

- allocates memory for the new program
- builds the Program Segment Prefix (PSP) at the lowest area of this memory (paragraph aligned)
- loads the program above the PSP
- sets up appropriate registers, i.e. segment registers and the stack and transfers control to the new program.

For .EXE programs, the EXEC function may also do some additional processing like passing parameters from parent to child through the environment block. (See Chapters 8 and 10 for more details of the EXEC function.) Both the .COM and .EXE programs are referred to as Transient Programs since they are brought into memory, executed and subsequently discarded after their job is done. They only own the memory allocated to them and have full control over all system resources while they are executing. The external (or extrinsic) commands provided by DOS are of this type and are loaded and executed through COMMAND.COM using the EXEC function. On a proper exit, both these types of programs would normally release the memory which was allocated to them on loading. This released memory may be subsequently used to load other programs. In Figs. 3.1 and 3.2, we have shown simple examples of a .COM and a .EXE program. Both these programs do the simple task of echoing the key pressed on the keyboard to the screen. These are discussed in greater detail in Sec. 3.2.2 and 3.2.3, respectively.

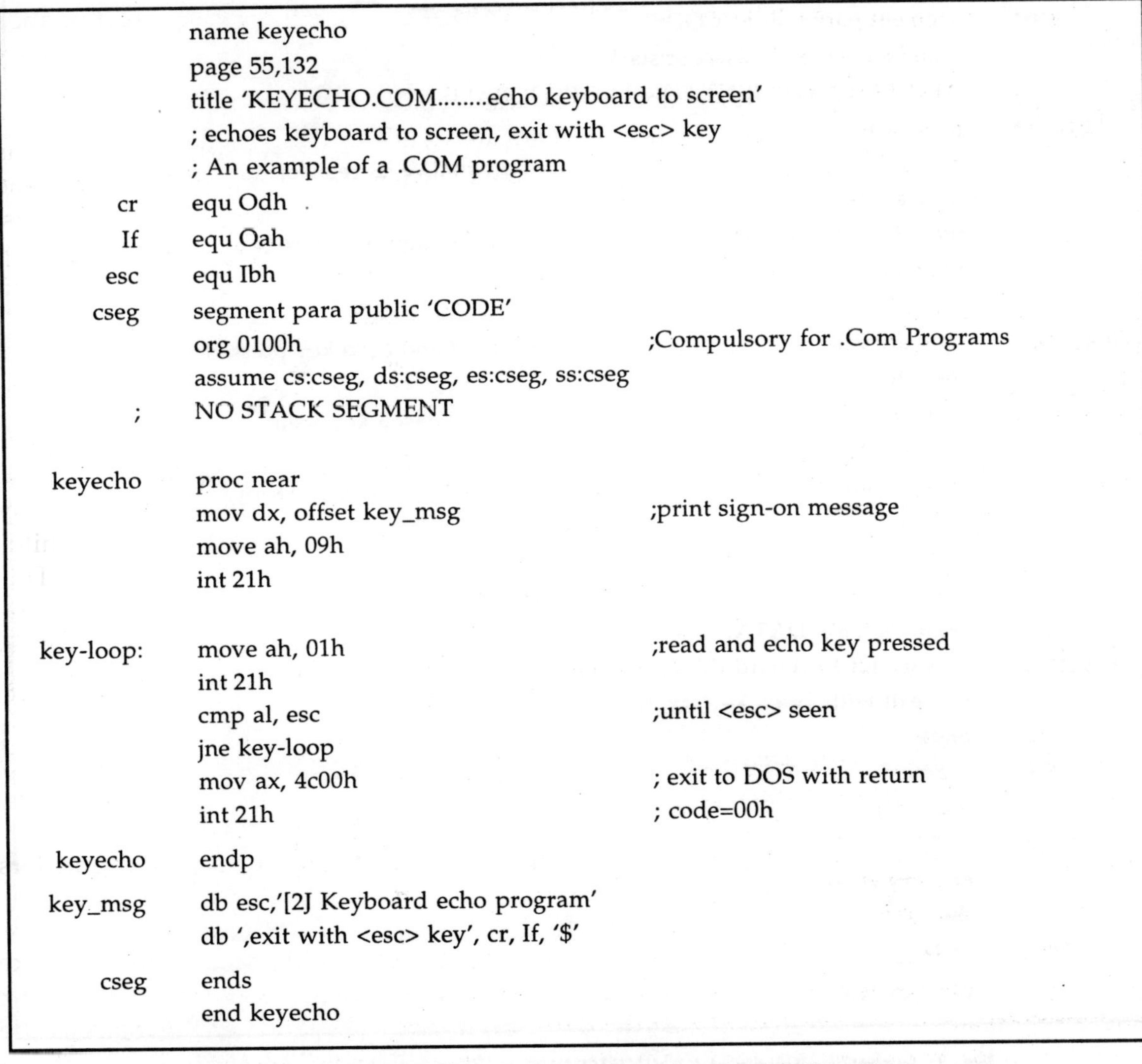

```
            name keyecho
            page 55,132
            title 'KEYECHO.COM........echo keyboard to screen'
            ; echoes keyboard to screen, exit with <esc> key
            ; An example of a .COM program
      cr    equ Odh
      If    equ Oah
     esc    equ Ibh
    cseg    segment para public 'CODE'
            org 0100h                           ;Compulsory for .Com Programs
            assume cs:cseg, ds:cseg, es:cseg, ss:cseg
       ;    NO STACK SEGMENT

 keyecho    proc near
            mov dx, offset key_msg              ;print sign-on message
            move ah, 09h
            int 21h

key-loop:   move ah, 01h                        ;read and echo key pressed
            int 21h
            cmp al, esc                         ;until <esc> seen
            jne key-loop
            mov ax, 4c00h                       ; exit to DOS with return
            int 21h                             ; code=00h
 keyecho    endp
 key_msg    db esc,'[2J Keyboard echo program'
            db ',exit with <esc> key', cr, If, '$'
    cseg    ends
            end keyecho
```

Fig. 1. Assembly listing of KEYECHO.COM, an example of a .COM program

```
            name keyecho
            page 55,132
            title 'KEYECHO.EXE..... ..echo keyboard to screen'
            ; echoes keyboard to screen, exit with < esc > key ;
            An example of a .EXE program
cr          equ 0dh
If          equ 0ah
esc         equ l bh
cseg        segment para public 'CODE'
            assume cs:cseg, ds:dseg, ss:stack
;           NO ORG STATEMENT FOR .EXE PROGRAMS
keyecho     proc near
            mov ax, dseg                    ; initialize ds register
            mov as, ax
            mov dx, offset key-msg          ; print sign-on message
            mov ah, 09h
            int 21h
key_loop:   mov ah, 01h                     ; read and echo key pressed
            int 21h
            cmp al, esc                     ; until <esc> key seen
            jne key_loop
            mov ax, 4c00h                   ; exit to DOS with return
            int 21h                         ;code = 00h
keyecho     endp
cseg        ends
dseg        segment para 'DATA'
key_msg     db esc, `[2J Keyboard echo program'
            db', exit with <esc> key', cr, if, `$'
dseg        ends
stack       segment                         ; para stack `STACK
            dw 64(?)
stack       ends
            end key echo
            dw 64(?)
stack       ends
            end key echo
```

Fig. 2. Assembly listing of KEYECHO EXE. an example of a EXE program

1. The Program Segment Prefix (PSP)

The Program Segment Prefix or PSP is a 256-byte data structue which is loaded by DOS before the transient program is loaded. It occupies offset 0000H-000FFH from the beginning of the segment used by DOS for loading the transient child program. It is paragrpah aligned and serveilance following purposes-

- provide linkages to DOS for use by the transient program.
- save information needed by DOS for its own purposes. These are typically the interrupt vector addresses of the parent program for the termination handler (INT 22H), the ^C interrupt (INT 23H) and the critical error handler (INT 24H). Assuming that the child program may have modified these vectors, DOS restores them from the values stored here when it return from the child to the parent program.
- save information which the transient program might need, eg. the command tail for the command invoking the child program.
- provide two default File Control Blocks (FCBs) which the child program may use if it is using the FCB-type calls for accessing files.

Format and Contents of the PSP (Offset addresses from beginning of load area) 2-byte values are stored in byte reversed fashion

Field	Offset	Contents
#1	00-01H	instruction INT 2011, terminate program (see Sec. 7.5)
#2	02-03H	segment address of end of allocated memory
	04H	reserved
#3	05-09H	long call to the DOS function dispatcher, otherwise provided through INT 21H command
#4	OA-ODH	original value of the termination handler(INT 22H) interrupt vector
#5	OE-11H	original value of ^ C (INT 23H) interrupt vector
#6	12-15H	original value of critical error handler (INT 24H) interrupt vector 16-2BH reserved
#7	2C-2DH	segment address of environment block (inherited from the parent program)
	2E-4FH	reserved
#8	50-52H	INT 21 H, RETF (far return) instructions
	53-54H	reserved
#9	55-5BH	extension for default FCB #1
	5C-6BH	default FCB #1
#10	65-6BH	extension for default FCB #2 (note overlap with default FCB # 1)

	6C-7FH	default FCB #2
#11	80-FFH	buffer for command tail and default buffer for disk transfer area (DTA)
	80H	length of command tail (not including the terminating <cr> character)
	8I-xxH	the command tail (ASCII string terminating with <cr>, ie. ODH, character)

[Consider the command 'EDIR KEYECHO*'. Here, the command tail is KEYECHO.* which will be stored as 09H 4BH 45H 59H 45H 43H 48H 4FH 2EH 2AH 0DH starting from 80H. EDIR.COM or EDIR.EXE would be the program to be executed.]

The user is strongly advised not to modify the program's PSP locations PSP:0000—PSP:005BH This may prove disastrous, if done without due care.

From the viewpoint of a user, the most useful PSP field is #11 since it contains the command tail. The command tail (if any) contains the switches, file name or other parameters that are required by the transient program. Note that redirection, if present in the command, is not passed on via the command tail to. the user's transient program. This is because redirection is the responsibility of the parent program and is supposed to be transparent to the transient child program. As illustrated earlier, the command tail as entered by the user is an ASCII string separated from the program name by a blank; intermediate blanks or commas are not deleted. Note that this is stored in the PSP as a count byte followed by an ASCII string terminating with the < cr > character; The count byte does not include the terminating < cr >.

Field #7 of the PSP is also useful since it contains the address (paragraph aligned, ie. xxxx0) pointing to a copy of the program's environment block, inherited from the parent by the child. The environment block consists of ASCII strings describing the environment of the program. This may be used by the child program to find its own inherited environment. One should avoid changing directly the environment of the program while it is executing. More details of the environment block may be found in Sec. 10.2.2.

Apart from the above, the other fields of the PSP are either meant for use by DOS or are relics of the CP/M parentage of the DOS operating systems. The significance of some of these fields and their purpose are described below.

The PSP's fields # 4,5 and 6 contain the parent program's vectors for INT 22H, INT 23H and INT 24H as described earlier. In case these vectors are modified by the child program, DOS restores them on returning from the child program to the parent. A transient child program can modify its parent's vectors for these interrupts by modifying these fields appropriately. This is an extremely non-standard usage and should be strictly avoided.

For terminating a child program, DOS recommends the use of either Function 31 H, INT

21H (terminate & stay resident, ie. KEEP) or Function 4CH, INT 21H (terminate, ie. EXIT). Both these techniques provide a return code which may be interrogated by the parent following return or examined from a batch file. Other methods of termination are—

- INT 20H or Function 00H, INT 21H Both these techniques are equivalent. They cannot always be used with .EXE programs since they require that the CS register must have the segment address of the PSP's origin when they are called. This cannot always be ensured for large .EXE programs.
- INT 27H Terminate & stay resident. This suffers from the same problem as INT 20H above.

The two methods given above should not be used with .EXE programs. In general, their use should be avoided with DOS versions 2.0 or higher.

Apart from the above, the PSP's fields # 1,3,8 provide some more exotic ways of terminating a program. This may be done as—

- Jump to PSP:0000H Since this location contains the INT 20H instruction, this will terminate the program.

- Set AH = 00H, 31H or 4CH, set up other registers as required for INT 21H functions 00, 31H or 4CH and then either jump to PSP:0050H or to PSP:0005H.

Note that these two methods are also not recommended.

Function calls to DOS are typically called by setting the appropriate function no. in AH, setting up other registers as needed, and then executing the INT 21H instruction. The PSP's field #3,8 may be used for some more exotic ways of invoking these function calls. Specifically, doing all other things as before except issuing of the INT 21H instruction, one can—

- Jump to PSP:0005H. If used, control will not return to the transient child program. Should not be used except for terminating the program.
- Far call to PSP:0050H. This will return control to the transient child program since PSP:0050H contains the instructions INT 21H followed by RETF (far return).

Obviously, neither of these two methods are preferred since there is no reason why the program cannot itself issue the INT 21H instruction directly.

DOS provides space in its PSP for two default FCBs for application programs which use FCB-type calls for accessing files. Since most modern application programs will use Handle-type calls for file operations, the default FCBs of fields #9,10 are virtually useless for DOS versions 2.0 or higher. If no Disk Transfer Area (DTA) is specifically set up using Function IAH, INT 21H, field #11 will be used as the default DTA. In this case, disk operations will destroy the command tail. Therefore, the program should properly save the command tail elsewhere or process it before any disk operations are done.

Recall that field #3 is a long call to the DOS function dispatcher. (This is what the INT 21H instruction does.) The call is set up such that PSP:0006, 0007 (ie. the offset of the called address) indicates how much of the 64K code segment is allocated upto FFFOH. If more than 64K is available, then the total memory allocated is given in number of paragraphs (16-byte units) in field #3 of the PSP.

2. *Features of .COM Programs*

In Figs. 3.1 and 3.3, we have given two examples of assembly language programs which are used to obtain the respective .COM program. The assembly language program is entered with an ASM extension and is assembled to produce an object file with the same name but with an OBJ extension. This object file is then linked to produce a linked file with the EXE extension. This step is enough for .EXE programs and the resultant file with this extension can directly be run. For programs written for final rendition into a .COM program, one more step is necessary. This uses the EXE2BIN external command provided by DOS to convert the EXE file into one with the COM extension. This final file with the COM extension can then be run as a .COM program by entering its name (ie. from COMMAND.COM) or calling it through EXEC from another program.

```
                name showpsp
                page 55,132
                title 'SHOWPSP.COM'
cr              equ 0dh
If              equ 0ah
blank           equ 20h
esc             equ Ibh
cseg            segment para public 'CODE'
                org                             0100h
                assume cs:cseg, ds:cseg, es:cseg, ss:cseg
showpsp         proc        near
                mov dx, offset show-msg         ; display sign-on message
                mov ah, 09h
                int'2Ih
                xor bx, bx                      ; clear ax register
show—loop:      mov dh, 10h
show—loop 1:    xor ax, ax                      ; clear ax register
                mov al, [cseg+bx]
                call conv—byte                  ; byte in AL converted to CH-CL.
                mov ah, 02h
                mov dl, ch                      ;display CH
                int 21 h
                mov ah, 02h
                mov, dl, cl                     ;display CL
```

Fig. 3 Contd.

```
                int 21h
Black           mov ah, 02h
                mov, dl, cl           ; diaplay space
                int 21h
                inc box
                cmp bh, 01h           ;loop 256 times for entire PSP
                je show—end
                dec dh
                jnz show_loop 1
                mov ah, 02h           ;put < cr > < if > after 16 bytes
                move dl, cr
                int 21h
                mov ah, 02h
                mov, dl, If
                int 21h
                jmp show_loop
show-end        mov ah, 02h
                mov dl, cr
                int 21h
                mov ah, 02h
                mov dl, If
                int 21h
                mov ax, 4c00h
                int 21h
showpsp endp
ascii           proc near             ; ASCH conversion routine
                add al, 30h
                cmp al, 39h
                jle asciil
                add al, 7
ascii:          ret
asciil:         ret
conv_byte       proc near             ; convert byte into two     ASCII
                xor ah, ah
                mov cl, 10h
                div cl
                call ascii
                mov ch, al
                mov al, ah
                call ascii
                mov cl, al
                ret
```

Fig. 3 Contd.

```
conv_byte        endup
show-msg         db          esc, `[2J'
                 db          `PSP Contents', cr, `$'.
cseg             ends
                 end         showpsp
```

PSP Contents

00	CD	20	00	A0	00	9A	F0	FE	ID	F0	2F	01	98	4B	3C	01
10	98	4B	EB	04	98	4B	98	4B	01	03	01	00	02	FF	FF	FF
20	FF	FF	FF	FF	FF	FF	FF	FF	FF	FF	FF	FF	67	4C	E6	FF
30	87	4C	14	00	18	00	87	4C	FF	FF	FF	FF	00	00	00	00
40	00	00	00	00	00	00	00	00	00	00	00	00	00	00	00	00
50	CD	21	CB	00	00	00	00	00	00	00	00	00	00	20	20	20
60	20	20	20	20	20	20	20	20	00	00	00	00	00	20	20	00
70	20	20	20	20	20	20	20	20	00	00	00	00	00	00	00	00
80	01	20	0D	68	6F	77	70	73	70	2E	65	78	65	20	73	68
90	6F	77	70	73	70	2E	63	6F	6D	0D	70	2E	61	73	6D	0D
A0	00	00	00	00	00	00	00	00	00	00	00	00	00	00	00	00
B0	00	00	00	00	00	00	00	00	00	00	00	00	00	00	00	00
C0	00	00	00	00	00	00	00	00	00	00	00	00	00	00	00	00
D0	00	00	00	00	00	00	00	00	00	00	00	00	00	00	00	00
E0	00	00	00	00	00	00	00	00	00	00	00	00	00	00	00	00
F0	00	00	00	00	00	00	00	00	00	00	00	00	00	00	00	00

Fig. 3. SHOWPSP.COM, a program displaying its own PSP and the resultant display.

The COM programs are stored in disk files with the COM extension and contain the absolute memory image of the actual program to be run. They are directly loaded by DOS, without any relocation or error checking. DOS directly transfers control to location 0100H of the loaded program (in the current segment) for its execution. Note that this location at 0100H corresponds to the location immediately after the 256-byte PSP. The .COM programs load faster and are stored more compactly as disk files than equivalent .EXE programs. DOS creates the PSP from segment:0000H to segment:00FFH, loads the actual program from segment:0100H, sets up the segment registers appropriately and transfers control to the instruction al segment:0100H. The reader should now realize why .COM programs are always written with origin specified as 0100H by the ORG 0100H assembler directive. In addition, the program should be written such that all code and data areas lie in one 64K segment. The program should not define the stack segment and the programmer should ignore the corresponding warning from the linker (ie. Warning: no stack segment)

For .COM programs, on loading, DOS initializes all segment registers —ie. CS, DS, ES, & SS—to point to the base of the PSP (ie. CS:0000 = PSP:0000). It also loads the IP register with 0100H to point to the first instruction of the .COM program. The stack pointer register SP is initialized to the top of the segment, ie. offset OFFFEH. In case this high setting is not allowed because of lack of memory, it is instead set as high as the available memory will allow. In addition, DOS pushes two bytes (ie. a word) of 00H on the stack. This allows program termination with a NEAR RETURN instruction. Such a return, gets the next instruction from PSP:0000H. This instruction is INT 20H which terminates the program. This method of program termination should, however, be avoided.

If a .COM program is being built from separate object modules, the programmer should note that—

- All procedures must be near since the .COM program cannot exceed 64K in any case.
- Only one of them must have the ORG 0100 statement. This is the module which will gel control from DOS and must be linked first.
- All modules must specify the same code-segment name and the same class name (ie. public).

Actually, a .COM program can use at most 65278 bytes of memory (65536-256 bytes of PSP-2 mandatory bytes of stack). This not only includes all its code and data but also the maximum stack area it might use. For larger programs, the programmer has no choice but to go for the .EXE program format. Note that this restriction comes from the fact mentioned earlier that the total volume of a .COM program cannot exceed one 64K segment (65536 bytes). Perversely enough, even though it cannot use more than 64K bytes, DOS allocates all of the remaining transient program area to it. This implies that, if a .COM program wants to load and execute another program, it must reduce its memory allocation via Function 4AH, INT 21H to the minimum it requires including its requirement of stack. The stack itself will also have to be relocated into this reduced memory if the .COM program reduces its memory allocation to less than one 64K segment.

DOS provides a myriad of different techniques to lerminate a .COM program. As mentioned earlier, the recommended methods are to use Function 4CH, INT 21H or Function 31 H, INT 21H. Other methods presented while describing the features of the PSP (Sec. 3.2.1) may also be applied. In addition, one can end a .COM program with a mere NEAR RETURN (RET) instruction. This is possible because of the 0000H word pushed on the stack before control is given to the .COM program and the fact that location 0000H in the current segment has the INT 20H instruction for terminating a program.

Terminations which provide a return code (i.e. Functions 4CH or 31H, INT 21H) are preferred since the return code may be monitored by the parent program being returned to.

This may be used by the child program to inform its parent about its execution status on return. If the execution of the transient program is invoked from a batch file, then, on termination, the next instruction (if any) of the batch file will be done. The return code set by the above functions may also be examined by the batch file through its conditional instructions.

3. *Features of .EXE Programs*

In Fig. 2, we have given an assembly language program which can be executed as a .EXE program after assembly and linking. Unlike .COM programs, .EXE programs do not need the EXE2BIN utility to provide an executable program file. Note that the way of writing the assembly language program essentially determines if it can be run as a .COM or a .EXE program. This is evident if one compares the program of Fig. 1 with that of Fig. 2. Both programs achieve the same function but are different in several ways. This is elaborated in greater detail in this section.

Unlike COM programs, .EXE programs can be of any size upto whatever memory is available in the Transient Program Area (TPA). The corresponding assembly language program (with ASM extension) must specify its code, data and stack segments. The program should not have an ORG statement. This is because the exact loud location of the .EXE program is decided by DOS when the program is loaded. The program should end with a statement of the type 'end xxxxx'. The loader ensures that after the .EXE program is loaded control is transferred to the statement labelled xxxxx. This should be the first executable instruction of the .EXE program. If the .EXE program is larger than 64K bytes, it is the user's responsibility to ensure that the various procedures of the program are appropriately declared to be either NEAR or FAR in nature.

One can also generate a .EXE program file by linking together several modules using the linker program. As before, procedures should be NEAR or FAR depending on their naming conventions and the size of the program. Note that, in this case, only one module must define the stack segment and only one module should have the 'end xxxxx' type of statement. Here too, after loading, DOS will transfer control to the statement labelled xxxxx.

The typical loading pattern of the .EXE program (after loading is done by DOS) is—

Low memory	—	PSP
	—	Code
	—	Data
High memory	—	Stack (stack grows towards low memory)

After loading a .EXE program, DOS will initialize—

CS:IP — to the program's entry point specified by the end statement mentioned earlier.

DS and ES — to the beginning (base) of the PSP. Note that the PSP is loaded in a paragraph aligned fashion starting from an address of the type xxxx0H.

SS:SP to point to the top of the stack area. The register SS is initialized to the segment with the stack attribute and SP to the size of this segment.

The above steps are such that the user must properly initialize the DS register in his program so that it points actually to his data segment. This is the reason for the instruction sequence—

```
mov ax, dseg
mov ds, ax
```

in the program of Fig. 2. For programs which may expect a command tail, the PSP of the program needs to be examined from location PSP:0080H onwards. This is conveniently done through the DS and ES registers which initially point to the segment address of the PSP. Note that if the DS register is to be used for this purpose, storage or processing of the command tail should be done before the user initializes DS to the segment address of the data segment as mentioned earlier. The size of the stack area to be used must also be explicitly declared in the assembly language program. The user may choose to initialize this stack area with a fixed byte (typically 00H) or to leave it uninitialized. (Initializing may help in estimating stack growth during actual execution by means of a memory dump done after the program terminates). Examples of stack initialization are given below—

```
(a)   stack   segment   para stack 'STACK'
              dw        64 dup (0)            ; initialize with 00
      stack   ends
(b)   stack   segment   para stack 'STACK'
              dw        64 dup (?) ;          no initialization
      stack   ends
```

The .EXE program should always terminate with either Function 4CH, INT 21H (terminate with return code) or Function 31 H, INT 21H (terminate with return code but stay resident). No other type of termination should be used.

In Fig. 4, we have shown the actual format and contents of a .EXE file. Note that apart from the code, data and stack segments , the file contains 512n (n = 1, 2...) bytes of a 'loading header' at its beginning; here n is decided by the number of relocatable instructions in the program. The loading header is created by the linker from the information provided by the programmer in his assembly language program. The information provided in the loading header is used by DOS tor loading the.EXE program from the .EXE disk file.

Fig. 4 shows the contents of the .EXE file from its initial value (i.e.offset 0000H). The first two bytes are 4DH, 5AH indicating that this is a file containing a .EXE program. The actual size of the file is given in locations 0002H-0005H. The file size (in bytes) is divided by 512; locations 0004H, 0005H give the integer result of this division and the remainder is stored in locations 0002H, 0003H. The next field in locations 0006H. 0007H contains the number of items in the relocation table, i.e. the number of items in the program that need to be relocated. The actual size of the loading header (in paragraphs) is stored in locations 0008H, 0009H. The memory allocation desired for the program is given in the next two fields in units of paragraphs. If possible, DOS tries to give the program, on loading, the maximum allocation desired. If this is not possible, it tries to allocate to the program as much memory as it can. If this is less than the minimum allocation desired by the program, the program cannot be loaded and the loading fails. The fields at locations 000EH, 000FH, and 0010H, 0011H specify the values to which the SS and SP registers, respectively are to be initialized following load. The contents of locations 0012H, 0013H contain a check-sum for the file. This is useful to verify if the file has become corrupted or not. The initializing values of the IP and CS registers are contained in locations 0014H, 0015H and 0016H, 0017H respectively. Locations 0018H, 0019H specify the offset in the file to the first relocation item. Location 00IAH contains an overlay number. As shown in Fig. 4, the .EXE file also contains a

OFFSET	CONTENTS (2-byt values stored byte-reversed)	
0000H-01H	4DH, SAH .EXE file indicator	
0002H-03H	mod 512	File length
0004H-05H	multiples of 512 bytes	
0006H-07H	No. of items in relocation table	
0008H-09H	Header Size in paragraphs (16-byte units)	
000AH-0BH	min. allocation	Memory allocation for the program
000CH-0DH	max. allocation	
000EH-0FH	segment displacement of stack area	stack definition
0010H-11H	initial value of SP (stack top)	
0012H-13H	2-byte checksum	
0014H-15H	initial value of IP (offset to start)	code definition
0016H-17H	segment displacement of code area	
0018H-19H	offset (in file) of first relocation item	
001AH	Overlay number (0 for resident portion)	
	RESERVED (variable length)	
	Relocation Table	
	RESERVED (variable length)	
	Program and Data Segments Stack Segment	

Fig. 4. Contents of EXE file (including header and program).

relocation table to properly locate the relocatable items in the file during load. It also contains the code, data and stack segments of the actual program. As can be easily realized, these contents of the loading header help in properly loading the program and initializing various registers. The user as such will probably not be interested directly in its contents. One exception to this is probably the memory allocation fields. If a .EXE program does not load, the user may want to check these fields to determine their contents and take appropriate steps.

3. Device Handling by DOS

The PC supports a number of devices with which it does I/O in order to get or send data. It loads the device drivers (software interfacing the PC to the device) for a number of devices as part of itself. The user may add other devices and get their corresponding drivers loaded by specifying them properly in the CONFIG.SYS file at boot. Some special commercial devices to be interfaced to the PC come with their own software device drivers; for others, the user may have to write his own software. Apart from floppy drives and hard disks (for the PC-XT), the other standard devices supported by DOS are—

CON	for the console with keyboard as the input and the video display as the output
PRN	for the printer
AUX	for the serial port 1 (or COM1)
CLOCK	for the clock device
NUL	for the null device or the 'byte bucket'. Data output to this device is simply discarded

An additional RAM-disk or extended keyboard and display support may also be provided by including the statements VDISK.SYS and ANSI.SYS in the CONFIG.SYS file as shown earlier in Sec. 3.1. DOS also supports redirection. Once redirection has been established, I/O for a device will always get channelled from that device to the one to which it has been redirected. Of course, redirection previously established may also be cancelled at will.

Another interesting feature of DOS is the fact that it tends to treat devices and files in an equivalent fashion. Like files, a device has to be opened before one can do I/O with it. Once the required I/O is done, the device is closed like a file. Commands intended for files are generally also applicable to devices making their handling extremely easy.

DOS classifies devices into two categories, block devices and character devices. Block devices are those which transmit bulk data, typically to or from a mass storage device. Floppy drives or hard disks are devices of this type. Character devices, on the other hand transfer data, one byte at a time. Typical examples of such devices are the keyboard and display (CON), the printer (PRN), the serial ports COM1 and COM2 and the null device (NUL). We will describe these two types of devices in greater detail in this section.

1. Block Devices

As mentioned earlier, these devices transfer data in blocks (i.e. a large number of bytes at a time) typically to or from mass storage devices like disks or tapes. Depending on the type of the device, random access of data is possible (i.e. from anywhere in the device, without any requirement to move sequentially to the desired area where the data is stored). This, for example, is possible with disks but is not possible with tapes. Even if random access is not possible, it is still possible to support such devices under DOS.

The device driver for a block device provides the software interface to that device for bulk data transfers. It is possible that the same device driver supports more than one physical device, or conversely, that one physical device looks like more than one logical device. Access to a logical device is by means of letters assigned as 'drive designators', e.g. A, B, C, D etc... Character devices may be referred to by assigned names (just as files). This is not possible with block devices. As far as non-disk block devices are concerned, they are treated very much like disk devices, e.g. they are assigned drive letters for access and the access mechanism is the same as that followed for disk-type block devices. For access, each block device must store within itself a File Allocation Table (FAT) and a root directory through which access must be made to the other contents of the device. These devices support data storage in the form of files, allowing for subdirectories and a hierarchical file structure.

DOS provides two types of functions for access to data stored in these block devices in the form of files. Data can be accessed either through File Control Blocks or FCBs (for FCB-type access) or through a numerical Handle (for Handle-type access). The FCB is a special data structure used to access a file. This approach is a relic of the CP/M parentage of DOS and was the only file-access method available in DOS version 1.0. In newer DOS programs, this approach is rarely used since it is complex and, moreover, does not support the hierarchical file structure. FCB-typc access methods can only access files in the current subdirectory of the designated drive. (See Sec, 3.4. for more information on the hierarchical file structure.)

The Handle functions provide a UNIX-type file access mechanism. Virtually all operations (and more) that can be done with FCBs can also be done through the Handle functions. These are recommended for DOS versions 2.0 and higher and will be exclusively used by us in our examples. They are simple to use und provide direct support tor the hierarchical file structure. Their error reporting is also considerably better than that of the FCB functions. Access in this case is through a single 16-bit number referred to as the Handle. This number is provided by DOS when a file (or device) is opened. Subsequent read/write/append operations on this file are done by using the handle and not the file name. (The same file can be assigned two handles, if needed.) Closing the file releases the handle which can subsequently be reassigned by DOS to another file (or device) on an open request. The data structures needed for access are internal to DOS and are not accessible to the user.

For block devices, DOS typically provides the device drivers for the system's floppy and/or fixed drives. Additional block deviced may be interfaced by devices drivers provided through the CONFIG.SYS file. For example, the line

device = vdisk.sys 256 256 64

in the CONFIG.SYS file installs a 256KB RAM-DISK in the system (provided it has sufficient RAM). The user can write his own driver with a .SYS extension and include that in his CONFIG.SYS file to interface more exotic block devices to the system:

Character devices may operate in either cooked or raw mode. This depends on whether the data byte accessed is to be examined and possibly modified or is to be passed unchanged. These modes are not relevant for block devices since they access data in blocks and take no action on the contents of the data itself.

DOS provides a large number of file manipulation functions through the INT 21H services. These are available for both FCB and Handle type of accesses, though the latter functions are strongly recommended. The important services for both types of access mechanisms are summarized in Fig. 5. For directly reading or writing to a logical sector on a disk, the DOS interrupts INT 25H and INT 26H may also be used. These DOS services directly use the BIOS (see Sec. 3.1) to provide these lower level accesses. Similar services are also available through the ROM-BIOS interrupt service INT 13H for the floppy drives. (The reader should note that whereas the ROM-BIOS service refers to a disk location in terms of the side no., track no. and sector no. the DOS services use a single logical sector no.

FCB type function	Handle type function	Operation
16H	3CH, 5AH, 5BH	Create File
0FH	3DH	Open File
10H	3EH	Close File
13H	41H	Delete File
17H	56H	Rename File
14H, 21H.27H	3FH	Read
15H, 22H, 28H	40H	Write

Fig. 5. File operations provided by the INT 21 H functions

2. *Character Devices*

These devices transfer data one byte at a time either from or to the PC. They also require software device drivers to interface to the PC. However, unlike block devices, a character device can only interface to one hardware unit. A character device can be operated in either cooked or raw mode; the operating mode can be selected through the IOCTL function provided by Function 44H, INT 21 H.

Cooked Mode. In this mode, during output, DOS checks the keyboard between the output of each byte to see if CNTRL-C (^C) has been pressed. It branches to the ^C handling routine on detecting ^C. During input, DOS places each byte in its internal buffer checking for both ^C and the carriage return character < cr > If the input is from the console device (CON), the characters are echoed to the screen. It branches to the ^C handling routine on detecting the ^C character. Otherwise, input to DOS's internal buffer is continued until either the requested number of charaters are received or a <cr> character is encountered; the contents of the internal buffer are then transferred to the calling program. Note that the ^C handling routine provided by DOS essentially aborts the ongoing program and returns control to its command processor (e.g. COMMAND.COM or the user's shell). The user can substitute his own ^C handling routine by changing the ^C Interrrupt Vector to point to his own routine.

Raw Mode. In this mode, the requested number of bytes are read or written without checking for ^C or any other character. The corresponding device driver does not return control to the calling program until all bytes are read or written.

Character devices can be handled just as files either through the FCB-type functions or the Handle-type function calls. (The latter are recommended. DOS treats files and devices almost equivalently.) For the keyboard and display (CON), the serial ports COMl and COM2 and the printer (PRN), special INT 21H functions are also available in DOS.

For its standard devices, DOS provides the following predefined handles—

0	for	standard input device	(CON)
1	for	standard output device	(CON)
2	for	standard error device	(CON)
3	for	standard auxiliary device	(AUX)
4	for	standard list device	(PRN)

These handles may be directly used without opening the device. If they are not needed, the device may be closed and the handle returned to DOS. Note that in this case, DOS may subsequently reassign that handle to another file or device; in any case, once the standard handle has been relinquished, the program will have to open the device once again for DOS to assign it a fresh handle. Duplicate handles may also be.obtained, e.g. for CON by opening CON again. Note that the handle calls support I/O redirection. If any of the standard devices are redirected to a file or device, I/O will be done with that file/device instead of the original one. Without redirection, the keyboard is the standard input device, the display is the standard output and error device, the serial port COMl is the standard auxiliary device and the printer LPT1 is the standard list device.

In case redirection has been done, one can overcome its effect by—

- cancelling redirection appropriately
- for console, serial ports and printer, by using the direct INT 21H functions tor these devices rather than their standard handles and handle-type access calls

- closing or ignoring the standard handles and getting new handles for the redirected device

The number of simultaneously open handles for a process cannot exceed twenty including the five standard handles. Moreover, the number of simultaneously open handles must be less than xx as specified in the line—

FILES = xx

in the CONFIG.SYS file. If this line is not present, the limit xx is eight by default. It can be put as high as 255 by 'FILES = 255 Note that this will get fixed at boot.

At the lowest level, the user may take over the I/O operations from the device drivers provided by DOS. This can be done by polling the device status in the user's own routines. A possibly more elegant method is to find out the hardware interrupt associated with the device and point its interrupt vector to an interrupt service routine written by the user for that device. This routine will then do I/O directly with the device without going through the standard device driver. As mentioned in Chapter 4, this approach is most desirable for the serial ports since it can significantly speed up I/O with them. It may also be desirable for the video display. At a somewhat higher level, the user may substitute his own device drivers for the default drivers given by DOS for its standard devices. These .SYS drivers may then be installed in the system through appropriate entries in the CONFIG.SYS file.

3. Driver Installation Sequence

If no additional drivers are specified in the CONFIG.SYS file, the resident device drivers are installed in the following sequence—NUL, CON, AUX, PRN, CLOCK, resident block devices, resident character devices. If the CONFIG.SYS file specifies additional device drivers to be installed then the installation sequence becomes—NUL, installable character devices, CON, AUX, PRN, CLOCK, resident block devices, resident character devices, installable block devices.

The built-in block device drivers cannot be superseded by user-specified drivers; one can only add supplemental device drivers to support additional block devices. However, the built-in character device drivers, may be superseded by user-specified device drivers. The latter are given the same logical device name in their device header as the device to be superseded. This works because, for character devices, DOS examines the list of installed drivers first before it looks at the list of built-in device drivers.

The CLOCK device, mentioned above, is a special device for recording date and time information. To read/set this device, a 6-byte sequence is needed.

2-byte days (LO.H1) 16-bit integer for no. of days elapsed since 1-1-80

1-byte minutes

1-byte hours

1-byte seconds/100

1-byte seconds

4. File Structure of DOS

DOS versions 2.0 and higher support a UNIX like hierarchical file structure starting from a root directory and extending down in tree fashion to other subdirectories. Any directory (root or sub) may contain files or other subdirectories. The current directory (root or sub) is taken as the default directory. Files can be created or stored directly in the root directory. However, in order to store files in a subdirectory, the subdirectory itself must be created; this is also true if a subdirectory (rather than a file) is to be created in a subdirectory. The contents of a subdirectory (files or other subdirectories of this subdirectory) must be erased before the subdirectory itself can be deleted. An example of a typical hierarchical structure is shown in Fig. 6. The path of a file is the sequence of subdirectories (separated by \) that have to be gone through in order to reach the subdirectory containing the file. This can be done either from the root directory or from the current directory. For example, referring to Fig. 6, assume that the current subdirectory is WSTAR and the file of interest is Letter 1. The path to this file may be specified as—

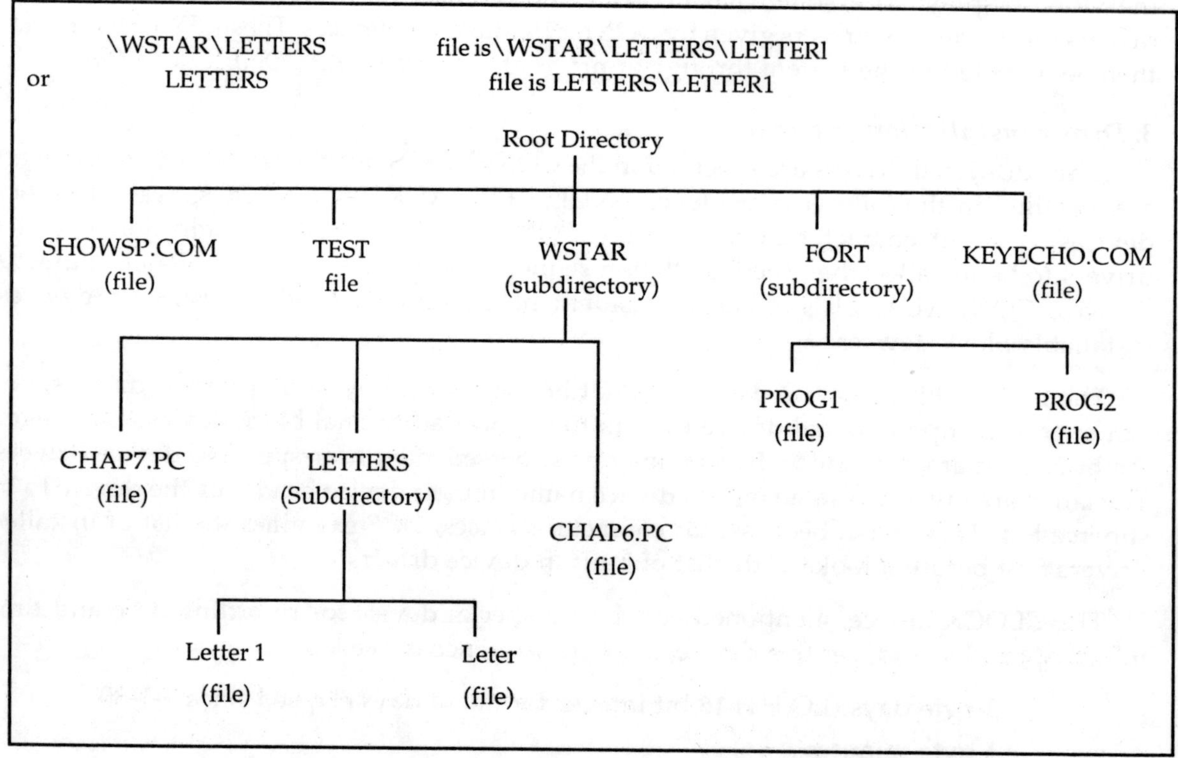

Fig. 6. An example of hierarchical file organization under DOS

DOS version 1.0 did not support the hierarchical file structure and used only the root directory. File accesses here can only be done through FCB-type function calls. Higher DOS versions support both the FCB and Handle type of calls for accessing files/devices.

For the handle type of calls one can use the handles provided by DOS for accessing the standard devices. For other devices or files, a handle has to be obtained from DOS by an open request. This handle may be used for subsequent file operations. Closing the file or device effectively releases the associated handle to DOS which can assign it subsequently to another file/device.

In Fig. 7, we give a program SHOW.ASM (which leads to the program SHOW.EXE) as an example of using handle-type functions. Here these functions are used for all read and write operations. I/O with the console also uses these functions with DOS's predefined handles assuming that I/O redirection bas not been done. The user is prompted for the name of the file to be displayed. An attempt is made to open the desired file. If it cannot be opened, the program

```
                name show
                page 55, 132
                title 'SHOW.EXE....display contents of file'
cseg            segment para public 'CODE'
                assume cs:cseg, ds:dseg, ss:stack
show            proc near
                mov ax, dseg                       ; point ds to data segment
                mov ds, ax                         ; & dx to offset of message
                mov, dx offset show_msg
                mov ah, 40h;                       display sign-on message & query
                mov bx, 000 1h                     ; user for file-name
                mov cx, show_msg_len
                int 21h                            ; display with standard handle 01
                mov dx, offset file_name
                mov ah, 3fh                        ; get and store file-name reading
                mov bx, 0000h                      ; keyboard with standard
                mov cx, 50h                        ; handle 00
                Int 21h
                mov bx, ax                         ; null terminate the ASCII string
                mov [file_name + bx -- 2], 00h     ; for file-name
                mov ax, 3d02h                      ; open file
                mov dx, offset file_name
                int 21h
                jnc show 1                         ; on error, terminate
                jmp show_end                       ; else continue
show 1:         mov handle, ax                     ; store handle from open
```

Fig. 7 Contd.

```
show 2:      mov bx, handle              ; read file with handle and
             mov ah, 3fh                 ; and store in file_buf
             mov cx, 0400h
             mov dx, offset file_buf
             int 21h
             cmp ax, 0000h
             je show_fin
             push ax                     ; save no. of bytes read on stack
             xor bx, bx
             mov cx, ax
show3:       mov al, [file_but + bx]
             and al, 7th                 ; make high-order bit = 0
             mov [file_buf + bx],al
             inc bx
             loop show3
             pop cx
             push cx
              mov ah, 40h
             mov bx, 0001 h              ; display - file buf using handle 01
             mov dx, offset file_buf
             int 21h
             pop ax
             cmp ax, 0400h
             jne show—term
             jmp show2
show-term:   mov ah, 3eh
             mov bx, handle              ; close file
             int 21h
             mov ax, 4c00h               ;terminate
             int 21h
show—fin:    xor bx, bx                  ; display last block, if needed
             mov cx, 0400h               ; and terminate
show—fin 1:  mov al, [file_buf + bx]
             and al, 7th                 ; make high-order bit = 0
             mov [file_buf + bx], al
             inc bx
             loop show_finl
             mov ah, 40h
             mov bx, 0001 h              ; display file - buf using handle 01
             mov cx, 0400h
             mov dx, offset file_buf
```

Fig. 7 Contd.

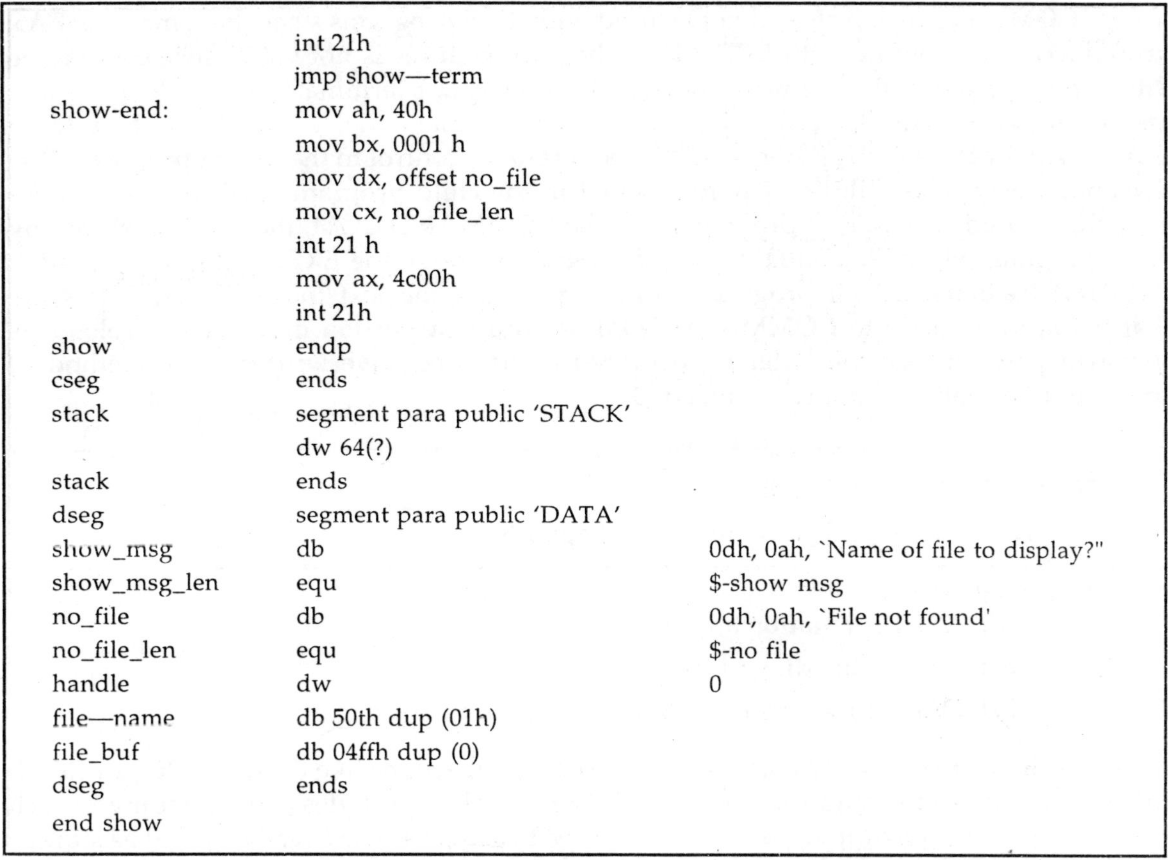

```
                int 21h
                jmp show—term
show-end:       mov ah, 40h
                mov bx, 0001 h
                mov dx, offset no_file
                mov cx, no_file_len
                int 21 h
                mov ax, 4c00h
                int 21h
show            endp
cseg            ends
stack           segment para public 'STACK'
                dw 64(?)
stack           ends
dseg            segment para public 'DATA'
show_msg        db              0dh, 0ah, `Name of file to display?"
show_msg_len    equ             $-show msg
no_file         db              0dh, 0ah, `File not found'
no_file_len     equ             $-no file
handle          dw              0
file—name       db 50th dup (01h)
file_buf        db 04ffh dup (0)
dseg            ends
end show
```

Fig. 7. SHOW.EXE, A program displaying a file's contents using handle type calls

terminates with an error message. If it can be opened, the contents of the file are displayed with the high-order bit reset in every byte. Once the entire file has been displayed, the program terminates after closing the file. The user may find it useful in this context, description of the INT 21H functions 3DH-40H and 4CH. A more detailed version of this program, incorporating further modifications.

5. The DOS Interrupts (INT 20H-2FH)

In this section, we give the details, of the various DOS interrupts that are available. Note that in the following description, CY indicates the carry flag.

INT 20H Terminate program

Call with CS = segment address of the PSP

Returns nothing

This interrupt is absolutely identical to Function 00, INT 21 H. This was the typical way to end .COM programs. It should not be used with .EXE programs since these may use FAR procedures. Terminating with INT 20H in these procedures is not valid since CS may be different from the PSP's segment address. This interrupt terminates the child program, restores the vectors for the termination handler, ^C handler and the critical error handler to their original values in the parent program and returns control to the parent program. This does not always close files which are opened in the child program. Such files should be explicitly closed. The parent program could be COMMAND.COM, the user's shell or any other program which 'spawned' the child program through the EXEC call (Function 4BH, INT 21H). If a batch file is in progress, control is passed to the next line of the batch file. Note that if return is made to COMMAND.COM, its resident portion may have to reload its transient part, in case the latter is corrupted or has been overwritten. This method of program termination is not recommended.

INT 21H DOS Functions 00H-63H

These are described in detail in Chapter 8.

INT 22H, 23H.24H

INT 22H Termination address

INT 23H ^C handler address

INT 24H Critical error handler address

These three are not really meant to be interrupt instructions like the other DOS or ROM-BIOS interrupts and should never be issued directly. The four bytes corresponding to each one in the CPU's interrupt vector table (i.e.4*type to 4*type + 3) are really treated as storage locations where the segment and offset addresses of these important routines are stored. This storage is done as per the convention followed by the CPU in storing interrupt vectors in its interrupt vector table.

The interrupt vector for INT 22H in locations 00088-0008BH contain the address of the parent program's instruction which receives control when the child program terminates. Note that this address is also stored in Field #4 of the child program's PSP. For INT 23H, the locations 0008C-0008FH stores the address of the ^C handler routine of the parent program; this address is also given in Field #5 of the child program's PSP. This is the routine which receives control when a ^C is encountered during I/O with a character device in the cooked mode. (If the BREAK flag is turned ON, the checking for ^C is done whenever any I/O operation is done by the operating system.) The user may change this interrupt vector by Function 25H, INT 21H to point to his own ^C handler. On termination, DOS will restore the parent program's value for this vector from the value stored in the PSP. These comments are also valid for the interrupt vector for INT 24H which is stored in locations 00090-00093H. This routine is given control whenever a hardware error (eg. parity error in RAM) or any other critical error is encountered.

It should be emphasized that none of these interrupt vectors (or for that matter, any interrupt vector) should be modified directly. The DOS service provided by Function 25H, INT 21H should always be used to do this in a safe fashion.

INT 25H Absolute disk read operation

Call with AL = drive no. of disk to be read with A = 0, B = 1, C = 2 etc.

DX = starting logical section no. to be read

CX = number of consecutive logical sectors to be read

DS:BX = segment:offset address of the memory area to be used to store the data read Returns with

(a) If successful, CY = 0 und the above buffer contains the data read from the disk

(b) If unsuccessful, CY = 1 and AH - error code

The error codes are—

01H if bad command

02H if bad address

03H if write-protect fault

04H if requested logical sector is not there

08H if failure in DMA operation

10H if bad CRC indicating data error

20H if the controller failed

40H if the seek failed

80H if the attachment did not respond

This interrupt instruction leaves the CPU's segment registers unaffected but may change all other registers. The user should take care to store registers appropriately before calling this interrupt. On return, the stack has two extra bytes containing me original FLAGS, and SP should be incremented either with POPF or ADD SP,2 in order to properly clear the stack. The other register's may be saved on the stack provided they are restored from the stack only after the above stack clearing has been done.

The reader is referred to Sec. 9.1 for the details of how to compute the logical sector no. from the numbers for side, track and sector and vice versa

---

INT 26H Absolute disk write operation

This function should be used with extreme care since it may irretrievably damage the contents of floppies or hard disks.

Call with AL = drive no. of disk to write in with A = 0, B = 1 C = 2 etc.

DX = starting logical sector no, to be written

CX = number of consecutive logical sectors to be written

DS:BX = segment:offset address of the memory area storing the data to be written Returns with

(a) If successful, CY = 0, ie. the data was written

(b) If unsuccessful, CY = 1

And AH=error code

Same error codes as for INT 25H

The comments made about CPU registers and stack for INT 25H are also valid for this interrupt.

The reader is referred to Sec. 9.1 for the details of how to compute the logical sector no. from the numbers for side, track and sector and vice versa.

INT 27H Terminate and stay resident

Call with CS = segment address of the PSP

DX = relative offset from the base of the PSP of the last byte of the program to be kept + 1

Returns nothing

This terminates the child program (like INT 20H) but retains a part (or whole) of it in memory so that it does not get overlaid by the next program loaded by DOS. Only a maximum of 64K bytes can be kept in this fashion. Moreover it is recommended for use with only .COM programs for the same reason as INT 20H. From both these reasons, this should not be used for .EXE programs. In any case, it is preferable to use Function 31 H, INT 21H to terminate but stay resident. The child program must have the portion to keep resident in the beginning and the DX register specifies the offset in the code segment of the first byte beyond the portion to be kept resident. Anything left resident by INT 27H will typically stay resident as long as DOS is also resident. Several programs may be left resident in this way. This programming technique is complicated and may cause the various resident programs to interfere with each other. This service may be used to retain interrupt handling routines (except those for INT 22H, 23H, 24H) that are required to stay permanently resident. These routines may be for new interrupts or replacements for the routines provided by DOS. INT 27H may also be used to retain programs and data that other programs may want to use or establish a data area to be used for communications between different programs.

Like INT 20H, this interrupt terminates the child program, restores the vectors for the termination handler, ^C handler and the critical error handler to their original values in the parent program and returns control to the parent program. This does not always close files which are opened in the child program. Such files should be explicitly closed. The parent program could be COMMAND.COM, the user's shell or any other program which 'spawned' the child program through the EXEC call (Function 4BH, INT 21 H). If a batch file is in progress, control is passed to the next line of the batch file. Note that if return is made to COMMAND.COM, its resident portion may have to reload its transient part, in case the latter is corrupted or has been overwritten. This method of program termination is not recommended.

INT 28H-2EH Reserved

INT 2FH Print Spooler, only available in DOS 3

Call with AL = Function code

DS:DX = segment: offset address of the beginning of the packet address for Function 01

= segment:offset address of the beginning of null terminated ASCII string specifying the file to be printed for Function 02

Function 00H get status

01H submit file for printing to print queue

02H remove file from print queue

03H cancel all files from print queue

04H hold print jobs to allow status to be read

05H cancel Function 04H, ie. cancel hold print

Returns with (a) If successful, CY = 0

In addition, for Function 00H

AL = 00H nut installed but can be installed

01H not installed und can not be installed

FFH printer is installed

and for Function 04H

DX = error count

DS:SI = segment:offset address of print queue

(*b*) If unsuccessful, CY = 1 and AX=error code

The error codes are--

01H invalid function code

02H file to be printed not found

03H path specified not found

04H too many files are simultaneously open

05H access is denied

08H queue is full

09H spooler is busy
0CH file name is too long
0FH invalid drive was specified

This function may be used to submit a file to the print spooler's queue for printing. It may also be used to remove a file from the print queue or for reading the status of the printer. The various options possible are chosen through the function code specified in the AL register.

For Function 0, the status of the printer is returned in AL as shown. Function 1 is used to submit a file for printing. For this DS:DX points to a 5-byte packet. The first byte specifies the level. (The function of this byte is not evident.) The remaining four bytes contain the segment and offset address pointing to a null terminated ASCII string (without * or ?) completely specifying the file to be printed. Function 2, on the other hand, can take the wild card characters * and ? in the file specification. Function 3 removes all files from the print queue including the one currently being printed. Function 4 freezes the print queue so that its status may be determined. It does not stop the printing but will prevent a file which has just finished getting printed from being removed from the print queue. It returns with DS:SI pointing to a data base describing the current contents of the print queue. This data base contains a 64-byte string for each entry in the queue and ends with an additional 0 byte. Each 64-bit string contains a null terminated ASCII string giving the name of a file in the queue. Function 5 merely unfreezes the print queue frozen by Function 4. This unfreezing will also get done if any of Functions 0-3 is issued following Function 4.

PROBLEMS

1. Repeat the EXPLORER program of Problems 1 and 2, Chapter 6 using the DOS services of INT 25H and INT 26H. Note that these require logical sector numbers to be specified rather than three-dimensional coordinate system of side, track and sector numbers required by the corresponding ROM-BIOS services. Allow the user to specify the drive (A, B, C, D) which should be examined by the EXPLORER program.
2. Write your version of the program SHOWPSP in the EXE format. This should display its own PSP as in the program shown in the example SHOWPSP.COM. Augment the display for every line by printing on the last 16 rows of the display the ASCII equivalents of each of the 16 bytes displayed on that line. Run this program with different parameters in the command tail and note its effect in the display. (In this case, the parameters will be dummy ones since SHOWPSP does not require any command tail.) Introduce redirection appropriately in the command line invoking SHOWPSP and check.
3. Write a program DUPL.EXE to duplicate a floppy disk using the DOS services of INT 25H and 26H. This program is required to do a blind vector by sector copy of the entire diskette and should appropriately prompt the user to exercise one of the following options-

copy a floppy in drive A to another floppy in drive A. In this case, the program should read sectors from the source diskette in drive A, ask the user to put in the target diskette und press any key to copy these sectors to the target diskette.

- copy a floppy in drive A to another in drive B.
- provide a verify option which may be exercised by the user to do a read-after-write test on the target floppy. The data read back in this test should be compared with the data written; in case of mismatches, the mismatched locations (logical sector numbers and the offset within that) should be displayed and the user should be given the option of trying to write once again or quitting.

Use a buffer large enough to read half of a DSDD diskette in one shot. Therefore two read-&-write cycles should be enough to complete the copy operation. The verify option, if exercised, should also be done within these two cycles.

4. We always recommend that you use the DOS services EXIT or KEEP of INT 21H in order to end a program. Though this rule should be strictly followed when writing a piece of software for public consumption, it may not be a bad idea to actually try out the other program terminations that are possible and verify their operation. Pick up any of the earlier programs that you might have written and try out different termination techniques to see if they work or not.

4

The DOS Functions of INT 21H

Most of the functions and services available in DOS are invoked through the INT 21H instruction. These provide a variety of services to user programs such as manipulation of files and directories, device I/O, reading the keyboard or writing to the display, loading and executing another program or loading overlays through EXEC, refined I/O control through the IOCTL function, manipulating the clock or terminating a program. Even if an alternative approach is provided through equivalent ROM-BIOS calls or even other INT n instructions, this is the preferred method of implementation. Using them ensures that the user's program will run on any computer (not just PCs or its compatibles) operating under DOS. This guarantee is not there if ROM-BIOS calls are used. The INT 21H services provide functions 00-63H some of which are reserved by DOS and are not user-accessible. Appendix I gives a list of the DOS functions available through the INT 21H services.

The typical way of invoking the INT 21H functions is to load the AH register with the number (in binary) of the function to be invoked and other registers as specified for the particular function in question. The instruction INT 21H is now executed to do the job that the function is required to do, Other procedures do exist of calling these functions but are rather arcane and should not be used. Some of these are—

load function no. in AH and other registers as appropriate and execute a long call to PSP:0050H for DOS 2.0 and above

for functions 00-24H, load the function no. in CL and other registers as appropriate and execute an Intrasegment call to PSP:0005H. This method destroys register AX.

Except for the EXEC function provided by Function 4BH, the Function 59H and the DOS 2.25-specific Function 63H, all other DOS functions provided through INT 21H preserve all registers across the function calls other than those which are used to return the result. The success or failure codes of a function are typically indicated by the Carry flag (CY) and/or the AL register on return. More specific error codes may be returned by some functions through the AX register. The reader should examine the details of the function for specific effects.

We give below, in sequence, the functions available through INT 21H. The reader is requested to read this carefully before actually using any of them.

Function 00H Terminate Program

Call with AH = 00H

CS = segment address of the PSP

Returns nothing.

This function is *absolutely identical in effect to the INT 20H instruction*. This was the typical way to end .COM programs. It should not be used with .EXE programs since these may use FAR procedures. Terminating with Function 00H, INT 21H in these procedures is not valid since CS may be different from the PSP's segment address. This interrupt terminates the child program, restores the vectors for the termination handler, the ^C handler and the critical error handler to their original values in the parent program and returns control to the parent program. This does not always close files which are opened in the child program. Such files should be explicitly closed. The parent program could be COMMAND.COM, the user's shell or any other program which 'spawned' the child program through the EXEC call (Function 4BH, INT 21H). If a batch file is in progress, control is passed to the next line of the batch file. Note that if return is made to COMMAND.COM, its resident portion may have to reload its transient part, in case the latter is corrupted or has been overwritten. *This method of program termination is not recommended.*

Function 01H Input Character from Standard Input Device and echo to Standard Output Device

Call with AH= 01H

Returns with AL= 8-bit ASCII code of input character

This function waits until a character is available for reading. If no redirection has been done, it waits until a key is pressed on the keyboard, displays the corresponding ASCII character on the display and returns with the 8-bit ASCII code tor the character in AL; with I/O redirection, the input and the echo output are done with the devices to which the redirection has been done. The wait could be a disadvantage since other instructions cannot be done during this wait-time. For keys with extended ASCII codes (e.g. F1-F10). the value returned in AL is 00H. This function should then be called again for the extended code (e.g.3BH-44H for keys Fl-FI0, respectively). If the input is the ^ C character, INT 23H is executed. This ^ C handler routine will usually terminate the on-going program.

Example: To read and echo keyboard (assuming no redirection)

```
mov ah, 01 h
int 21 h                    ; read keyboard
```

```
          cmp al,00
          jz again                     ; read again for extended code
             mov ah, 0ffh              for normal keys AH — FFH and
             jmp exit                  ; and ASCII code in AL
again:    mov ah, 01h ; read again
             int 21h                   ; for extended codes AH = 00H
             mov ah, 00H               ; and extended code in AL
exit:     nop ;                        exit from keyboard read
```

Function 02H Display Character to Standard Output Device

Call with AH = 02H

DL = 8-bit ASCII code of character to be displayed

Returns nothing

The character whose 8-bit ASCII code is given in DL is displayed on the screen; in case of redirection, the character is sent for display to the device to which the standard display device has been redirected. If ^C is detected after the character is output, then the ^C handler routine, INT 23H, is executed.

Example: to write $ on screen

```
mov dl, '$'
mov al,02h
int 21h
```

Function 03H Input Character from Standard Auxiliary Device (i.e. Serial Port COM 1, if not Redirected)

Call with AH = O3H

Returns with AL = 8-bit ASCII code of input character

The standard auxiliary device is the serial port COM1, unless it has been redirected. This redirection may be done by the MODE command of DOS. The default setting of COM1 is 2400bps, no parity, 1 stop bit and 8 bits/character. This can also be changed through the MODE COM1 command, the appropriate ROM BIOS interrupt (Function 00H, INT 14H) or by directly reprogramming the serial device INS 8250. The input in this mode from COM1 is unbuffered and data may be lost if it is coming too fast. This and other I/O errors (i.e. parity etc.) are not reported by this function call. For this function, an INT 23H is executed whenever ^C is detected. Instead of using this function, the user will probably do better to use Function 02H, INT 14H of the ROM-BIOS It will probably be even more advantageous to read the data and error status of the serial port COM1 directly through one's program. The advantages offered by this latter approach are greater speed and flexibility in reading and controlling COM1.

Function 04H Output Character to Standard Auxiliary Device (i.e. Serial Port COM1, Unless Redirected)

Call with AH = 04H DL = 8-bit ASCII code of character to be output

Returns nothing

This outputs on the standard auxiliary device, AUX, the character whose ASCII code is in DL. If ^C is detected, DOS executes the INT 23H instruction to execute the ^C handler. The default options mentioned for Function 03H are also applicable here. This function is slow and does not report the device status. In case the output device is busy, the function waits until it is free and then outputs the byte. This could be a disadvantage since other instructions cannot be done during this wait-time. It may be more advantageous to use Function 01H, INT 14H of the ROM-BIOS from considerations of speed and status reporting. For even higher speeds and greater flexibility of operation, direct control of COM 1 is recommended.

Example: To read from standard auxiliary device and echo the dala back to it.

```
mov ah, 3h
int 21h
mov dl, al
mov ah, 4
int 21h
```

Function O5H Print Character on the Standard List Device (i.e. First Parallel Port LPT1, Unless Redirected)

Call with AH = O5H DL = 8-bit ASCII code of character to be printed

Returns nothing

This prints on the printer LPT1 (unless the standard list device has been redirected) the character whose 8-bit ASCII code is given in DL. As before, this incorporates ^C detection by executing INT 23H if ^C is detected. If the printer is busy, the function waits until it becomes free and can accept the character. The status of the printer cannot be polled which may be a distinct disadvantage.

Function 06H Direct Character I/O with Console, (i.e. Input from Standard Input Device or Output to Standard Output Device. I/O May be Redirected)

Call with AH = 06H

DL = 00-FEH ASCII code of character to output

FFH input character and put it in AL

Returns with —

(a) For output operation, nothing is returned

(b) For input operation,

(*i*) if character is available, Zero Flag = 0 and AL = 8-bit ASCII code

(II) if no character available, Zero Flag = 1

For input of characters with extended ASCII codes, this function must be called twice. The first time it returns 00, indicating an extended ASCII character whose actual code is obtained the second time this call is issued.

This does not incorporate ^C detection (i.e. raw mode of operation). If the standard devices are redirected, the direct I/O provided by this function will be done with the devices to which I/O has been redirected.

Function 07H Input Character from Standard Input Device Without Echoing it and Without Checking for ^C

Call with AH = 07H

Returns withAL = 8-bit ASCII code of input character

This function waits' until a character is available for reading. If no redirection has been done, it waits until a key is pressed on the keyboard and returns with the 8-bit ASCII code for the character in AL; with I/O redirection, input, is done from the device to which the redirection has been done. The wait could be a disadvantage since other instructions cannot be done during this wait-time. For keys with extended ASCII codes (e.g. F1-F10), the value returned in AL is 00H. This function should then be called again for the extended code (e.g. 3BH-44H for keys F1-F10, respectively). ^C is not checked for during this function call.

Example: To read and echo keyboard to display (assuming no redirection)

```
mov ah, 07h
int 21 h ;          read keyboard
mov dl, al
mov ah, 06h
int 21h ;           and output to display
```

Function O8H Input Character from Standard Input Device Without Echoing it but with Checking for ^C

Call with AH = O8H

Returns withAL = 8-bit ASCII code of input character

This function waits until a character is available for reading. If no redirection has been done, it waits until a key is pressed on the keyboard and returns with the 8-bit ASCII code for the character in AL; with I/O redirection, input is done from the device to which the redirection has been done. the wait could be a disadvantage since other instructions cannot be done during this wait time. For keys with extended ASCII codes (e.g. Fl-F10), the value returned in AL is 00H. This function should then be called again for the extended code (e.g. 3BH-44H for keys Fl-F10, respectively). *If ^C is pressed, the INT 23H instruction is executed to call the ^C handler routine; this is its only difference with Function 07H*

Example: To read and echo keyboard to display (assuming no redirection)

```
mov ah, 08h
int 2In                    ; read keyboard
mov dl.al
mov ah, 06h
int 21h ;                  , and output to display
```

Function 09H Output a String of ASCII Characters to the Standard Output Device (ie. the Display, Unless Redirected)

Call with AH = 09H

DS:DX = segment:offset address of string to be displayed, the string should terminate with an extra '$' (ASCII code 24H)

Returns nothing

Given a string of ASCII characters terminating with a $, this function prints the string on the standard output device if the starting address of the string is specified in DS and DX in terms of its segment and offset addresses. The terminating $ is not primed. Any ASCII character other than $ can be printed by specifying its ASCII code as part of the string. The output may be redirected by redirecting the standard output device.

Example: To print 'Hello!' on the screen (no redirection)

```
mov ax, seg displ
mov ds, ax
mov dx, offset displ
 mov ah, 09h
int 21h
displ db 'Hello !','$'
```

Function OAH Inputs a String of Characters Upto und Including the Terminating Carriage Return Character <cr> from the Standard Input Device und Places them in a Designated Buffer

Call with AH = OAH

DS:DX = segment:offset address of beginning of buffer. 'Initialize [DS:DX], i.e. first byte of buffer, to the maximum number of characters that may be input to this buffer

Returns with-

(a) [DS:DX 4- 1], i.e. the second byte of the buffer, indicates the number of characters actually input, not counting the terminating <cr> (character 0DH)

(b) The input string, including the terminating <cr>, is stored from location [DS:DX + 2], ie. the third byte of the buffer, onwards.

This inputs a string from the standard input device upto the terminating <cr> in a user specified buffer. The input device may be redirected from the standard keyboard. If ^C is seen, the INT *23H instruction is executed.* The maximum number of characters to be accepted is specified us the first byte of the buffer and DOS in turn reports the actual number of characters received before the terminating <cr>. The buffer may be filled to one less than the maximum number of input characters specified; subsequent characters input are ignored und the bell is sounded till the terminating <cr> which ends the input sequence is received.

If no redirection has been done, this is a very powerful and useful function to get strings from the keyboard. All of the regular DOS editing keys may be used to edit the string as it is being entered. Keys with extended ASCII codes will contribute two bytes to the buffer, the first being 00h and the second the extended code.

Example: To read a string of 80 characters from keyboard (no redirection)

```
        :
        mov ax, seg buff
        mov ds, ax
        mov dx, offset buff
        mov ah, Oah
        int 21h
        :
buff    db 51h
        db 00h
        db 81 dup(?)
```

Function OBH Get Character "Available/Not Available" Status of the Standard Input Device (ie. Keyboard if No Redirection)

Call with AH = 0BH

Returns withAL = 00 if no character available

FF if character is waiting

If character has been input but has not yet been read, it reports "character waiting" until the character is actually read. *Detection of ^C will cause INT 23H to be executed.* This function may be used to find if a character is waiting before calling Function 01 H, 07H or 08H to ensure that a character is indeed available for reading.

Example: To read a character from keyboard only if one is available (no redirection) :

```
mov ah, 0bh        ; check status
int 21h
cmp al, 00
je no_char         ; go to no_char if no character
mov ah, 01 h       ; else read character and put in
int 21 h           ; register AL
```

Function 0CH Clear Buffer of Standard Input Device and then Invoke any of Functions 01 H, 06H, 07H, 08H or 0AH

Call with	AH	=	0CH
	AL	=	function no. to be invoked for input, one of 01 H, 06H, 07H, 08H or 0AH
	If AL	=	0AH, DS:DX must be specified as segment: offset of the input buffer and [DS:DX + 1] with maximum no. of characters that may be input

Returns with

If functions 01H, 06H, 07H or 08H invoked, then AL=8-bit ASCII code of character input If function 0AH invoked, then

(a) [DS:DX + 1], i.e. the second byte of the buffer, indicates the number of characters actually input, not counting the terminating <cr> (character 0DH)

(b) The input string, including the terminating <cr>, is stored from location [DS:DX 2], ie. the third byte of the buffer, onwards.

This function discards any keyboard character which might have been pressed before it was called; only characters entered after this function is called will be returned.

Function ODH Resets Disk in Drive A and Flushes all File Buffers

Call with AH = 0DH

Returns nothing

This resets the disk in drive A and flushes all the internal file buffers of DOS. This flushing implies that data stored in the buffers associated with the files opened on drive A are written back to the disk and the buffers are cleared. This, however, does not automatically close the files or update their directory entries and hence the data recorded may still be lost. For proper usage, close all files opened on the disk before issuing this function call. *This function does not change the default drive.*

Function OEH Selects Current Drive (i.e. Default Drive) and Reports the Number of Logical Drives in the System

Call with AH = OEH

DL = drive code (eg. 00 for A, 01 for B etc.)

Returns with AL = total no. of logical drives in the system (logical drives include floppy drives, RAM disks and hard disks. A hard disk with partitions may constitute two or more logical drives)

Note that DOS will report two drives for single-drive systems.

Function 0FH Open File Using FCB for Subsequent Read/ Write

Call with AH = 0FH

DS:DX = segment:offset address of FCB

Returns with

(a) If file not found, AL = FFH

(b) It file found, AL = 00H and appropriate FCB fields properly initialized by DOS.

Function 10H Close File using FCB

Updates directory entries appropriately for files which have been modified

Call with AH = 10H

DS:DX = segment :offset address of FCB

Returns with

(a) If file not found, AL = FFH

(b) If file found, AL = OQH and directory entry for file is suitably updated.

Function 11H Using FCB, Search for First Match for File in Current Directory

Wild card designators allowed in file name

Call with AH = 11H

DS:DX = segmentioffset address of FCB

Returns with

(a) If file not found, AL=FFH

(b) If file found, AL = 00H ; i.e. first file with a matching file name found in the current directory of designated drive.

Subsequent matches are found by repeated application of Function 12H.

Function 12H Using FCB, Search for Next Match for File with Matching Name

This can be used only if Function 11H has been previously successful for this file name.

Wild card designators allowed in file name

Call with AH = 12H
DS:DX = segment:offset address of FCB

Returns with

(a) If file not found, AL = FFH ; no more matching file names in the current directory.

(b) If file found, AL = 00H ; i.e. next file with a matching file name found in the current directory of designated drive.

Subsequent matches are found by repeated application of Function I2H.

Function I3H Using FCB, Delete File from Current Directory

Wild card designators allowed in file name. All files in the current directory with matching file names are deleted.

Call with AH = 13H
DS:DX = segment :offset address of FCB

Returns with

(a) If file not found, AL = FFH i.e. no matching files found or that all the ones found were read-only and could not be deleted.

(b) If file found, AL = 00H i.e. all files with matching names in current directory were deleted. (This does not delete read-only files.)

Function 14H Using FCB, Head next Sequential Record from File

File pointer is suitably incremented.

Call with AH = 14H
DS:DX = segment:offset address of FCB
Return with AL = 00 successful read
01 end of file has been reached
02 segment wrap in DTA (error!)
03 partial record successfully read at end of file

Function 1511 Using FCB, Write next Sequential Record to File

File pointer is suitably incremented.

Call with AH = 15H
DS:DX = segment: offset address of FCB
Return withAL = 00 successful write
01 disk is full
02 segment wrap in DTA (error!)

Function 16H Using FCB, Create New File (if it does not already exist) or Truncate Existing File to Zero Length

Call with AH = 16H
DS:DX = segment:offset address of FCB
Return with AL = 00 if operation successful
FFH if operation unsuccessful, i.e. no space in current directory

---

Function 17H Using Special FCB, Rename Files with Matching File Names in the Current Directory of Specified Drive

Wild card designators may be used.

Call with AH = 17H
DS:DX = segment:offset address of special FCB
The special FCB has a second file name from offset 0011H.
Return with AL = 00 if file(s) successfully renamed
FFH if operation unsuccessful, i.e. no matching file name or if new name matched the old name

---

Function 18H Reserved

Function 19H Get Drive Code of Default Drive

Call with AH = 19H
Returns with AL= drive code of default drive (0 for A, 1 for B, 2 for C etc.)

Function IAH Set Disk Transfer Area (DTA) Address

Call with AH = IAH
DS:DX = segment:offset address of the memory area lo be used as the DTA

Returns nothing

The default 128-byte DTA is the location from PSP:0080H onwards. This is used unless Function IAH sets up another DTA. This function must be used before the file-search functions 11H, 12H (FCB) or 4EH. 4FH (handle) are actually called.

Example: see program EDIR.COM.

Function 1BH Get Information about the Default Drive

Call with AH = 1BH

Returns with DS:BX = segment :offset address of byte containing the media ID of the FAT may not point into the actual FAT

AL = no. of sectors per cluster (cluster size)

CX = number of bytes in a sector

DX = number of clusters in default drive

Function 1CH Get Information about the Specified Drive

Call with AH = 1CH

DL = drive code (e.g. 0 for default, 1 for A, etc.)

Returns with DS:BX = segment:offset address of byte containing the media ID of the FAT may not point into the actual FAT

AL = no. of sectors per cluster (cluster size)

CX = number of bytes in a sector

DX = number of clusters in specified drive

Functions 1DH, 1EH, 1FH, 20H Reserved

Function 21H Using FCB, Read Random Record from File

Call with AH = 21H

DS:DX = segment:offset address of previously opened FCB

Return with AL = 00 successful read

01 end of file has been reached

02 segment wrap in DTA (error)

03 partial record successfully read at end of file

This read function reads on the basis of the random record field and the record size field of the FCB. The record of the specified size is read from the record position specified.

Function 22H Using FCB, Write into Random Record of File

Call with AH = 22H

DS:DX = segment: offset address of previously opened FCB

Return with AL = 00 successful write operation

01 disk full (error!)

02 segment wrap in DTA (error!)

This provides the random write function corresponding to the random read provided by its counterpart Function 21H, INT 21 H.

Function 23H Using FCB, Get the Size of the File in Terms of the Number of Records

The record size of field in the FCB must be specified

File size reported in bytes if record size is 1.

Call with AH = 23H

DS:DX = segment:offset address of unopened FCB

Return with—

(*a*) AL = 00 if matching file found in the current directory. The record size is reported in FCB's random record field at offset 0021H.

(*b*) AL = FFH if no matching file found.

Function 24H Using FCB, Set the Random Record Field in the FCB Previously Opened

Call with AH = 24H

DS:DX = segment; offset address of previously opened FCB

Returns with the random record field in the FC'B filled to correspond with the current sequential block and record fields of we FCB *Registers are not affected at all.*

This facilitates switching from sequential to random I/O lor a previously opened file.

Function 25H Set Interrupt Vector

Call with AH = 25H

AL = Interrupt Number

DS:DX = segment :offset address of new interrupt handler routine

Return Nothing

This is the recommended method of changing the interrupt vector for any of the CPU's interrupts. Directly writing into the RAM locations containing the corresponding vector is not recommended. The typical procedure is to first read the current vector for the interrupt through Function 35H and save it before actually changing the vector. Then, once the application requirements are over, the vector should be restored to its original value through a second call to Function 25H. This saving and restoration need not be done for the interrupts INT 22H, INT 23H, and INT 24H since DOS will itself restore their values from the program's PSP on program termination.

Example: Change COMl's interrupt (Type 0CH) vector to point to new routine new_com

```
mov ax, 350ch                 ; use Function 35 to get old vector
int 21h                       ; and save it in old_com_seg and
mov old_com_seg, es           ; old_com_oft for later use
mov old_com_off, bx
mov ax, seg new-com
mov ds, ax
mov dx, offset new-corn
mov ax, 250ch                 ; set new interrupt vector to point
int 21H                       ; to new-com
```

After the requirement for the changed vector is over, it should be restored to its original value.

```
mov ax, old_com_seg           ; restore vector from values
move ds, ax                   ; stored previously
mov dx.old-com_off
mov ax, 250ch
int 21h
:
:

old_com_seg dw 0
old_com_off dw 0
```

Function 26H Create a New Copy of Program's PSP

Call with AH = 26H

DX = segment address of memory to store new copy of the PSP

Returns nothing

This creates a new copy of the program's PSP at the specified memory address so that a new subprogram or overlay may be loaded. The segment paragraph of the new program is specified in DX. The current PSP is copied in locations at offset 00-FFH of the segment and this new copy is updated with the new memory and interrupt vector information. This docs not load the new program or gel it to execute. *This function is obsolete in DOS versions 2.0 and above which can do this job much better with the EXEC function, Function 4BH. INT 21H.*

Function 27H Using FCB, read one or more Records from File starting from a Random File Location.

The starting random record no. is taken from the previously opened FCB. To prevent segment wrap around the DTA set by Function IAH should be large enough.

This is similar to Function 21 H, except that more than one record may be read

Call with	AH	=	27H
	CX	=	number of record to be read
	DS:DX	=	segment: offset address of previously opened FCB
Return with	AL	=	00 successful read
			01 end of file has been reached
			02 segment wrap in DTA (error!)
			03 partial record successfully read at end of file
	CX	=	the number of records actually read

Function 28H Using FCB, Write one or more Record to File Starting from a Random File Location.

The starting random record no. is taken from the previously opened FCB.

Call with	AH	=	28H
	CX	=	number of records to be written
	DS:DX	=	segment:offset address of previously opened FCB
Return with	AL	=	00 successful write operation
			01 disk full (error!)
			02 segment wrap in DTA (error!)
	CX	=	number of records actually written

This provides the random write function corresponding to the random read provided by its counterpart Function 27H, INT 21H. Note that unlike Function 22H, one or more records may be written with this function.

Function 29H Purse File Name into the Field of an Unopened FCB

Call with AH = 29H

DS:SI = segment:offset address of null-terminated ASCH string specifying file name File must be in current directory of default or specified drive. This does not support a path name in the file specification.

ES:DI = segment:offset address of unopened FCB

AL — AL register bits 0-3 as follows

AL(0) 1 for ignoring leading separators

0 otherwise

separators are :.; = + /"[ ] and<tab>

AL(I) 1 if drive ID of FCB to be modified only if ASCH string specifics drive 0 otherwise, drive ID modified regardless

AL(2) 1 if filename already in FCB to be modified only if filename specified in ASCH string

0 otherwise, filename modified regardless

AL(3) 1 if extension already in FCB to be modified only if extension specified in ASCH string

0 otherwise, extension modified regardless

Returns with AL = 00 no wildcard characters encountered

01 wildcard characters in file name

FFH invalid drive

ES:DI = segment:offset of modified (unopened) FCB

DS:Sl = segment: offset address of first position after the filename just parsed.

Function 2AH Get Current System Date (day of month, day of week, month, year)

Call with AH = 2AH

Returns with AL = day of the week (with Sunday as 0)

DL = day of the month (1,2. ....31)

DH = month (1,2, ...12: Jan is 1)

CX = year (1980 through to 2099)

Function 2BH Set current system date (day of month, day of week, month, year)

Call with AH = 2BH

DL = day of the month (1, 2, ...31)

DH = month (1,2. .....12; Jan is 1)
CX = year (1980 through to 2099)

Returns with

(a) AL = 00 if date was successfully set

(b) AL = FFH if date specified was wrong and could not be set

---

Function 2CH Get current system time (hours, minutes, seconds, and seconds/100)

Call with All = 2CH

Returns with CH= hour (0, 1, 2, ..., 23)
CL = minutes (0, I, 2. ...... 59)
DH = second (0, 1, 2, ... 59)
DL = second/100 (0, 1, 2, ... 99)

Function 2DH Set Current System Time (hours, minutes, seconds und seconds/100)

Call with AH = 2DH
CH = hour (0, 1,2, ...23)
CL = minutes (0, 1, 2, ..., 59)
DH = seconds (0, 1, 2, ... 59)
DL = seconds/100 (0, 1,2, ... 99)

Returns with

(a) AL = 00 if time was successfully set

(b) AL = FFH if time specified was wrong and could not be set

---

Function 2EH Turn on/off Automatic Read-after-Write Flag for Disk Operations

Call with AH = 2EH
AL = 00H to turn off flag
01H to turn on flag
DL = 00H for DOS versions 1 and 2

Returns nothing

If the automatic read-after-write (i.e. verify) flag is ON, then data integrity of disk storage is increased. Then, after every write operation, DOS reads back the data written and compares the data read with the data written to verify its correctness. This is normally not required and the verify flag should be kept OFF. Keeping the verify flag ON slows down write operations on disks. The reader can find the current state of this flag by means of Function 54H.

Function 2FH Returns the Address of the DTA Currently in Use

Useful for FCB - type accesses

Call with AH = 2FH

Returns with ES:BX = segment:offset of the DTA currently used

Note that the default DTA is a 128-byte area starting from offset 0080H of the program's PSP. However, this default setting can be changed through Function IAH. DTAs are normally required for FCB-type file accesses. Handle-type calls need them only for the directory search operations of Functions 4EH and 4FH.

Function 30H Get the Current DOS Version Number

Call with AH = 30H

Returns with AL = major version no. (ie. 3 for DOS 3.1.)

AH = minor version no. units of 0.01 (ie. 0AH for DOS 3.1)

Function 31H Terminate but stay resident (KEEP)

Call with AH = 31H

AL = return code

DX = memory size to be reserved in paragraphs (16 byte units)

Returns nothing

This is an improved version of the service provided through the DOS interrupt INT 27H and should be the one used to terminate a child program. On termination, some of the memory allocated to the child program may be kept resident (i.e. not released). The number of paragraphs of memory to be retained in this fashion should be specified directly in DX. Starling from the beginning of the child program's memory allocation, the number of paragraphs specified through DX is retained and the rest released to the TPA. This function is meant to release only the memory that was initially loaded. Subsequent modifications, if any made to the memory allocation through Functions 48H-4AH are not released through this function.

The child program can pass a return code, specified in AL, to the parent. This return code should be chosen such that it may indicate to the parent the completion status (eg. successful/ unsuccessful) of the child. The parent program may find the return code passed by the child through Function 4DH, INT 21H. These return codes may also be tested in batch files through commands which test the ERRORLEVEL.

Apart from the fact that it provides a return code and may he used to retain more than 64KB of memory, this function of INT 21H is similar to the INT 27H instruction. The comments made in describing the latter are also applicable here.

Example: Terminate with return code of 00 but keep the first 32 KB of the program resident and release the rest

```
mov dx, 0800h
mov ax. 3100h
int 21h
```

Function 32H RESERVED

Function 33H Get/Set^C (or ^Break) flag

Call with	AH	=	33H
	AL	=	00H to get the status of the ^C flag
			01H to set the status of the ^C flag
For	AL	=	01, call with—
	DL	=	00 to turn ^C flag OFF
			01 to turn ^C flag ON
Returns with	DL	=	00 if ^C flag is OFF
			01 if ^C flag is ON

If the ^C flag is ON, DOS checks for ^C from the keyboard after any DOS operation. Otherwise, when the ^C flag is OFF, ^C is checked for only in those DOS functions which specifically incorporate this checking (typically some of the I/O operations).

Functions 35H Get Interrupt Vector

Call with	AH	=	35H
	AL	=	Interrupt Number
Returns with	ES:BX	=	segment:offset address of the current interrupt handler routine for the interrupt number specified (in AL)

This function should be used to get the current address of the interrupt handler routine corresponding to a particular interrupt. Rather than reading the vector directly from the vector table, this is the recommended method for getting the current vector. For applications which change the interrupt vector, the old value of the vector should be obtained through this function and saved before the new vector is put in through Function 25H. This is required so that, when the needs of that application are over the old vector may be restored from these saved values.

Example: See example given for Function 25H, INT 21H

Function 36H Get Disk's Free Space

Information provided regarding the space status of the disk in the specified drive. Among other things, this allows the space remaining on the disk to be calculated.

Call with AH = 36H

DL = drive code (eg. 0 for default, 1 for A, etc.)

Returns with—

(*a*) If valid drive specified—

AX = no. of sectors per cluster (cluster size)

BX = no. of clusters free on the disk

CX = number of bytes in a sector

DX = number of clusters in default drive

(b) If drive specified was not valid-AX = OFFFFH

This function is similar to that provided by Functions 1BH and I CH, except for the additional information provided in BX on the number of clusters on the disk which are still free. The number of free sectors will then be given by BX*AX and the number of free bytes of storage by BX*AX*CX.

Example: to get the number of free sectors in disk in drive B

```
mov ah, 36h
mov dl, 03h
int 21h
cmp ax, Offffh                    ; check for valid drive
je in_valid
mul bx                            ; no. of free sectors in AX
```

Function 37H RESERVED

Function 38H Get/Set country code of the system See Tech. Ref. Manual

Function 39H Create subdirectory using specified drive and path,

Call with AH = 39H

DS:DX = egment:offset address of a null-terminated ASCH string specifying the path for the subdirectory to be created (see example)

Returns with—

(a) If function succeeds, CY = 0

(b) If function fails. CY = 1

and AX = 3 if path not found

5 if access denied

AX gives the error code when the function fails.

This function creates the subdirectory specified by the path string if successful. It fails if—

(a) the parent directory is the root directory and it is full

(b) one or more elements specified in the path does not exist

(c) a subdirectory with the same name and path already exists. AX is reported as 3 for (b) and 5 for (a) and (c)

Example: Create subdirectory BOOK in subdirectory USER of the root directory in drive C

```
        mov ax, seg subdir
        mov ds, ax
        mov dx, offset subdir
        mov ah, 39h
        int 21h
        jc no-subdir
        :
        :
        :
        :
subdir  db      'C:\USER\BOOK'.
```

Function 3AH Delete Subdirectory Using Specified Drive and Path

Call with AH = 3AH

DS:DX = segment:offset address of a null-terminated ASCH string specifying the path for the subdirectory to be deleted (see example)

Returns with—

(a) If function succeeds, CY = 0

(b) If function fails, CY = 1

and AX = 3 Path not found

5 if access denied

16 if current directory

AX gives the error code when the function fails.

This function will delete the subdirectory specified in the ASCH string. It fails if—

(a) the subdirectory is not empty (i.e. still has files etc.)

(b) one or more elements of the path name does not exist

(c) the subdirectory specified is the current directory

Example: Delete subdirectory BOOK in subdirectory user of the root directory in drive C

```
mov ax, seg subdir
```

```
        mov ds, ax
        mov dx, offset subdir
        mov ah. 3ah
        int 21h
        jc no_subdir
        :
        :
        :
        :
subdir  db 'C:\USER \ BOOK',0
```

Function 3BH Change Current Directory

Call with AH = 3BH

DS:DX = segment:offset address of a null-terminated ASCH string specifying the path for the (sub) directory to be set as the current directory (see example)

Returns with—

(a) If function succeeds, CY = 0

(b) If function fails, CY = 1

and AX = 3 if path not found

AX gives the error code when the function fails.

This function will set the current directory to that specified in the ASCH string. It tails if one or more elements of the path name does not exist. The current directory may be found through Function 47H before Function 3BH is applied. This may be used to restore the old value of the current directory later.

Example: Set subdirectory BOOK in subdirectory USER of the root directory in drive C as the current directory. The old value of the current directory is saved and restored later.

```
mov ah.47h
mov d l,03h
mov si,.scg scratch
mov ds, si
mov si, offset scratch
int 21h
                        ; save current directory

mov ax, seg subdir
```

```
mov ds, ax
mov dx. offset subdir
mov ah, 3bh
int 21h                         ; change current directory
jc no_subdir
:
:
mov ax. seg scratch
mov ds, ax
mov dx, offset scratch
mov ah, 3bh
int 21h                         ; restore old directory
:
:
subdir db 'C:\USER\BOOK', 0
scratch db 64 dup (0)
```

Function 3CH Handle Type Call to Create New File or Truncate Old One

The file is opened if the function succeeds and a file handle is provided for further access.

Call with AH = 3CH

CX = attribute of file

00H for normal   01H for read-only

02H for hidden   04H for system

DS:DX = segment: offset address of null-terminated ASCH string specifying the file Returns with—

(*a*) If function succeds, CY = 0

and AX = file handle

(*b*) If function fails, CY = 1

and AX = 3 if path not found

4 if no handle available

5 access denied

AX indicates the error code in case of failure. Error code 5 indicates that either the directory (root, in this case) is full, or the file exists and has the read-only attribute.

This function is an example of a handle type file access mechanism. The complete file specification must be given in the specifying ASCH string either in the designated or default directory of the designated or default drive. The function fails if one or more elements of the path specification does not exist, if the file is to be created in the root directory and that directory is full, if the file already exists and has its read-only attribute set or if the current process has so many files/ devices open that DOS cannot give a handle for this file.

When successful, this function creates a new file as specified in the ASCH string (if it does not already exist), opens it and assigns it a file handle. If the specified file already exists, it is truncated to zero length (i.e. its previous contents are discarded) and opened and a file handle is assigned for further access to that file.

The file created with this function is given the read/write attribute. This can subsequently be changed through Function 43H.

Example: In subdirectory USER of drive C, create/'truncate to zero length' and open file TEST.ASM with normal attributes.

```
                mov ax, seg file-name
                mov ds, ax
                mov dx, offset file-name
                mov ah, 3ch
                xor cx, ex
                int 21h
                jc no-file
                mov handle, ax ;        save file-handle
                :
                :
                no-file:............
                :
                :
file-name       db'c:\user\test.asm', 0
handle          dw 0
```

Function 3DH Handle type call to open specified file

Call with AH = 3DH

DS:DX = segment:offset address of null-terminated ASCII string specifying the file

AL = see below for bits AL7-ALO

AL2-ALO =. access mode

000 if read only access to file

001 if write only access to file

010 if both read or write access to file

This specification of AL2-ALO is identical for both DOS 2 and 3. For DOS 2, other bits of AL (ie. AL7-AL3) may be set to 0. For DOS 3, the other bits of AL are specified as follows—

AL7 = inheritance flag

0 if child programs of current program will inherit the file

1 if file is to be kept private to the current program (not to be inherited)

AL6-AL4 = sharing mode

000 compatibility mode

001 deny read/write access mode

010 deny write access mode

011 deny read access mode

100 full access mode

AL3 = 0

Returns with—

(a) If function succeeds, CT = 0
and AX = File handle

(b) If function fails, CY = 1
and AX = 01H if file sharing not loaded
02H if file not found
03H if path not found or file does not exist
04H if handle not available
O5H if access denied
0CH invalid access code

This is the most general way to open files. To use it in its simplest fashion, ignore bits AL7-AL3 (set them as 0s) and call the function with the access mode specified in AL2-AL0; normally, this access mode will be set as read/write, i.e. AL2-ALO = 010. The more complicated usage of this call (with bits AL7-AI3 properly specified) is valid only with DOS version 3 and requires file sharing to be loaded through the SHARE command ol DOS. In typical usage these more complex access techniques are usually not needed and are not described further here.

This function will open any normal, system or hidden file with the specified name and will return a 16-bit file handle in AX which is to be used for further access to the file. The file will not be opened if any of the reasons for the error codes given above are satisfied. The read/write pointer of the opened file is set to zero pointing to the first byte of the file; its date and time stamp can now be accessed using Function 57H or its attribute may be read/set using Function 43H. In the sharing mode of DOS 3, the programs sharing the file get the same sharing and access restrictions for the file (ie. on inheritance) and, in case of sharing errors, the Critical Error Handler is invoked by DOS through INT 24H. It is worth noting that the typical DOS devices (eg. COM2, NUL etc.) may also be opened for .access with this function call.

Example : In subdirectory USER of drive C, open file TEST.ASM with for read/write access

```
          :
          :
          mov ax.seg file-name
          mov ds, ax
          mov dx. offset file-name
          mov ax, 3d02h
          int 21h
          jc no_file
          mov handle, ax          : save file-handle
          :
          :
no -file  :
          :
          :
file-name db'c:\user\test.asm', 0
handle    dw 0
```

Function 3EH Handle Type Call to Close file, Can Also be Used for Devices.

Call with AH = 3EH

BX = file handle (from previous open or create)

Returns with—

(a) If function succeeds, CY = 0 (ie. file closed and handle returned to DOS)
(b) If function fails, CY = 1
AX = 6 if handle not open or if it is invalid

This is the recommended way to close a file or device using its previously opened (or default from DOS) handle. The file buffers are flushed to the disk, the file is closed and its date and time stamps are appropriately modified if the file was modified. The file's entry into its directory is suitably modified and the handle is returned to DOS.

Example: In subdirectory USER of drive C, open file TEST.ASM with for read/ write access. Subsequently, close this file.

```
        :
        :
        mov ax,seg file-name
        mov ds. ax
        mov dx, offset file-name
        mov ax, 3d02h                   ; open file
        int 21h
        jc no_file
        mov handle, ax                  ; save file-handle
do whatever file access operations are required
        :
        :
        mov ah, 3eh                     ; close file
        mov bx, handle
        int 21h
        :
        :
file-name db'c:\user\test.asm'. 0
handle    dw 0
```

Function 3FH Handle Type Call to Read from File/Device

Call with AH = FH
BX = file handle (from previous open or create)
CX = no. of bytes to read (from present position of the associated file pointer)
DS:DX = segment:offset address of buffer area to store the data read from the file/ device

Returns with—

(*a*) If function succeeds, CY = 0

AX = actual no. of bytes read; AX will be different from the specified CX if—

(i) for a file, end of file has been reached,

(ii) for a character device in the cooked mode, a <cr> was encountered. The <cr> character is placed in the buffer.

(*b*) If function fails, CY = 1

and AX = 5 if access denied

6 if handle is invalid or is not open

AX contains the error code in case of failure.

This function reads the specified number of bytes from the file or device previously opened or created, whose handle is given in BX. The data read is transferred to the designated buffer.

For files, the file pointers are updated following a successful read; a subsequent read will read the sequentially next bytes in the file. Even if the function is successful, the count returned in AX may be different from the count specified in CX. This may happen if the end-of-file is reached; if AX = 00H, the file pointer was already at the end-of-file position when the read call was issued. For devices in the raw mode, this function will not check for ^C or carriage return <cr> Return from the function call will only happen when the requested number of bytes have been read. The calling program will have to wait till then. For devices in the cooked mode, the ^C handler will be called through INT 23H if a ^C is encountered in the data. This will usually terminate the input (and the program) and return control to DOS. If a <cr> is encountered, the input is terminated and the function returns control to the calling program. The input string, including the terminating <cr> is placed in the user's buffer.

Example: Read filename from keyboard, open it and transfer 1024 bytes from it to the designated buffer and close the file.

```
:
:
mov ax.seg file-name
mov ds. ax
mov dx.offset file_name
move ah, 3fh                  read filename from keyboard till <cr>
mov bx, 00                    : using std. handle for console
mov cx. 50h                   : put filename in 80-character buffer
int 21h
```

```
        mov bx, ax                      : put null termination on filename
        mov [file_name + bx_2], 00h     : for console, extra < If > goes
        mov ah.3ch                      : with the <cr >
        mov cx. 00h                     : open file
        int 21h
        mov bx, ax                      : store file handle in BX
        mov ax, seg buff                : read 1024 bytes from file to
        mov ds.ax                       :       buffer
        mov dx, offset buff
        mov cx, 0400h
        mov ah, 3fh
        int 21b
        mov ah, 3ech
        int 21h                         ; close file
        :
        :
        :
file_name db 50th dup (?)
buff      db 400h dup (0)
```

Function 40H Handle Type Call to Write to File/Device

Call with AH = 40H

BX = file handle (from previous open or create)

CX = no. of bytes to write (from present position of the associated file pointer)

DS:DX = segment:offset address of buffer area which has the data to be written

Returns with—

(*a*) If function succeeds. CY = 0

and AX = actual no. of bytes written; AX will be different from the specified CX if the disk's capacity has been reached

(*b*) If function fails, CY = 1

and AX = 5 if access denied

6 if handle is invalid or is not open

AX contains the error code in case of failure.

This function writes the specified number of bytes to the file or device previously opened or created, whose handle is given in BX. The data is transferred from the designated buffer to the file or device.

For files, the file pointers are updated following a successful write; a subsequent write will write into the sequentially next bytes in the file. Even if the function is successful, the count returned in AX may be different from the count specified in CX, if the disk gets full and cannot store all the bytes specified.

For devices in the raw mode, this function will not check for ^C at all. Return from the function call will only happen when the requested number of bytes have been read. The calling program will have to wait till then. For devices in the cooked mode, the ^C handler will be called through INT 23H if a ^C is encountered from the keyboard during character input. This will usually terminate the input (and the program) and return control to DOS.

Example: Read file name from keyboard, open it and transfer 1024 bytes from the designated buffer to it and close the file.

```
:
:
mov dx. seg file_name
mov ds. ax
mov dx, offsct file_name
mov ah, 3fh                  ; read filename from keyboard till <cr'.
mov bx, 00                   ; using std. handle for console
mov cx, 50h                  ; put filename in 80-character buffer
int 21h
mov bx, ax                   ; put null termination on filename
mov [fi]e_name + bx-2] 00h   ; for console, extra <If> goes
mov ah., 3ch                 ; with the <cr>
mov cx, 00h                  ; open file
int 21h
mov bx, ax                   ; store file handle in BX
mov ax, seg buff             ; write 1024 bytes from buffer to
mov ds, ax                   ; file
mov dx, offset buff
mov cx, 0400 h
mov ah, 40h
int 21h
mov ah, 3eh
```

```
          int 21 h                          ; close file
          :
          :
          :
file-name db 50th dup (?)
buff      db 400h dup (0)
```

Function 41H Handle Type Call to Delete Specified file

Call with AH = 41H

DS:DX = segment:offset address of a null-terminated ASCH string specifying the path and filename

Returns with—

(a) If function succeeds, CY = 0

(b) If function fails. CY = 1

and AX = 2 if file was not found
5 if access was denied

This deletes the file specified in the ASCH string in the designated or default directory of the default or designated disk. The complete file and path name must be specified; otherwise, the function fails. Wildcard characters and? cannot be specified in the filename. This function will not delete read-only files. To delete such a file, convert file to one with normal attributes using Function 43H; after this, the file may be deleted.

Example: Delete file BOOK in subdirectory USER of the root directory of drive C.

```
        mov ax, seg file
        mov ds, ax
        mov dx, offset file
        mov ah, 41 h
        int 21h
        jc error
        :
        :
file    db 'C:\USER\BOOK', 00
```

Function 42H Handle Type Call to Move file Pointer of a File Previously Opened

The pointer may be moved relative to its current value, the start-of-file or the end-of-file

Call with AH = 42H

AL = option code
00 positive offset from start-of file
01 positive/negative offset from current value
02 positive/negative offset from end-of- file
BX = file handle (from previous open or create)
CX:DX = MSB:LSB of byte offset by which to move pointer

Returns with—

(a) If function succeeds, CY = 0
and DX:AX = MSB:LSB of the new pointer location

The new pointer location specified in DX:AX is the absolute offset from the start-of-file.

(*b*) If function fails, CY = 1
and AX = 1 invalid option code
6 invalid or unopened handle

This function is used to move the file pointer to a new location using either of options 0, 1 or 2. Subsequent file access will be from this new location. An interesting use of this function is to get the file size as shown by the following example.

Example: get the file size using option 2 of Function 42h

```
        xor cx,cx                    ; CX = 0
        xor, dx, dx                  ; DX = 0
        mov bx, handle
; "handle" assumed to have the file handle from previous open or
; create
        mov ax, 4202h                ; option 2 of Function 42H
        int 21h
; MSB of file size in DX, LSB in AX
```

Function 43H Handle type call to get/set the attributes of the specified file

Call with AH = 43H
AL = 00 to get the attributes of the file
01 to set new attribute of the file
DS:DX = segment:offset address of a null-terminated ASCH string specifying the path and filename
If AL = 01, ie. the file attributes are to be changed, the new attributes are

specified in CX in the same format as the directory entry for this given in Sec.
For CX, bit 5 = 1 to set archive attribute
bit 2 = 1 to set system attribute
bit 1 = 1 to set hidden attribute
and bit 0 = 1 to set read-only attribute

Returns with—

(*a*) If function succeeds, CY = 0
For AL = 00, CX = attribute of file in the same format as shown above
For AL = 01, the desired attributes are set

(b) If function fails, CY = I
and AX = 1 if invalid AL option
2 if file was not found
3 if file docs not exist or path not found
5 if access was denied

This function may be used to read the current attributes of a file as well as to change the file attributes. The attributes that may be read or set are archive, system, hidden and read-only. The file and its path must be completely specified by a null terminated ASCH string pointed by DS and DX. Wildcard characters * and ? are not allowed in the file name. This function cannot be used to set/reset the volume or subdirectory bits of the attribute byte of a directory entry.

Example: Delete a user-specified file. If file is read-only or system, reset these attributes and then delete the file

```
mov ax, seg file_name
mov ds, ax
mov dx, offset file_name
mov ah, 3fh                    ; read filename from keyboard till < cr >
mov bx, 00                     ; using std. handle for console
mov cx,50h                     ; put filename in 80-character buffer
int 21h
mov bx, ax                     ; put null termination on filename
mov [file_name + bx-2], 00h    ; for console, extra <lf > goes
mov ax, 4300h                  ; with the < cr >
int 21 h                       ; read attributes of file
```

```
          and cl, 05h            ; check for read-only and system attrib.
          jz cont
          move cx, 0000h         ; reset attributes if set
          mov ax. 4301 h         ; Note DS:DX still points to the
          int 2Ih                ; the required file specification
cont:     mov ah, 4Ih            ; now delete the file
          :
          :
file_name db 50h dup (0)
```

Function 44H I/O Control for Devices Refer to Technical Reference Manual for Details

Function 45H Duplicate file Handle

Call with AH = 45H
BX = file handle (from previous open or create)

Returns with—

(a) If function succeeds, CY = 0
and AX = new duplicate file handle

(*b*) If function fails, CY = 1
and AX = 04H if no handle can be given
06H if handle invalid or is not open

This is a somewhat obscure and little-used function which may be used to force DOS to generate a duplicate file handle for a file or device which is already open with a valid handle. The only use documented for this function is to update the directory entry of an already open file without closing it. A duplicate file handle is forced with Function 45H and then either the old or the new handle is closed thereby updating the directory entry for the file. The file is, however, still open and may be accessed with the remaining handle. Note that the new handle's file pointer has the same value as that of the old handle; moreover, changing the file pointer for one of the handles through appropriate operation (read, write or move file pointer) will also correspondingly move the pointer associated with the other handle.

Example: To update an open file's directory entry without closing it. The old handle is asumed to be in the variable "handle"

```
mov ah, 45h
mov bx, handle
int 21 h                 ; duplicate handle in AX
```

```
jc error
mov bx, ax
mov ah, 3eh                ; close new handle to update the
int 21h                    ; file's directory entry
jc error
```

Function 46H Force Duplication of Handle

Call with AH = 46H
BX = old (existing) file handle
CX = new handle

Returns with—

(a) If function succeeds, CY = 0
(b) If function fails, CY = 1
and AX = 04H if no handle can be given
06H if handle invalid or is not open

This function duplicates a file handle in a manner similar to Function 45H. However, in this case, the user provides the specific duplicate handle wanted in CX. The function, if successful, forces this new handle to refer to the same file/device in the same position as the old handle in BX. As for Function 45H, the file can be referred to by either handle. File operations affecting the file pointer of one handle will also modify the pointer of the other handle. If the new handle desired (given in CX) when the function is called, is already assigned to a file/device, then that file/device is first closed. Only then is the handle made to refer to the same file/device as the handle in BX. This function is useful for redirection purposes as illustrated by the example given below.

Example: To dynamically redirect printer output to a file C:TEST.ELE

```
mov ah,45h                 ; force duplicate of standard list
mov bx, 04h                ; device's handle = 04
int 21 h                   ; and save in variable
jc error
mov old_handle, ax         : "old_handle"
mov ax, seg file_name
mov ds, ax
mov dx, offset file_name
mov ax, 3d02h              ; open file for read/write
int 21h                    ; and copy handle to BX
jc error                   ; and variable "handle"
```

```
        mov bx, ax
        mov handle, ax
        mov cx, 04h                   ; force it to duplicate to
        mov ah, 46h                   ; the standard list device
        int 21h                       ; handle = 04h
        jc error
        :
        :
;The standard list devices handle 04H is now closed.
;At this point any output directed to the standard list device
;will go to the file C:TEST.ELE
        :
        :
        mov ah, 46h                   ; restore handle 04H for
        mov bx, old_handle            ; the standard list device
        mov cx, 04h
        int 21h
        jc error
; The handle 04H associated with the file C:TEST.ELE is now
; closed and reassigned to the printer. At this point, "handle"
; refers to the file C:TEST.ELE, "old-handle" and handle = 04H
; refer to the standard list device.
        mov ah, 3eh                   ; close file handle "handle"
        mov bx, handle
        int 21h
        jc error
        mov ah, 3eh                   ; close handle "old_handle"
        mov bx, old_handle
        int 21h
        jc error
        :
file_name   db 'c:test. ele',0
old_handle dw 0
handle      dw 0
```

Function 47H Get Current Directory

Call with AH = 47H

DL = drive code (0 for default, 1 for A, 2 for B ..)

DS:SI = segment:offset address pointing to 64-byte scratch buffer to write the full path name of the current directory on return.

Returns with—

(a) If function succeeds, CY = 0

and the scratch buffer pointed to by DS:SI has a null-terminated ASCH string giving the full path name of the current directory

(b) If function fails, CY = 1

and AX = OFH for invalid drive

If the current directory of the drive happens to be the root directory, the first byte of buffer will be 00H (i.e. the null terminator). In any case, the path name generated by this function does not include the drive letter or a leading \ ;it is (rightly) assumed that the given path starts from the root directory and that the drive ID will anyway be there in DL.

Function 48H Allocate Memory

Call with AH = 48H

BX = number of paragraphs of memory to be allocated (one paragraph = 16 bytes).

Returns with—

(a) If function succeeds, CY = 0

and AX = segment address of the beginning of the memory block allocated

(b) If function fails, CY = 1

AX = 7 if memory control blocks destroyed
8 insufficient memory in TPA to provide the allocation requested

and BX = size in paragraphs of largest possible block that may be allocated

This function is used by a program to dynamically increase its memory allocation (provided sufficient memory is there in the TPA). The number of additional paragraphs requested is specified in BX. On a successful return, the AX register gives the paragraph aligned starting address (i.e. segment address) of the memory allocated to the request. Note that the allocated memory will then be from AX:0000H onwards. If the function fails because there is not enough memory in the TPA, the BX register returns the maximum number of paragraphs that may be allocated. If the program can do with this reduced allocation, then it should issue one more call to Function 48H with this size in BX.

Function 49H Release Allocated Memory

Call with AH = 49H

ES = segment address of block of memory to be released

Returns with—

(*a*) If function succeeds, CY = 0

(*b*) If function fails, CY = 1

and AX = 7 if memory control blocks destroyed
9 if incorrect segment has been specified in ES

This function releases only the memory allocated to the program through Function 48H. The memory segment address provided by a call to Function 48H should be specified in ES to have that block of memory released. Note that this function cannot be used to release the memory allocated to the program on loading (for that, Function 4AH must be used) or that obtained through Function 4AH. If the program tries to release memory it does not own (through Function 48H), then Error 9 is reported. See Chapter 10 for examples and use of this function.

Function 4AH Modify Memory Allocation

Call with AH = 4AH

BX = new size of memory allocation block (in paragraphs)

ES = segment address of block to be modified

Returns with—

(a) If function succeeds, CY = 0

(b) If function fails, CY = 1'

and AX = 7 if memory control blocks destroyed
9 if incorrect segment has been specified in ES
8 if insufficient memory for requested allocation

For Error Code 8 in AX, the register BX contains—

BX — sizc in paragraphs of largest possible block that may be allocated.

This function may be used to modify the memory initially allocated to a program on loading or by a call to Function 48H. It may be used by a program to dynamically increase/ decrease its memory allocation. If BX has a value less than the originally allocated block size, then the allocated memory shrinks; if it has more, then the allocated memory is increased. Note that interesting combinations can be done with the program's original loading allocation, the use of Functions 48H-4AH and final termination. For example, a program gets loaded with 32K bytes and subsequently asks for an additional 16K bytes through Function 48H. Function 4AH is then used to increase the added allocation from 16K bytes to 32K bytes through Function 4AH. Then Function 49H is used to release the added allocation. This releases the 32K bytes (current!) of added allocation leaving the program with only the original 32K bytes it had got on loading. This is released only when the program terminates.

Functions 48H-4AH, along with the allocation and release done on program loading and termination should be used with caution. Otherwise, unpleasant surprises and side-effects may happen.

Function 4BH Load and Execute Child Program or Load Overlay of Current Program (EXEC)

Call with AH = 4BH

AL = 00 if loading and executing child program from the current program (parent of the child)

03 if loading (only) overlay of the current program (overlay is not directly executed)

ES:BX = segment.'offset address of the base of the memory area containing the parameter block

DS:DX = segment:address of the null-terminated ASCH string, without wildcard characters, fully specifying the file with either COM or EXE extension that is to be loaded (and executed for the load & execute child option)

The parameter block contains—

For AL = 00 Load & execute child

(low memory)	segment address of environment block	2 bytes
	offset address of command tail	2 bytes
	segment address of command tail	2 bytes
	offset address of FCB #1	2 bytes
	segment address of FCB # 1	2 bytes
	offset address of FCB #2	2 bytes
(high memory)	segment address of FCB #2	2 bytes

All double byte values are stored in byte reversed fashion.

For AL = 03 Load overlay of current program

(low memory) Segment address of paragraph aligned memory address, overlay is to be loaded from this address onwards2 bytes

(high memory) Relocation factor for overlays stored in .EXE format 2 bytes

Returns with—

(a) If function succeeds, CY = 0

and all registers, except CS and IP, are destroyed on return. This includes the stack pointers,. SS and SP.

Function 4CH Terminate with Return Code (EXIT)

Call with AH = 4CH

AL = return code to be passed to the program to which this returns

Returns nothing (exits to the parent program of this program)

This is the approved way of terminating a program in versions 2 and 3 of DOS and is not available in DOS 1.0. This has been extensively earlier and is the only method that can be used for large .EXE programs. This returns to the parent program with a return code which may be interrogated by the parent through Function 4DH. The parent program to which this returns will be the one which loaded und executed the current program through EXEC (i.e. its parent program). This can be COMMAND.COM (in which case its transient portion may have to be reloaded) or any other program. If a batch file is currently in progress, then the next command line of the batch program is fetched und executed; the butch program can interrogate the return code through ERRORLEVEL and its IF type of conditional commands. *Program termination, other than Functions 31H or 4CH, should be avoided in all new programs.*

To summarize, this function does the following—

- restores the vector for INT 22H, termination handler, from PSP:C00AH
- restores the vector for INT 23H. '^C handler, from PSP:000EH
- restores the vector for INT 24H, critical error handler, from PSP:0012H
- flushes all file buffers of files opened by the terminating program
- terminates program and returns to the parent by transferring to the termination handler address.

We repeat that all new programs for running under DOS should use either Function 31H or 4CH to exit.

Function 4DH Get Return Code of Child Program after its Termination

Call with AH = 4DH

Returns with AH = 00 for normal termination through Function 4CH
01 for termination through ^C, INT 23H
02 for termination due to critical error INT 24H
03 for termination through Function 31H (i.e. portion of child program is still resident)

AL = return code specified while terminating by Functions 4CH or 31H

The parent program can use this function to find the way the child program (called through EXEC) terminated. The return code specified in the terminate functions 4CH and 31H of the child are reported in AL when this function is called. The contents of the register AH specifies the exact way in which the child program terminated. *Note that this program may be called by a parent program only once (i.e. on return from EXEC to the parent program) to find the return status of the child.*

Function 4EH Search Directory for First Matching File and report various information about it

Call with AH = 4EH

CX = attribute specified for search (see later)

DS:DX = segment:offset address of null-terminated ASCH string specifying the file to be searched for in the default or specified directory

Before this function is called, the user must call Function IAH to set up the Disk-Transfer Area (DTA) at a user-specified address. The results of Function 4EH are returned in the DTA, as given below.

The file specification given in the ASCH string may contain the wildcard characters * and/or ?.

Returns with—

(a) If function succeeds, CY = 0

A file with name matching the given filename was found in the specified (or default) directory). The following information is reported in the DTA —

Offset (into the DTA from its base)

Bytes 00-14H reserved

15H attribute of matched file

16-17H file time of creation/update

18-19H file date of creation/update

1A-1BH least significant word of file size

1C-1DH most significant word of file size (Word values are stored in byte-reversed fashions. Note that file size is a 32-bit binary number)

1E-2AH filename and extension of matched file (The '.' between file name and its extension, if any, is part of the ASCH string returned in this area. The string terminates with null, 00H.)

(b) If function fails, CY = 1
and AX = 02H for invalid path
12H if no file with matching name was found in the default or specified directory.

It is important to note that the DTA to be used in the search by DOS must first be set up through Function IAH before calling this function. If the search fails, then no matching file exists with the given name and matching attribute in the specified or default directory. Otherwise, the DTA contents 1SH-2AH give information on the matched file.

If the attribute specified in CX is 00, only normal files will be searched for. If the volume label bit (Bit 3) is set, then only volume labels matched are returned. If any combination of the hidden, system or subdirectory attribute bits (Bits 1,2,4 respectively) are set, then the function will try to match all normal files as well as all other directory entries (other than volume label) which have these attributes. The archive bit and the read-only bit are not significant for the search.

The other information returned in the DTA following a successful call to this function gives the date and time stamp of the matched file and its size. The format of this information is exactly as given for the corresponding directory entry. The reader is referred for the format of these bytes.

If the file specification contains wildcard characters, then this function returns with only the first matching filename. Other matching filenames, if present, will have to be found through repeated application of Function 4FH.

Example: Search for all normal, hidden and system files with extension ASM in the subdirectory USER of drive C

```
mov ah, lah                  ; set up DTA at dta_buf
mov dx, seg dta_buf
mov ds, dx
mov dx, offset dta_buf
int 21h
mov ah, 4eh                  ; search for first match
mov cx, 07h                  ; with this attribute
mov dx, seg file_spec
mov ds; dx
mov dx, offset file_spec
```

```
                int 21h
                jc no_match_exit
                :
                :
match_again     mov ah, 4fh                 ; search for next match
                nt 21h
                jc match_over
                :
                :
                jmp match_again
                :
                :
match_over:
no_match_exit:
                :
                :
dta_buf         db 2bh dup (0)
file_spec       db'C:\USSER\*.ASM'00
```

Function 4FH Search Directory tor Next Matching File, Following a Successful Call to Function 4EH, and Report Various Information about it

Call with AH = 4FH

Before this function is called, the user must call Function IAH to set up the Disk Transfer Area (DTA) at a user-specified address, followed by a successful call to function 4EH. The results of Function 4FH are returned in the DTA, as given below.

The file specification given in the ASCII string may contain the wildcard characters * and/or ?.

Returns with—

(a) If function succeeds, CY = 0

A file with name matching the given filename was found in the specified (or default) directory) The following information is reported in the DTA—

Offset (into the DTA from its base)

Bytes	00-14H	reserved
	15H	attribute of matched file

16-17H	file time of creation/update
18-19H	file date of creation/update
1A-1BH	least significant word of file size
1C-1DH	most significant word of file size (Word values are stored in byte reversed fashions. Note that file size is a 32-bit binary number)
1E-2 AH	filename and extension of matched file (The '.' between file name and its extension, if any, is part of the ASCH string returned in this area. The string terminates with null, 00H).

(b) If function fails, CY = 1
and AX = 12H if no file with matching name was found in the default or specified directory.

Repeated call to this function to search for all matching files should conclude when the function fails (CY= 1,AX= 12H)

This function is used if the filename given in the corresponding previous call to Function 4EH had a wildcard character and the call was successful. This function searches for the same filename once again, with the same attributes, and returns information through the same DTA which was specified earlier through Function IAH for Function 4EH. The format and contents of this information is also the same as for Function 4EH. This function should be called repeatedly to yield all the matching files in the specified or default directory. This process concludes only when Function 4FH reports failure with CY = 1 and AX = 12H.

See Function 4EH and the example program EDIR.COM of Fig. 5 for examples on the use of this function.

Function 50H-53H RESERVED

Function 54H Get Verify state

Call with AH = 54H

Returns with AL = 00 if verify flag OFF
01 if verify flag ON

If the verify or automatic read-after-write flag is set, then every disk write operation is followed by a read to check the correctness of the data written. This flag can be turned ON/OFF: by Function 2EH or the DOS commands VERIFY ON and VERIFY OFF. This function, Function 54H, reports the current status of this verify flag.

Function 55H RESERVED

Function 56H Rename file

Call with AH = 56H

DS:DX = segment:offset address of null-terminated ASCH string specifying the file to be renamed.

ES:DI = segment:offset address of null-terminated ASCH string specifying the new name of the file being renamed.

Returns with—

(a) If function succeeds, CY = 0

The file with the given old name is renamed to have the new name.

(b) If function fails, CY = 1

and AX = 02H for file not found

03H for invalid path

05H for access denied (e.g. read-only file or new file already exists)

11H for not same device

On failure, AX contains the error code.

This function can not only change the name of a file but can also move it from one directory to another (root or sub). However, one cannot move the file from one drive or device to another, attempts to do that will report AX = 11H with the function failing. (Note that the RENAME command of DOS merely renames a file but cannot move it to a directory different from the original one.) Wildcard characters cannot be given for either the old or the new filenames and the drives, if specified, must be the same lor both. The function will fail if the two paths are not valid, the file with the old name cannot be found on the specified path or if the file to be renamed is a read-only file. The function also fails if a file with the same name and path as the new specification already exists. If this function is used to move a file from a subdirectory to the root directory of the same drive, then the function may also fail; this will happen if the root directory is full and cannot accommodate the new file.

Example: rename (and move) old file C:\USER\OLD.TXT to C:NEW.TXT

```
move ah, 56h
mov dx, seg old_file
mov ds, dx
mov dx, offset old_file
mov di, seg new_file
mov es, di
mov di, offset new_file
int 21h
jc error
```

; error only if old file is incorrectly specified or root ;
directory is full

```
            :

            :

old_file    db 'C:\ USER\ OLD.TXT', 00
new_file    db 'C:NEW TXT, 00
```

Function 57H Handle Type Call to Get or Set the Date and Stamp of a Previously Opened File

Call with AH = 57H
BX = file handle of previously opened file
AL = 00 if getting date and time stamp of file (reported on return in CX and DX) = 01 if setting data and time stamp of file

For setting the date and time stamp (AL = 01)—

CX = 16-bit new time stamp

DX = 16-bit new date stamp

Returns with—

(a) If function fails, CY = 1
and AX = 01H if invalid option indicated in AL when function was called 06H if handle in BX is invalid

(b) If function succeeds, CY = 0

For AL = 00, on return

CX = 16 -bit time stamp of file

DX = 16-bit date stamp of file

For AL = 01, the time and date stamps to the file are suitably modified to the specified values

This function may be used to read or change the date and time stamps of a file previously opened or created through a handle type call. The time and date stamps specified (AL = 01) or read (AL = 00) are the same as for the directory entry for this file and follow the same format as given in Sec. 9.1.3; the reader is referred to that section for more details. If a file is specifically opened or created to read its time and date stamp or to change it, then the user is advised to close it once this has been done.

Example: Get the date and time stamps of file C:OLD.TXT

```
mov ax, seg file_name
```

```
          mov ds, ax
          mov dx, offset file_name
          mov ax, 3d00h
          int 21h ;                  open file
          jc error
          mov handle, bx             ; store file handle
          mov ax, 5700h              ; get time stamp in CX
          int 21h                    ; and date stamp in DX
          jc error
          mov bx, handle
          mov ah, 3eh
          int 21h                    ; close opened file
          :
          :
handle    dw 0
file-name db 'C:OLD.TXT', 00h
```

Function 58H Get or Set Memory Allocation Strategy

Call with AH = 58H

If getting strategy, AL = 00
current strategy code reported on return in AX
If setting strategy, AL = 01
and BX = strategy code to be set

Returns with—

(a) If function fails, CY = 1
and AX = 1 indicating invalid option exercised through AL on call

(b) If function succeeds. CY = 0
If strategy code was being set, nothing else is returned
If strategy code was being read (AL = 00), then-
AX = current strategy code

The strategy code defines the particular way in which DOS would look for free memory to be assigned on a request for memory block allocation. The strategy codes and their implications are —

00	first fit	DOS searches available memory blocks from low to high addresses and assigns the first block found to be large enough to satisfy the allocation request (i.e. lowest block)
01	best fit	DOS searches all available memory blocks in memory and assigns the smallest block found to be large enough to satisfy the allocation request (smallest block)
02	last fit	DOS searches available memory blocks from high to low addresses and assigns the first block found to be large enough to satisfy the allocation request (highest block)

Function 59H Extended Error Reporting Function

Call with AH = 59H
BX = 00H
Returns with AX = extended error code
BH = error class
BL = recommended action for the reported error
CH = error locus (i.e. device where error occurred)

The contents of registers CL, DX, SI, DI, BP, DS, and ES are destroyed by a call to this function. The user should take adequate steps to save the required registers before calling this function and restore them afterwards.

The details of the errors reported by AX, BH, BL, and CH are given in the Appendix II to this chapter.

Function 5AH Create Temporary File

Call with AH = SAH
CX = attribute of temporary file

00H	normal
01H	read-only
02H	hidden
04H	system

DS:DX = segment:address of null terminated ASCH string specifying the path name of the directory which will contain the temporary file.

Returns with—

(a) If function fails, CY – 1
and AX = 3 path not found 5 access denied

(b) If function succeeds, CY = 0
and AX = file handle for the temporary file
DS:DX = segment:offset address of null-terminated ASCH siring completely specifying the temporary file created

There is nothing temporary about a file created with this function. Such a file has to be explicitly closed and deleted when its requirement ends (unless, of course, the file is still needed). The temporary file created will have the attributes specified in CX while calling. The DS:DX address points to the string containing the path name to be used to create to file; a null string implies that the current directory OD the current drive is to be used for the temporary file. On calling, the string pointed at by DS:DX must be ready to have the DOS-created file name to be attached to it. This implies that 12 additional bytes of memory must be there for the filename and extension which will be filled in by this function. If the temporary file is being created in a root directory, it might also fail if the root directory is full.

Function 5BH Create New File

Call with AH = 5BH
CX = attribute of file to be created
00H normal
01H read-only
02H hidden
04H system
DS:DX = segment:address of null terminated ASCII string specifying completely the file to be created

Returns with—

(a) If function fails, CY = 1
and AX = 03 path not found
04 no available handle
05 access denied
50H file to be created already exists

(b) If function succeeds, CY = 0
and AX = file handle for the new file

This function is similar to Function 3CH; the only difference is that Function 5BH fails if the file to be created already exits. In contrast, in such a situation, Function 3CH will truncate the original file to zero length. This may be very undesirable if the user has unfortunately specified the wrong file name and does not really want the original file to be truncated to zero. In all other respects, the two functions are exactly identical.

Function 5CH-5FH are intended for use with networking and are not of interest to us here.

Function 60H-61H arc RESERVED

Function 62H Get the Address of the Current Program's PSP

Call with AH = 62H

Returns with BX = segment address of the current program's PSP

The reader should recall that the PSP is loaded in a paragraph aligned fashion when a program is loaded for execution. This function returns the segment address of the PSP in BX. Therefore, on returning from this function, the base of the PSP may be found at the address BX:0000H. The program's PSP has been described earlier. The reader should refer to that for the format of the PSP and the meaning of its various fields; these fields are specificd us offsets relative to the base of the PSP.

Function 63H is peculiar to DOS. 2.25 alone and is not of interest to us here

APPENDIX I

A list of the DOS functions available through INT 21H (partly organized on the basis of class)

00H	Terminate Program

Character I/O

01H	Input character from standard input device and echo to standard output device
02H	Display character to standard output device.
03H	Input character from standard auxiliary device.
04H	Output character to standard auxiliary device
05H	Print character on standard list device
06H	Direct character I/O with console
07H	Input character from standard input device without echoing or checking for ^C
08H	Input character from standard input device without echoing but with ^C checking
09H	Output ASCH string to standard output device
0AH	Input ASCH string from standard input device
0BH	Get available/not available status of standard input device
0CH	Clear buffer of standard input device and invoke any of the functions 01 H, 06H, 07H 08H or 0AH
0DH	Reset disk in drive A
0EH	Select current drive and report the number of logical drives in the system

FCB Type File Access Calls

0FH	Open file
10H	Close file
11H	Search for first matching file
12H	Search for next matching file
13H	Delete file
14H	Sequential file read
15H	Sequential file write
16H	Create new file/Truncate existing file to zero length

17H	Rename file
21H	Random file read
22H	Random file write
23H	Get file size in terms of number of records
24H	Set the file's random record field
27H	Read one or more records from file
28H	Write one or more records to file
29H	Parse filename into the fields of an unopened FCB
18H	RESERVED
19H	Get drive code of default drive
IAH	Set Disk Transfer Area (DTA) address
1BH	Get information on the default drive
1CH	Get information on the specified drive
36H	Get the specified disk's free space
1DH-20H	RESERVED
25H	Set interrupt vector
35H	Get interrupt vector
26H	Create new copy of program's PSP
62H	Get the address of the current program's PSP
2AH	Get current system date
2BH	Set current system date
2CH	Get current system time
2DH	Set current system time
2EH	Turn ON/OFF verify flag (automatic read-after-write)
54H	Get state of verify flag
2FH	Get address of DTA in use
30H	Get current DOS version number
31H	Terminate but stay resident (KEEP)
4CH	Terminate (EXIT)

4DH	Get return code of child following its termination
32H	RESERVED
37H	RESERVED
38H	Get/Set country code of the system
39H	Create subdirectory in specified drive and path
3AH	Delete subdirectory in specified drive and path
3BH	Change current directory
47H	Get current directory

Handle Type File Access Calls

3CH	Create new file/Truncate existing file to zero length
3DH	Open file/device
3EH	Close file/device
3FH	Read from file/device
40H	Write to file/device
41H	Delete specified file
42H	Move file pointer of previously opened file
43H	Get/Set the attributes of the specified file
45H	Duplicate file handle
46H	Force duplication of handle
4EH	Search for first matching file
4FH	Search for next matching file
56H	Rename file
57H	Get/Set date and time stamp of previously opened file
5AH	Create temporary file
5BH	Create new file
44H	I/O Control for devices (IOCTL)
48H	Allocate more memory
49H	Release allocated memory
4AH	Modify allocated memory

58H	Get/Set memory allocation strategy
4BH	Load and execute child program or Load overlay (EXEC)
50H-53H	RESERVED
59H	Extended error reporting for DOS functions
5CH-5FH	For use with networking
60H-61H	RESERVED
63H	Peculiar to DOS 2.25

APPENDIX II

Extended Error Information Reported by Function 59H. INT 21H

Subsequent to an unsuccessful call to any INT 21H function, or following the INT 24H instruction, Function 59H, INT 21H may be called with AH = 59H and BX = 00H, in order to get more details on the type or error and remedial moves suggested by DOS for the error in question. Thee are reported by the registers AH, BH, BL and CH on return from Function 59H as follows-

AX	=	Extended error code
BH	=	Error class code
BL	=	Code for remedial action recommended by DOS
CH	=	Error locus code

The specific codes each of these listed below;

Extended Error Code (Reported in AX)

00H	NO ERROR
01H	invalid function code (i.e. for subfunction of the function)
02H	file specified was not found
03H	path specified was not found
04H	no handle available (too many files/devices are open)
05H	access denied (e.g. write operation on read-only file)
06H	invalid handle is specified
07H	control blocks of the memory are destroyed
08H	insufficient memory in TPA for the function to work
09H	invalid memory block address specified
0AH	invalid environment (invalid string in SET command)
0BH	invalid format
0CH	invalid access code for file/device
0DH	invalid data
0EH	RESERVED
0FH	invalid drive code specified
10H	attempt made to delete current directory

11H	different device (e.g. in the RENAME Function 56H)
12H	no further files can be found
13H	attempt to write on write-protected diskette
14H	unknown ID specified for unit
15H	drive not ready
16H	unknown command requested
17H	CRC error reported on disk data
18H	bad request structure length
19H	disk seek error
1AH	unknown media
1BH	sector specified on disk not found
1CH	no paper in printer
1DH	error in write operation
1EH	error in read operation
1FH	general failure
20H	file sharing violation (for network functions)
21H	file lock violation (for network functions)
22H	disk changed improperly
23H	no FCB available for use
24H-4FH	RESERVED
50H	file already exists
51H	RESERVED
52H	cannot create specified subdirectory
53H	failure in INT 24H, Critical Error Interrupt Handler

Error Class (Reported in BH)

01H	not enough resource for function requested (e.g. storage or channels)
02H	temporary situation; function may be tried again later
03H	unallowed authorization
04H	error in system's DOS itself

05H	hardware failure in system
06H	failure in DOS (e.g. for missing configuration files)
07H	error in application program (user's fault)
08H	file or item requested was not found
09H	bad format in file or item
0AH	interlocked items or files
0BH	error in the disk media
0CH	unknown error class

Recommended Action Advised by DOS (Reported in BL)

01H	retry function now
02H	retry after waiting
03H	request user to fix error (e.g. change disks)
04H	abort application program but close files and clean-up!
05H	abort immediately
06H	ignore error
07H	retry after user has fixed error (i.e. code 03H)

Error Locus (Reported in CH)

01H	unknown location of fault
02H	error in block device (e.g. one of the drives)
03H	error on the network
04H	error in serial device
05H	error in memory

PROBLEMS

For all of the following problems and other problems elsewhere, make a judicious choice as to whether ANSI.SYS, ROM-BIOS or direct video control should be used for display purposes. Do not make a Choice which overkills. Your program should be able to run both on a standard MA or on a CGA/EGA system.

1. Write a program CHATTR to be called with a file name in its command tail to display and change the attributes of the specified file. CHATTR should first check to see if the file exists (with any attribute). If it does, its attributes should be displayed and the user should be given the option of changing these attributes or of quitting without changing anything. If the file does not exist, the user should be prompted to enter another file name or quit. (Note that the file name may contain a path specification or may use a default path.)

   If the user wants to change attributes, the program should allow him/her to change the file's attributes to any combination of READ-ONLY, HIDDEN and SYSTEM. After changing the file's attributes, the program should verify that the change has indeed been made and should display the new attributes to the user. It should then give the user the option of quitting or of changing the attributes of another file.
2. Having written the program CHATTR of Problem 1, a natural requirement would be to write a program which can implement the equivalent of DOS's DIR command regardless of the attributes of the files in the directory. Write such a program EXTDIR which will work exactly like the DIR command except that instead of displaying the date and time of file creation/update, it should display the attributes of the files. The example program EDIR.COM given in the text may be of some help in writing EXTDIR.
3. For disks implementing subdirectories, one would like to have a program which shows directly the directory-subdireciory structure of the disk starting from its root directory. Write a program HIERARCH to do this. Starting from the root directory. HIERARCH should show all the subdirectories in the root directory as well as subdirectories of other subdirectories. You can make the program more elaborate (and useful) by allowing some means of displaying to the user all the files in a specified directory within HIERARCH. If you do this, allow the user to specify by means of a switch whether all files will be shown or only files, with normal attributes.
4. In Problem 3, we described how a WORDSTAR file may be changed to normal ASCH text. Implement a program SHOWWRD to do this conversion. Note that this will be an extension of the program SHOW given as an example in the text. Allow the user to specify the source and object file/device for SHOWWRD in the command line itself.

Ideally, SHOWWRD should probably be written as a DOS Filter. For the moment, if you want to write a version of SHOWWRD (say SHOWWS) as a filter, ensure that all your I/O commands are done using the DOS Handle-type functions with the standard handles for console input and output. For a filter, the command line would look like

SHOWWS < xxx.yyy > zzz.www

5. Recall that for each timer tick, the ROM-BIOS causes INT 1CH to be executed al the end of its own timer operations. At boot, the PC's vector for INT 1CH points to an instruction IRET providing a do-nothing routine for this interrupt.

   Write and execute a program CLKDISP which when run provides a stop-watch function using the timer-tick interrupt by providing your own ISR for INT ICH und changing its original interrupt vector to point to your own ISR. (Use DOS functions to change this interrupt vector and change it back to its original value before you exit CLKDISP.) The stop-watch should be started and stopped by the FI key. Pressing F2 should freeze the stop-watch display but keep the stop-watch running internally; normal display should resume on pressing F2 once again. The < esc > key should be used to exit CLKDISP and return to the main program. Use your imagination to provide an interesting display of elapsed time on the slop-watch as per the above description. Display elapsed time in hours, minutes, seconds and tenths of seconds. Use graphics modes for display in case your requirements call for a graphics screen.

6. One problem with the COPY command of DOS is that it does the copy regardless of whether the target file already exists or not. It would be definitely advantageous to have a CHKCOPY program which first checks to see if the target file exists and proceeds normally with the copying operation in case the file is not found. In case the de is found, it should query the user whether the existing file should remain as it is, whether it is to be overwritten or whether the new data is to be appended to the existing file. (It would be even better if switches can be used in the command line to signal these options.) Write CHKCOPY to achieve this. Apart from the above features, CHKCOPY should perform as far as possible like the COPY command (including its ability to accept the wild-card characters ? and * in the file specifications).

   Instead of writing CHKCOPY in its full gory detail, a more elegant solution would be to do the required preprocessing, reload a fresh copy of COMMAND.COM and pass on the appropriate COPY command to it. Once the COPY has been done, exit from the new copy of COMMAND.COM to return to CHKCOPY and then exit CHKCOPY to return to its parent program. This can certainly be done. Can you think of how this might be implemented?.Note that if this is done, you can simplify some of your programs by getting a lot of work done through existing DOS commands.

5

The COBOL Language

COBOL is the acronym of Common Purpose Business Oriented Language. As the name suggests, it is a language ideally suited for developing programs for pure business purposes. It is also known as the "English Language" language because of its close similarity to the natural language `English'.

Programs written in COBOL almost read like the English language. It has certain reserved words for specific purposes and tasks, while data names, etc. can be coined by the programmer almost at will.

COBOL, unlike BASIC, is essentially a file oriented programming language. This is the reason that BASIC is considered to be a learner's language. The understanding of COBOL would become very simple to person who has been exposed to some sort of file handling on computers.

COBOL programs are usually written on coding sheets as it is much easier to transfer a program from a coding sheet to punched cards and the chances of errors are also reduced to a great extent. However, with the advent of the microcomputers and keyboards, punched cards are not essential for inputting COBOL programs. Rather, they are directly entered through the keyboard and then saved on a disk magnetic tape to later compilation.

If the coding sheets are used, one line of program on the coding sheet represents the information to be entered on one punched card. There are 80 columns on each line of the coding sheet.

Columns 1-6 to specify page and line numbers

Column 7 to enter the continuation symbol

Columns 8-11 Margin A

Columns 12-72 Margin B

Columns 73-80 Program Identification Cols.

Each Cobol program line is assigned a six digit identifying number which is ignored by the compiler and this is entered in these columns.

Column 7 is used to entér a hyphen which signified that the previous line is being continued on the current line.

Margin A is used to start all the division, section and paragraph names.

Margin B is used to enter the statements of the procedure and other divisions. However, it is not compulsory for the statements to start exactly from Column 12. They may begin anywhere in Margin B.

The columns from 73 to 80 are ignored by the compiler and may by used for the programmer's reference.

Organisation of a COBOL Program

A COBOL program is quite different from a BASIC program. It is divided into four parts or four divisions. These divisions have to be entered in a certain sequence. This sequence is as follows:

1. IDENTIFICATION DIVISION
2. ENVIRONMENT DIVISION
3. DATA DIVISION
4. PROCEDURE DIVISION

COBOL programs should be standardly written in capital letters. The first two divisions do not do much in implementing the program. Rather, they are meant for identifying the programmer's name and the computer system on which the program is going to be implemented. The DATA division holds all information about the various files to be used and the various data types. i.e., constants and variables required by the program. The PROCEDURE division contains the program proper, i.e., the commands and procedures to be carried out.

In a COBOL program, division are, at times, broken down into sections and at times, the sections are broken down into paragraphs. All the divisions do not use this form of breakdown. However, if this from of breakdown is need, the hierarchy is as follows:

Division

Section

Paragraph

Statement

Word

COBOL RESERVED WORDS

COBOL reserved words are words specific to the COBOL language which are meant to carry out a certain kind of function. These words have a preassigned meaning. They always have to be present in a COBOL statement. They can be compared with the keywords used in BASIC. They range from 280-300 depending upon the type of compiler being used.

Example:

MOVE

PERFORM

OCCUR

CONSTANTS OR LITERALS

Data which always holds a constant value is also knows as a literal in COBOL. The literal does not have any name as it represents itself. i.e. the value of the literal is the literal itself. Literals can be divided into three types, namely,

1. Numeric
2. Non-numeric and
3. Figurative

Numeric literals are those which can be formed with the digits only and they hold a numeric quantity which can be used for any mathematical operation. A numeric literal may have a sign on the left hand side. This sign may either be the minus or plus sign. There should not be any blank space between the sign and the literal. If there is no sign, the number is assumed to be a positive one. The numeric literal may have one decimal point to represent real numbers. A decimal point must not be the last character of the literal or it will be assumed to be a period which may cause vague errors in the program. If there is no decimal point, it is assumed that number is an integer.

Non-numeric literals are those that do not any values. These characters have to be bounded by quotations " ". The only restrictions to the type of characters that can be place with the quotation marks is the quotation mark itself. However, there are certain compiler versions which allow the quotation character to be used as a part of the character literal. The maximum length of the non-numeric literal is dependent upon the type of compiler and computer being used.

Example:

"RATE"

"TWENTY"

"18.75"

The third examples does not represent a numeric literal, even though it is made up of numerical digits. Since it has been bounded by quotation marks it is a non-numeric literal and should be treated as one.

Figurative constants are literals which represent values that are frequently used in the program. They are given some fixed names and when the computer recognises these names, it replaces them with the corresponding values of the figurative constants. These are standardised according to the type of computer and compiler being used.

Example:

ZERO, ZEROS, ZEROS

SPACE, SPACES

QUOTE, QUOTES

The literal ZERO represents the value 0. The literal SPACE represents blank spaces, either one or many depending upon the variable it is being used with. QUOTE represents the quotation marks.

VARIABLE DATA NAMES

The data name gives reference to the storage space in the memory. These data names are also known as variables or identifiers. The reason for this is that these data names can be assigned different values at different points in the program. These variables are usually defined in the DATA DIVISION and referenced in the PROCEDURE. In certain cases, the data name may have to be subscripted. There are certain rules which have to be followed in creating data process. They are as follows:

1. The data name should not be a reserved word.
2. The name can be upto 30 characters long and can have digits 0-9 or from A-Z and the hyphen (-) character. However, the name cannot begin or end with the hyphen.
3. Blanks are not permitted in the data name.
4. The same data name cannot be used for two different purposes in the program, i.e. it must be unique.

Example:

WIND-UP

EMPLOYEE-COUNTER

SALARY

DIVISIONS OF COBOL

IDENTIFICATION DIVISION

The IDENTIFICATION DIVISION is the first division of any COBOL program. It is also the simplest and least significant of the COBOL divisions. There may be several paragraphs of this division but it does not have any sections. Of the various paragraphs, the first one is the most essential. The other paragraphs are optional and may be omitted.

The first paragraph, which is also the most important one is known as

PROGRAM - ID

In this part of the IDENTIFICATION DIVISION, the program's identifying name has to be given. The rules regarding the program name are the same as those used for data names. The method of writing the program name is as follows:

PROGRAM-ID. PAYROLL.

Here, PAYROLL is the name of the program developed. There has to be at least one blank following the period in PROGRAM-ID. The program name should also end with a period. The period is not counted as a part of the program name.

The rest of the optional paragraphs in the IDENTIFICATION DIVISION are listed below.

AUTHOR xxxxxxx.
INSTALLATION. xxxxxxx
DATE-WRITTEN, xxxxxxx
SECURITY, xxxxxxx
REMARKS xxxxxxx

The xxxxxxx, represents a dummy entry made against the paragraph. The AUTHOR paragraph denotes name of the author, which may be given. The DATE-WRITTEN and the DATE-COMPILED may contain the date on which the program was written and when it was compiled. The SECURITY may have a password. The REMARKS paragraph is just an extra paragraph, in case the programmer wishes to enter certain earmarks.

ENVIRONMENT DIVISION

The ENVIRONMENT DIVISION in a program tells what is the name of the computer being used and it also assigns hardware devices to the files which will be manipulated. This division always follows the IDENTIFICATION DIVISION. This is the most machine dependent division of all the 4 divisions.

It is divided into two sections, namely the CONFIGURATION SECTION and the INPUT-OUTPUT section.

CONFIGURATION SECTION

This section is further divided into three paragraphs, out of which two are essential and one is optional. The two essential paragraphs are SOURCE-COMPUTER and the OBJECT-COMPUTER.

The first paragraph specifies the name of the computer the name of the computer being used to compile the program and the second paragraph will indicate the name of the computer system on which the program will be executed. The second paragraph may also have an extra statement called the MEMORY SIZE, followed by an integer which denotes the amount of storage necessary for the object program. This extra statement is an optional feature.

The third paragraph of this is also an optional feature and has the name SPECIAL-NAMES. This may be used for relating some hardware names to user specific mnemonic names.

INPUT-OUTPUT SECTION

This section contains information regarding the files to be used in the program. It is divided into two paragraphs. They are the FILE CONTROL and the I-O-CONTROL paragraphs. The FILE-CONTROL paragraph is essential in almost all programs, while the I-O-CONTROL paragraph is again on optional feature of depending upon the various parameters.

The FILE-CONTROL paragraph names each file and identified the medium on which file is stored or will be stored. For each file used there must be a FILE-CONTROL entry, which will name the file and assign a peripheral device which holds that particular file. The files must all be unique. The word OPTIONAL may be used with input files, which means that the particular file may be not be present. If the OPTIONAL word is not used, it is essential that the files mentioned, be present when the program is run.

Example:

```
Input-Output Section.
File-Control.
Select Paymaster Assign to Reader.
Select Paysheet Optional Assign to Reader.
Select Payreport Assign to Printer.
```

The I-O-CONTROL paragraph is used for handling of multiple magnetic tape files. This paragraph contains a MULTIPLE TAPE statement, which identifies the various tape files used in the program.

Example:

```
I-O-CONTROL.
MULTIPLE FILE TAPE CONTAINS
PAY-FILE REPORT FILE.
```

This completes a description of the first two divisions of the COBOL program. Presented below is an example of the first two divisions of a COBOL program.

Example:

```
IDENTIFICATION  DIVISION.
PROGRAM-ID.EXAMPLE.
AUTHOR D VASWANI.
SECURITY. CHECK.
ENVIRONMENT DIVISION.
CONFIGURATION  SECTION.
SOURCE  COMPUTER. PDP 11.
OBJECT  COMPUTER.  PDP 11.
MEMORY  SIZE  20K.
INPUT-OUTPUT  SECTION.
FILE-CONTROL.
SELECT  PAYMASTER  ASSIGN  TO  READER.
SELECT  PAYSHEET  OPTIONAL   ASSIGN TO READER.
SELECT  PAYREPORT  ASSIGN  TO  PRINTER.
I-O-CONTROL.
MULTIPLE FILE TAPE CONTAINS
PAY-FILE FULL REPORT FILE.
```

DATA DIVISION

The DATA DIVISION is the next division to be written in any COBOL program. Any data item to be used at any point in the program has to be described in the DATA DIVISION. It is further divided into 3 sections namely:

1. FILE SECTION
2. WORKING-STORAGE SECTION
3. REPORT SECTION

Before we continue with the detailed description of the various sections of the DATA DIVISION, it is essential to have a brief understanding of what are files and file structures. The importance of knowing file structures early on is important in COBOL, since it basically is a file oriented before handed language.

Files and File Structures

A file is a collection of related "data records". Data records are made up of "fields" and fields are made up of characters. To understand this more clearly, let us take an example of an employee records file.

In a business concern there are 100 employees. A file has been created which holds are detailed information on all the employees The details of a particular person are as follows: It will consists of the employees serial number, age, address, job code, date of employment and salary. Since we have to store information of 100 employees, the file will have 100 records, i.e. 1 record per person. Each record will contain all the details of one employee, Each record will be further sub-divided into 5 fields, as the record has been broken into 5 different entities consisting of the number, age, etc. Each file will further be made up of a number of characters, depending upon what kind of information it holds.

FILE SECTION

This section describes the files used for input as well as output. The file description mist begin with the word FD, followed by the file name. The file name must be identical with the file name given in the SELECT clause of the ENVIRONMENT DIVISION. The FD entry allows the programmer to give a number of clauses, of which many are optional. The essential clause is the file name as mentioned before. Hence, the FD entry is its most simplest form consists only of the word FD followed by the name of the file.

Example:

FD PAYROLL.

The file name should end with a period, in case no other clauses are entered. In case other entries are to be made, the period should come after the last entry. The period is not counted as a part of the file name. The label records clause tells us whether the file has labels or not. Labels appear at the beginning and end of the file, signifying the start ad end. They are knows as the header label and the trailer label. These records appear only on tape or disk file. The syntax of this clause is as follows:

LABEL RECORDS ARE STANDARD. or

LABEL RECORDS ARE OMITTED.

The first one is used it label records are present, while the second one is used if there are no label records.

Since the files on tape or disk cannot be seen with the naked eye, it is preferable to check out if the file being used is the correct one. For this, the VALUE of ID clause is used. This clause specifies the name given in quotes. Only if the name given in this clause and the name in the header label, match, further access is allowed. Other wise the file cannot be opened and an error results.

Example:

VALUE OF ID IS "PAYSHEET".

The next clause which may have to be included in the FD entry, is the type of recording mode. The recording mode of files on tapes may be binary or BCD (binary coded decimal).

Example:

RECORDING MODE IS BINARY

A further addition can be made on this clause regarding the density of recording the information. It may be stored on high density or low density. This would be entered as follows:

RECORDING MODE IS BINARY LOW-DENSITY

The next clause which can be given, is the number of records in each block on the tape. This part has been explained clearly in Section 1 of the book, It specifies how many records are there in each block.

Example:

BLOCK CONTAINS 50 RECORDS.

The next clause that may be included is the size of the record, i.e. how may characters is the record made up of. If the record would consist of 135 characters, the syntax of this clause will be.

RECORD CONTAINS 135 CHARACTERS

The last clause, which is optional, defines the records contained in the file. This record is generally described in full detail immediately following the FD entry.

Example:

DATA RECORD IS SALARY

Except the last two clauses, the other clauses are usually used for tape or disk files. An example of the FD entry with various clause entries is given below.

Example:

```
DATA DIVISION

FILE SECTION.
FD PAYMENT
LABEL RECORDS ARE STANDARD
VALUE OF ID IS "PAYSHEET"
RECORDING MODE IS BCD LOW-DENSITY
BLOCK CONTAINS 40 RECORDS
RECORD CONTAINS 122 CHARACTERS
DATA RECORD IS SALARY
```

Immediately following the FD entry, the description of the record or records contained in the file have to given. This is known as the record description. This record name may be entered with the FD entry as an option. The record description consists of the record name, the divisions of the records into fields and further subdivisions of each field, if necessary, along with the type and length of data contained in each field.

This breakup of the record structure is systematically denoted by assigning level numbers. The entire record is always given level 01. Field of the record may be assigned any level number from 02 to 99. As the fields are sub-divided, the level number increases. There are certain special level numbers used for specific purposes. These are 49, 66, 77 and 88.

Taking the previously mentioned record structure, we can observe that the record is broken into 5 fields. If we name the record as Employee-Descrip and the fields as SNO, AGE, ADDRESS, JOBCODE, DATE-EMP and SALARY, the record description would be as follows:

```
01 EMPLOYEE-DESCRIP
02 SNO
02 AGE
02 ADDRESS
92 JOB-CODE
02 DATE-EMP
02 SALARY
```

As the record name is EMPLOYEE-DESCRIP, it is given level 01. The fields are in turn given level 02. This level could as well have been 05 or 39, or any other number between 02 and 49, except the special levels. If the field DATE-EMP is further broken down into the year, month and day with the names YEAR, MON & DAY the record description would be,

```
01 EMPLOYEE-DESCRIP
________
________
02 DATE-EMP
04 YEAR
04 MON
04 DAY
```

The DATE-EMP FIELD has been sub-divided into three fields, which have level numbers higher than the level of the DATE-EMP field. Again this level number could be any number between 03 and 49, except the specials. In case the precious level was 05, the next level has to be greater than 05. The fields are therefore divided into two types.

1. Group Field and
2. Elementary Field

A group field is one which has been further broken down into different fields, while an elementary field is one which cannot be further sub-divided. In our example, all the fields except DATE-EMP are elementary fields. The further breakdown of DATE-EMP, i.e. Year, Month and Day are also elementary fields.

Besides giving the record name and its structure, the characteristics of the data has to be specified in the record description. This is done with the help of the PICTURE clause. This clause follows the field name. After the word PICTURE, a string made up of specific characters is given. This string is a dummy representation of the type of data to be stored in the particular record. One important point to be noted is that the PICTURE clause is to be used only with elementary fields and not with group fields.

The first characteristic it defines is the type of data, i.e. numeric, non-numeric, etc. The digit 9 is used to represent numeric data, the symbol X to represent character data and the symbol A to represent alphanumeric data. The symbol V is used to indicate the position of the assumed decimal point. The symbol S is used to indicate if the data item has a sign value or not. If the symbol does not exist, then it is assumed that it is a positive quantity.

Certain rules have to be followed in defining the data item with these symbols.

1. There is no specific symbol to indicate the size of the data item. A four digit numeric item may be specified by '9999' or '9(4)'. Both the methods of representation are correct.
2. In the case of an alphabetic item the picture can contain only the symbol A.
3. In the case of a numeric item, the picture may contain only the symbol 9, V &S. The symbol V and S can appear only and S can only be leftmost character.
4. In the case of an alphanumeric item, picture may contain all 'X's or a combination of 9, A and X.

Example:

PICTURE 9999 a four digit numeric

PICTURE 99V99 a four digit numeric with a decimal point after second place.

PICTURE AAAAAA a six character string

PICTURE S999V9 a four digit signed numeric with decimal point after the three digits

PICTURE 9(3)V9 a four digit numeric with decimal point after 3 digits

PICTURE AAA99X a six character alpha-numeric

PICTURE A(8) an eight character string

Along with the PICTURE clause another optional clause, i.e. the USAGE clause may be used. The USAGE clause is entered after the PICTURE clause has been made. It may define the data item to be one of two types. These are known as the COMP and DISPLAY types. If the item will be used very frequently for calculations, then it should be specified as a COMP item. Even if it is not specified as a COMP item, the computation will be carried out, but it will be much slower. Hence, to enhance the speed of the program, certain items which will be regularly used for frequent calculations can be defined as DISPLAY. However, it should be remembered that Comp items cannot be printed out in reports. They have to be converted into the Display type before they can be used for printing in reports, etc.

Example:

```
05 PAYSCALE  PICTURE 9999V99 USAGE  COMP.
```

Given below is a complete record description of our hypothetical file structure.

```
01 EMPLOYEE-DESCRIP.
02 SNO PICTURE 999.
02 AGE PICTURE 99.
02 ADDRESS   PICTURE A(3).
02 JOB-CODE  PICTURE XXX.
02 DATE-EMP.
05 YEAR        PICTURE 99.
05 MON         PICTURE 99.
05 DATE        PICTURE 99.
```

WORKING-STORAGE SECTION

This section describes the various data items which are used as temporary storage areas during the processing of the program. These are independent data items along with their sub-divisions, which are in no way related to the data items described in the FILE SECTION. Data items like loop counters, program headings, report headings, etc. are defined in this section. Again the data items are divided into Group Items and Elementary Items, like in the FILE SECTION. The data items in the WORKING-STORAGE SECTION are also assigned level numbers. The rules for assigning level numbers are slightly different from the FILE SECTION. The elementary items are given either the special level number 77 or may be given level number 01. Group items always begin with level number 01 and the sub-division may have any greater level number besides the special levels.

These items also have a PICTURE clause in the same manner as in the FILE SECTION. The USAGE clause can also be used in this section just as in the FILE SECTION. Besides the USAGE and PICTURE clauses, one additional clause known as the Value clause may be assigned as an optional feature. The VALUE clause follows the PICTURE clause and is given only for elementary items. An entry is made after the word VALUE and this entry signifies the actual value held by the data item.

Example

```
77 PAYSCALE  PICTURE 999V99 VALUE 100.
```

The numeric variable Payscale now has the value 100 stores against it. Similarly, characters variables can also have character values.

Group items are entered almost similar to the File Section. The group item is given level 01 and succeeding elementary items, a higher level number. A group item very commonly used in COBOL is the detail line of a report which may consist of various items.

Example:

```
WORKING-STORAGE  SECTION.
01 DETAIL-LINE.
02 NUMB PICTURE 99 VALUE IS SPACES.
02 NAME  PICTURE  A(10) VALUE  IS  SPACES.
```

Presented below is a complete example of an hypothetical WORKING STORAGE SECTION.

```
WORKING  STORAGE  SECTION
77 TOTAL  PICTURE 9(4) V9 (2) VALUE  ZERO.
77 HEADING  LINE  PICTURE  A (4) VALUE IS "COST"
77 EMP-COUNTER  PICTURE 9(3) USAGE  COMP.
01 DETAIL-LINE.
02 NUMB  PICTURE 99  VALUE  IS  SPACES
02 NAME  PICTURE  A (10) VALUE  IS  SPACES.
```

One important point to be mentioned is an explanation of the COBOL reserved word FILLER. The word FILLER is used from specifying an unused area on a card file or a blank area in a particular field or record. It contains a PICTURE clause specifying the size of the blank area. It is usually of the alpha-numeric type. It may be used in the FILE SECTION or the WORKING-STORAGE SECTION in the description of a data item or a file record. FILLER, an itself, is an elementary field or item containing blanks equal to its size.

Example:

```
01 PAY-SHEET.
02 EMPNO  PICTURE 99999.
02 FILLER  PICTURE  X(30).
```

```
02 NAME  PICTURE A(10).
02 ADRES  PICTURE  X(20).
02 FILLER  PICTURE  X(35).
```

A record called PAY-SHEET of 100 characters has been defined and its breakup is given, out of which 65 spaces are blank. They have been specified by the reserved word FILLER.

REPORT SECTION

The REPORT SECTION is used for writing out reports on certain files, with the help of the COBOL report writer. However, reports can be written without the report writer. Using the report section makes the task much easier and facilitates writing the report. The REPORT SECTION consists on a RD clause, which consists of the report description very much similar to the FD in the FILE SECTION. This defines the name of the report, the logical size of the report page, the number of lines to appear on a page, the heading lines and the footing line.

The RD entry is followed by the report description entry just like the record description in the file section. This has a description of the various report items or the report. Each report item will have a level number. Again there can be group items or elementary items.

Example:

```
REPORT  SECTION.
RD FINAL-REP.
PAGE 45 LINES.
HEADING 4.
02 TYPE  REPORT-LINE.
02 COLUMN 4 PICTURE 9(3) SOURCES NO
02 COLUMN 20 PICTURE A(10) SOURCE  NAME
```

PROCEDURE DIVISION

This is the most important division of the COBOL program. It is in this division that the program logic and computational steps are written to arrive at a solution to the problem. This division consists of statements, which specify the operations to be performed by the computer. These statements are formed with COBOL words and literals or variables.

The procedure division always begins with the words PROCEDURE DIVISION, as in the other divisions. A number of procedures may follow, each having a procedure name. Each procedure must have a unique procedure name. A procedure name may be made up of upto 30 characters within the framework of rules laid down for giving variable names. A period must follow every procedure name.

Optionally, the PROCEDURE DIVISION may be divided into sections. Sectionalising provides better documentation but is not compulsory. Section names are also created with the same rules as for procedure names. The COBOL word SECTION and period must follow the section name to signify a section.

Example:

```
PROCEDURE  DIVISION
FIRST-PART  SECTION.
GETT-PROC.
xxxxx
xxxxx
GIVE-PROC.
xxxxx
xxxxx
SECOND-PART  SECTION.
```

This section name in above example are First-Part and Second-Part, while GETT-PROC and GIVE-PROC are procedure names. The xxxxx represent dummy commands.

The PROCEDURE DIVISION may consist of as may sections as desired. Each section may further include as many procedures as required. A procedure may, in turn, be composed of one statement or several hundred statements. The procedure names are also referred to as paragraph names and the procedures as paragraphs. Each statement of a procedure has to end with a period. The period signifies the end of a statement. A statement may continue for more than one line. Statements should ideally be indented under the procedure names. This is not essential but highly desirable as it makes documentation and understandability very easy. Also, every new statement should begin on a new line for the same reasons.

Each statement of the PROCEDURE DIVISION always begins with a COBOL verb. The verb is a COBOL reserved word which designates the particular action that the statement will perform. An example of a PROCEDURE DIVISION is given below. It will not be possible for the student to completely understand the example, as the action of COBOL verbs has not yet been explained.

Example:

```
Procedure  Division
First-Part  Section.
Open-Files.
Open  Input  Pay-Sheet
Output  Pay-Report.
```

Move 1 to Counter.
Calculate.
READ PAY-SHEET
At End
Go to Complete.
Complete.
Close Pay-Sheet
PAY-REPORT.

THE MOVE STATEMENT

The MOVE statement is its most elementary form causes data to be copied from one memory location to another. The general syntax of the MOVE command is:

MOVE xxxxxx TO xxxxxx

Where xxxxxx are dummies for different variables. The action that takes place is that contents of the first variable xxxxxxx are copied to the second variable specified. The first variable is known as the sending variable while the second variable is known as the receiving variable xxxxxx can be fields of a certain record instead of being standard variables.

Example:
MOVE PAY-SHEET TO NEW-PAY-SHEET
MOVE 10 TO NEW-PAY-SHEET
MOVE "ALPHA" TO TEMP-STORE
MOVE 53 TO OLD-PAY, NEW-PAY, SALARY

A slight change is noticed in the second and third example. Here the sending part is not a variable, nor is it a field. A literal itself is moved to the receiving variable or field. In the last example, the literal 53 is being copied to 3 different variables or fields. Hence, the receiving variables are multiple in number. One important point to be noted is that if the sending part is a variable or a field, it remains unchanged. In case it a literal, there is no question of the value changing.

Rules regarding data movement by the MOVE verb:

1. The contents of the sending field are moved to a singular or multiple receiving field or fields. The contents of the sending field always remain unchanged.
2. The sending field cannot be more than one, while the receiving fields may be multiple.
3. Data movement cannot occur from numeric to alphabetic or from alphanumeric or alphabetic to numeric.

4 When the sending field is numeric and the receiving field is also numeric or numeric dinted, the data movement is called numeric data transfer. If both the fields are of the same size, the receiving field becomes an exact copy of the sending field. If the sending field is smaller than the receiving field, then the receiving field area is filed-in from the right-most position and the areas left blank are filled-in with zeros. If the sending field is larger than the receiving field, the receiving field loses the left most digits of the sending field. A warning is also given that part of the data is lost. Hence, the rule is that the movement of the integer portion of the sending field with respect to the receiving field is from right to left, while the movement of the decimal portion is from left to right.

5. When both the sending and receiving fields are alphabetic or alphanumeric, the data movement is called as alphanumeric data transfer. In such cases, if both the fields are equal in dimension, hen an exact copy is made. If the sending field is smaller than the receiving field then the receiving field is filled in from left to right and the extra spaces are filled-in with blanks. If the receiving field is smaller, then the data is lost from the right and a warning is issued. Hence, the rule is the movement of data from the sending field with respect to the receiving field is from left to right.

   Example:

1. Value of A is 1234 and B is PICTURE 9999. If the command is MOVE A TO B, then the value of B after the transfer will be 123.
2. If B is PICTURE 9(7) and the same command is used, the value of B will be 0001234.
3. If B is PICTURE 999 and the same command is used, then the value of B will be 234.
4. If A is 234.45 and B is PICTURE 99V99 and the same command is used, then the value of B after the command will be 23.45.
5. If B is PICTURE 9V99, then the value B after the command will be 3.45.
6. If B is PICTURE 99V9, then the value of B after the command will be 3.45.
7. If B is PICTURE 999V999, then the value of B after the command will be 023.450
8. If A is "PACK" and B is PICTURE A (4), the value of B after the command will be "PACK"
9. If B is PICTURE A(8), then value of B after the command will be "PACK".
10. If B is Picture A(2), then the value of B after the command will be "PA".

This is the simplest form of the MOVE verb. There are a few optional features which can be used with the MOVE verb, which change the outcome of the data movement slightly.

MOVE CORRESPONDING

This is an optional feature which can be used with the Move command, if it is used for transfer of data from one group field to another group field. The syntax of the command is as follows:

MOVE CORRESPONDING xxxxxx TO xxxxxx

In the above, the first xxxxxx represents the sending group field and the second xxxxxx represents the receiving group field. This command specifies that all the identical elementary data items from the sending field are copied over to the corresponding elementary data items in the receiving field. Hence, instead of using separate MOVE statements for each elementary data item, a single MOVE CORRESPONDING statements can be used more efficiently. In the normal course of events, it is always preferable to have unique names for elementary data items in the whole program. However, in certain instances it is preferable to have common names as it makes the data transfer simpler.

Example:

MOVE CORRESPONDING SER-NUMB TO NEW-SER-NUMB

where both the group fields are described as follows:

```
01 Ser-Numb
02 Part-1  Picture 9(3)
02 Part-2  Picture 9(2)
02 Part-3  Picture 9(4)
01 New-Ser-Numb
02 Part-1  Picture 9(3)
02 Filler  Picture X(2)
02 Part-2  Picture 9(2)
02 Filler  Picture X(3)
02 Part-3 Picture 9(4)
```

The above mentioned command will move the elementary data items of SER-NUMB into the appropriate locations in NEW-SER-NUMB. Here, the corresponding data items are appearing in the same order in both the group fields. This is not necessary. They may be in different orders in both the fields and still the data movement will take place properly. One important point to be noted is that only the common elementary data items in the receiving group field will be altered while the other areas will remain the same.

EDITING OF DATA ITEMS

Now that we have learnt to transfer data items from one field to another, we can now go to learn another important aspect of data transfer. This is known as editing. What essentially happens is that the format of the data being moved from one place to another is altered according to the programmer's specifications. We have already seen that data is automatically altered when the MOVE command is used in certain condition. Editing of data gives us more control of the output of data in reports or when the MOVE command is being used.

There are various characters which are used in the PICTURE clause of the receiving data item to indicate what sort of editing function has to be carried out. The various characters are:

Z *$ - + CR DB., B and /

We shall now see the functions carried out by each of these characters.

Z Zero Suppression

The edit character Z has the same meaning as that of a 9 in the PICTURE clause, except that insignificant leading zeroes in the source data, if any, in the positions indicated by Z are suppressed. It is quite obvious that Z cannot appear to the right of any 9. The lower case V represents the assumed location of the decimal point.

Example:

PICTURE of receiving field	Value Moved	Edited Value
ZZ999	05987	5987
ZZ999	00052	052
ZZ999	1v68	001
ZZZV99	038v4	3840
ZZZVZZ	0v1	1
ZZZVZZ	0	(BLANK)

The edit character * has a function similar to the Z, character except that instead of putting blanks, it puts the * character in place of the zero.

Example:

PICTURE of receiving field	Value Moved	Edited Value
**999	05987	6987
**999	00052	**052
**999	1v68	**001
***V99	038v4	*3840
***V99	0v769	***76
***V**	0v1	**0*1
***V**	0	*****

$ Currency Sign

A single currency sign can appear at the leftmost position of a PICTURE entry. If it does, the edited data will have a $ character inserted at the position specified by the $.

Example:

Picture of receiving field.	Value Moved	Edited Value
$ZZ999	05987	$5987
$**999	00052	$**052
$**999	1v68	$**001

It can be used in combination with the previously defined editing characters.

Minus Sign

A minus sign can appear at the left-most or the right-most position of the PICTURE entry. Depending on its position, a minus sign appears in the edited data value on the right-most position or a the left-most position, if the value is negative. If the value is a positive quantity, only a space will appear.

Example:

PICTURE of receiving field	Value Moved	Edited Value
-ZZ999	-05987	-5987
**999-	-00052	**052-
**999	1v68	**001

+Plus Sign

A plus sign has the same meaning as the minus sign, except that a plus sign appears instead of the minus sign when the number is a positive quantity. However, if the quantity is negative, a minus sign will be inserted, which is unlike the minus sign, where a blank is inserted, if the item is positive. One important point to note is that in case both these signs are not used there will be no indication that the data, which has been moved is positive or negative.

Example:

PICTURE of receiving field	Value Moved	Edited Value
+ZZ999	-05987	-5987
**999+	00052	**052+
+**999	1v68	+**001

CR & DB Credit and Debit Signs

The above two characters CR & DB may occur only on the rightmost position of the PICTURE entry. Their functioning is quite identical to the position of the PICTURE entry. They will appear in the edited data only if the data value being moved is negative and they appear on the rightmost-position of the edited value. In all other cases they are replaced by blank spaces.

Example:

PICTURE of receiving field	Value Moved	Edited Value
ZZ999CR	-05987	5987CR
**999DB	-00052	**052DB
**999CR	1v68	**001

The Decimal Point

The decimal point which is the same symbol as a period, may be inserted only once on the PICTURE entry. If there is a data value 23v45 to be printed out on a report, it should appear as 23.45 to give a proper meaning to its value. The v denotes only an hypothetical location of the decimal point for calculations: In fact, the data item 23v45 requires only four storage locations. Hence, the period sign may be used in the PICTURE clause while editing, to obtain the actual decimal point.

Example:

PICTURE of receiving field	Value Moved	Edited Value
ZZ99.99	96v32	96.32
999.99	23v12	023.12
Z99.99	12v03	12.03

Comma Character

A comma is quite often used while editing. A common is inserted into the edited data item at whichever position is appears in the PICTURE entry. The comma can be used more than once. When it is used in conjunction with the Z character or *, the comma will be suppressed if any suppression takes place to the right of comma. The comma cannot be the rightmost or the leftmost character in the PICTURE entry.

Example:

PICTURE of receiving field	Value Moved	Edited Value
99,99	3124	31,24
99,999	12	00,012
Z,ZZZ	231	231
*,***	13	**13

B Blank Insertion

The appearance of the character B any where in the PICTURE entry causes a space to be entered at the particular location in the edited data item.

Example:

PICTURE of receiving field	Value Moved	Edited Value
99B99	3124	31 24
99B999	12	00 012
ZBZZZ	231	231
*B***	13	**13

/Slash Insertion

The appearance of this character anywhere in the Picture entry causes the / to be inserted in the edited data item. It can appear more than once. It is quite useful when editing data items that represent dates. However, this function, many a times, is not available on the newer compilers.

Example:

PICTURE of receiving field	Value Moved	Edited Value
99/99/99	863124	86/31/24
99/999	12	00/012
Z/ZZZ	231	231

This completes a review of most of the editing functions. However, there remains one more aspect of using some of these.

Floating Insertion

We noticed that when the $ and the - and + symbols were used on the leftmost and rightmost sides of the PICTURE entry, blank spaces were left between the editing symbol and the actual data value when the size of the value being moved was lesser then the PICTURE description of the receiving field. To avoid this blank spacing in between the sign and the actual data on the left side, we can use the floating insertion method. Here, the editing symbol appears in multiples on the left hand side and behaves in the same way as the Z character, except that an extra symbol appears on the left hand side of the edited data value.

Example:

PICTURE of receiving field　　Value Moved　Edited Value

$$$999	05987	$5987
$$$999	00052	$052
$$$999	1v68	$001
999	-05987	-5987

Rules to be Observed While Editing

1. Symbols + - CR DB and the operational character S are mutually exclusive and only one of these may appear in a PICTURE entry.
2. As floating insertion characters $ + - S and * are mutually exclusive, i.e., if - is used as a floating insertion $ cannot be used in the same manner. However, $ may still be used as a regular editing character and thereby occupy the leftmost position.
3. Besides the regular editing characters, the PICTURE entry may contain the operational characters 9 and V. However, both the period sign and V are not permitted to gather in a PICTURE entry.
4. The editing characters plus the operational characters have to be considered to determine the size of the edited data item.
5. Only the B editing character can be used while editing alphabetic data items.
6. Two editing characters B and / can be used in the case of alphanumeric data.

ARITHMETIC COMMANDS

Let us classify COBOL programming statements who certain groups. Any COBOL statement falls into one of three groups. These are:

1. Imperative Statements
2. Conditional Statements
3. Compiler Directing Statements

An imperative statement is one which directs the object program to take a specific action during execution. The MOVE command we have learnt, forms an imperative statement.

A conditional statement is one which directs the object program to examine the truth value of condition and to take subsequent action depending upon the truth value. We shall learn conditional statements, when we learn the IF statement.

Compiler directing statements are those which are used to direct the COBOL compiler. These statements are not used in the object program. They can be compared to the immediate mode commands of BASIC. These statements many a times vary between system to system and compiler to compiler.

The arithmetic commands which we shall learn are imperative commands. These commands, when used, generate imperative statements, i.e., immediate action is taken as soon as these statements are read. They are used to perform computations variable or literal numeric data items. There are five main arithmetic commands. These are:

1. Add
2. Subtract
3. Multiply
4. Divide
5. Compute

The verb ADD is used to find the sum of two or more numbers and to store this to a particular variable. The ADD statement can be used in two different formats. The first format of the ADD statement in its simplest form is.

Add A to B

Where A is either a numeric literal or a numeric variable having some data value, while B has to be a numeric variable. In this case, the value in A is added to the value in B and the sum is stored in B.

The first value can be replaced by multiple values in the following fashion.

ADD A,B,C, TO D

In this format, the values in A,B and C are added to value of D and the sum stored in D. In both the above cases, the old value of D is lost. However, in certain cases, it is necessary to retain both the values and also the sum which is calculated has to be stored. In this case, the second format of the ADD statement is utilised. This is as follows.

ADD, A,B GIVING C

In this format, the word GIVING is used instead of To and an extra variable has to be used where the calculated sum has to be stored. In this case, the total of A and B is found and the sum stored in C. More than two variables or literals or a combination of variables and literals can be used before the word GIVING. Similarly, more than one variable can be used after GIVING, in the following fashion.

ADD, A, B, C, D, GIVING E,F

Here, the sum of A,B,C and D is found and stored in E as well a F. A very important rule to follow is that word To cannot be used when GIVING is used and vice versa. Another point to be noted is that wherever variables are being used, they should have had been previously defined in the DATA DIVISION.

Example:

ADD BONUS TO MONTHPAY. ADD PAY, BONUS, COMMISSION GIVING MONTHPAY.

Besides these regular formats of the ADD statement, there is an optional feature which may or may not be used. This is the word ROUNDED. This word can be added at the end of the statement in both the formats. The result is that the value obtained is rounded off, in case the result does not fit in the specification of the variable in which it has to be stored.

Example:

ADD BONUS TO MONTH PAY ROUNDED

In this example, if the value of BONUS is 57.291 and the value of MONTH PAY is 10.15, the actual answer is 67.441. If we assume that the PICTURE OF MONTH PAY has specified it to have only two places after the decimal, we would lose some degree of exactness in the answer. Using the ROUNDED option causes the answer to be rounded off, and the rightmost digit is left alone or increased by one, depending upon the digit which has been eliminated. Here the new value of MONTH PAY would be 67.44.

The Subtract Statement

The subtract verb is used to subtract one, or the sum of two or more numbers from one or more numbers, and store it. This can also be used in two formats. The first format is.

Subtract A from B

In this, the value of A will be subtracted from the value of B and the result stored in B. This is similar to the To format of the ADD statement. Again multiple variables can be used either before the word From or after the word From. This is demonstrated in the following examples.

Subtract A FROM B,C,D

In the first example, the values of A and B will be first added and the sum subtracted from C and stored in C. In the second example, A and B are added and the sum first subtracted from C and the result stored in C. The same procedure is carried out for D. The third example is similar to the second one, except that only the value of A is subtracted first from B and the result stored in B, then a gain A is subtracted from C and the result stored in C and then the same process is carried out for D.

Just like the ADD statement, in this format, the first value may be a literal or a variable, but the values after the word FROM must be variables. Also the old values of the variables in which the result is stored or lost. To prevent this from happening, the second format of the SUBTRACT statement is used. It is as follows,

Subtract A from B Giving D

Here the value of A is subtracted from B and stored in D. Again, multiple values can be used in place of A, B as well as D. The ROUNDED option may be used for the same purpose as the ADD statement.

The Multiply Statement

This statement causes one or more multiplicands to be multiplied a multiplier. This also has two formats, just like the ADD and SUBTRACT statements. The first format is,

Multiply A by B

Here, the word BY is used instead of FROM or TO. The value of A will be multiplied with B and the result stored in B. Again multiple values can be used by the ADD and SUBTRACT statements, multiple values cannot be used before the word BY. Only one variable or literal can be multiplied with multiple variables following the word BY.

Multiply A by B,C,D

The value of A is multiplied by B and the result stored in B, then A is multiplied by C and stored in C and finally the same is repeated with D. However, in all the above examples, the old values of the variables appearing after the word By are lost. To prevent this from happening the second format is used.

MULTIPLY A BY B GIVING D

MULTIPLY A BY C,D GIVING G, H

This is similar to the GIVING format of the ADD and SUBTRACT statements. In the first example, A is multiplied with B and the result stored in D. In the second, A is multiplied by C and the result stored G, and C multiplied by D and the result stored in H. In case multiple variables are used after the words BY and GIVING, care has to be taken that there are in equal number of variables in both the places, as in the second example.

Example:

MULTIPLY MONTH PAY BY 12 GIVING YEAR PAY.

This rounded option may be used alongwith the MULTIPLY statement in the same fashion.

The Divide Statement

This is more or less similar to the MULTIPLY verb, except that it carries out the function of dividing one number by another, instead of multiplying. This has three different forms rather than two. The first for is as follows.

Divide A into B

In this form, the value of B is divided by A and the result stored in B. This is the simplest form of the DIVIDE Statement. Multiple variables can be used following the rules of the MULTIPLY statement in the following manner.

Divide A into B, C

The value of B is divided by A and the result stored in B and then C is divided by A and the result stored in C. Multiple variables or literals cannot be used before the word INTO. In the second form of the DIVIDE statement, the word GIVING is used just as in the other case.

Divide A into Giving D

Here, C is divided by A and the result is stored in D. In this form, multiple variables are allowed before and after the word GIVING, following the rules of the MULTIPLY statement.

Divide A into C,D Giving P, Q

In the above example, C is divided by A and the result stored in P and D is divided by A and the result stored in Q. In all the above examples of the DIVIDE statement, we have noticed that in case there is a remainder left after the division, no provision has been made for it. The third format of the DIVIDE statement takes care of this. The form is as follows.

Divide A into B Giving Remainder D

In this case B is divided by A and the result is stored in C and the remainder, if any, is stored in D.

Example:

DIVIDE 12 INTO TOT PAY GIVING PAY

In some compilers, the syntax of the DIVIDE statement can be slightly modified and the word INTO is replaced by the word BY. However, care should be taken that when the word BY is used, the first value is divided by the second value, unlike the INTO word where the second value is divided by the first value.

Example:

DIVIDE TOT MARK BY TOT SUB GIVING A VERAGE.

DIVIDE TOT SUB INTO TOT MARK GIVING A VERAGE.

Both the statements mean the same thing. The variable value TOT MARK is divided by the variable value TOT SUB and the results stored in the variable AVERAGE.

The ROUNDED option may be similarly used with the DIVIDE statement, if desired.

The Compute Statement

The COMPUTE is the most powerful of all the arithmetic verbs. It can, in fact, be used to carry out all the functions previously mentioned and many programmers prefer using the COMPUTE statement instead of the other arithmetic statements. It causes entire equations to be evaluated. This general format is,

COMPUTE variable = (arithmetic expression)

The COMPUTE verb has the following meaning. The arithmetic expression on the right of the equal sign is evaluated and the result obtained, is stored in the variable on the left hand side. The data items on the right hand side may be numeric literals, numeric variables or a combination of both. The left hand side must be a numeric variable. The different arithmetic symbols are used to make up an arithmetic expression on the right hand side. + - * and / are used to indicate add, subtract, multiply and divide. The symbol ** is used to indicate exponentiation. These symbols are knows as operators. These are quite similar to those used in BASIC. Certain rules have to be followed fro developing arithmetic expressions.

Rules for Arithmetic Expressions:

1. The arithmetic expression may consist of two or more literals or variables, joined by the specified arithmetic operators.
2. There must be at least one space following and preceding the operator.
3. No two arithmetic operators can follow each other consecutively.
4. Parenthesis may be used to specify the order of operations. When parenthesis are used, the portion of the expression enclosed in the brackets is evaluated first. When parenthesis are used within parenthesis, the evaluation proceeds from the least inclusive pair to the most inclusive pair.
5. If parenthesis are absent, the order is from left to right with exponentiation first, followed by division and multiplication, and then subtraction followed by addition.

The following is an example of the COMPUTE statement.

COMPUTE AVERAGE = (MARK1 + MARK2 + MARK3)/3.

The Rounded option may be used for the same purpose, as is used in the other arithmetic statements. The syntax of using it is as follows,

COMPUTE ROUNDED AVERAGE = (MARK1 + MARK2 + MARK3)/3.

On Size Error

Now that we have completed a study of the various arithmetic verbs and their different formats, we can now learn an important clause that can be used with all the arithmetic statements. This is knows as the ON SIZE ERROR clause.

If, after an arithmetic, operation, the result exceeds the largest value that can be connodated in the result field, an error occurs and this is known as the ON SIZE ERROR. If the ON SIZE ERROR clause is used with any of the arithmetic statements, the programmer has to specify the action desired in case the error occurs. This clause is written at the end of any arithmetic statement, and is followed by the action which has to be taken if the error occurs.

Example:

ADD PAY TO TOT PAY ON SIZE ERROR

GO TO ERR MESSAGE.

Notice that the period is at the end of the complete statement. In case the size of the value obtained after the addition is greater than the size of the variable, TOT PAY, control will be transferred to the ERR MESSAGE procedure. We have not yet learnt the GOTO statement but right now the student can assume that it just means transfer control. In case the ON SIZE ERROR was not given, the data item would have been stored in TOT PAY with loss of characters from the left hand side, which would make the calculations absolutely wrong.

INPUT/OUTPUT STATEMENTS

The Input and Output verbs are meant for transfer of data between files, and CPU, the operator and the CPU, and between the operator and the file. Hence, these verbs deal with reading some form of data into the memory and outputting data from the memory. The input and output may be to and from files or the computer user. There are six verbs meant for such functions. Out of these, the first are for file handling and the last two are for interaction with the user. These are as follows.

1. Open
2. Close
3. Read
4. Write
5. Accept and
6. Display

The Open Statement

Before any data can be read or written onto a file, the file has to be opened. This is done with the help of the OPEN verb. The file to be happened has to be specified and also whether it is going to be in the input mode i.e. if data is going to be read from it or the output mode. i.e. if data is going to be written on it. A file once opened with the OPEN verb will remain open until it is close with the CLOSE verb. The general form of the OPEN statement is as follows.

```
OPEN  INPUT xxxxxxx
OUTPUT xxxxxxx.
```

The words INPUT and OUTPUT are COBOL reserved words used in the OPEN statement for specifying if the file is going to be in the INPUT mode or the OUTPUT mode. In case either of INPUT or OUTPUT files have to be opened, the word which is not required can be omitted. It is also possible to separately write the word OPEN for every file that is opened, but this is an unnecessary procedure.

Example:

```
1. Open Input Master-File
Output Report-File.
2. Open Input Pay-File.
Bonus-File
Divid-File
Output Pay-Sheet
Tax-form.
```

Notice the period at the end of the last entry. This signifies the end of the OPEN statement. It is very important to enter the period at the end of the statement.

The Close Statement

The CLOSE statement is used when the processing of a certain file is complete and it will not be required again the program. It is important to note that only those files can be closed which have been previously opened in the same program. If this is not the case, an error will result. However, it is important to close all open files at the end of the program or some data may be lost. Once a file is closed, it can be subsequently opened by using the OPEN statement again. Unlike the OPEN statement, the nature of the file, i.e. INPUT and OUTPUT need not be mentioned with the CLOSE statement. The general form is as follows;

CLOSE xxxxxx

xxxxxx represents the name of the file which has to be closed. Single or multiple files may be closed with a single CLOSE statement.

Example:

Close Master-File

Close Pay-File

Bonus-File

Divid-File

Pay-Sheet

Tax-form.

The Read Statement

The READ statement gets the next available logical record from an input file or an input device to the computer memory. The word logical has been stressed because, when a file is being read for the first time, the first record of the file will be read into the memory. Then next time, the READ command is executed, the second record of the file is input into the memory. In this fashion, each successive record of the file is input till the end of the file is encountered. It is at this point that the other part of the READ statement comes into play. The general form of the READ statement is as follows:

READ xxxxxxx AT END GO TO yyyyyyy

Here, xxxxxxx represents a file on some input device and yyyyyy represents some procedure. The verb GO TO has not yet been explained. It means that control is transferred to the procedure specified in yyyyyy. The words AT END mean that when the end of field is encountered, instead of a record being read, control is transferred to the procedure specified. The word GO TO yyyyyy are not compulsory. They may be optionally replaced by any other imperative statement. This means that some action which should take place on encountering the end of file has to be specified in the READ statement. The important point to be remembered is that the statement following AT END has to be an imperative one only.

Example:
Read Master At End
Go To Finish.
Read Master At End Move 5 To Counter
Go to Finish.

Besides the standard form of the READ statement, wherein the record is read into the computer's memory, another form exists wherein the record may be directly read into some other variable specified in the data division of the program. The format of this modification is as follows.

READ MASTER INTO NEW-MASTER AT END GO TO FINISH

Here, the record is read from the input file and, instead of just being stored in the computer memory, it is stored in the record specified by NEW-MASTER. The word INTO and a record name has to be used before the words AT END. A very important point to be noted is that the name specified before the word INTO is a file name, while a record or variable name is specified after the word INTO. This same procedure can be carried out by using the READ statement in its general form and then using a MOVE statement to transfer the contents of the record read into the new record.

THE WRITE STATEMENT

The function of the WRITE statement is to transfer information from a record in memory or from a record a file to an output device. The WRITE statement can exist in several forms. The simplest form of the WRITE statement is:

WRITE xxxxxxxx

In this form, the record specified by xxxxxx is simply sent to the default output device or any output device which has been previously specified. The above syntax is standardly used for printing out data on a printer. In case different devices used, the syntax may vary slightly. Discussing all the various devices is beyond the scope of this book and hence the WRITE statement will be described here only with reference to the printer output device. An important point to not is that xxxxxx represents a record name and not a file name, as is the case in the READ statement. The second format of the WRITE statement is as follows:

WRITE xxxxxx FROM yyyyyyy

Where xxxxxxx represents a record name, while yyyyy may be a record name or a variable previously defined in the DATA DIVISION and stored in the computer's memory. Here, the data is picked up from yyyyyy and written onto xxxxxx and then sent to the output device. In the first format, it is essential that the record name contain some data, else a blank record will be sent to the output device, while in the second format, the data is picked up from the second record or variable, temporarily transferred to the first specified record and then sent to the printer. An important point to be noted is that after the WRITE statement is executed, the data held in the record, which is written, is lost.

Example:

WRITE PAY OUT

WRITE PAY-OUT FROM HEADING.

Besides the above two formats, there are a few more optional features which may be used to control the output on the printer. These are the words BEFORE, AFTER, ADVANCING. LINE LINES and NEXT PAGE. The general format of using these commands is as follows:

WRITE xxxxxx BEFORE ADVANCING yyy LINES

or or

AFTER NEXT-PAGE

The words BEFORE and AFTER are written top-down, signifying that either of them may be used, as also LINES or NEXT-PAGE. xxxxx represents a record which has to be sent to the printer. yyy is a numeric integer literal or a variable. If the BEFORE clause is used, the record is printed out and then the page advanced by the number of lines specified in yyy. If AFTER is used, the page is advanced first and then the record is printed out. In case the record has to be printed on a new page, instead of using the yyy literal and the word LINES or LINE, the word NEXT PAGE is used, which automatically advances the stationary to the top of a new page.

The Accept Statement

The ACCEPT statement is used whenever a small amount of data has to be read in from the c if an action is dependent upon the operators input. This statement can also be used to read-in data like the day, time etc. from the operating system. The general form of the ACCEPT statement is,

ACCEPT xxxxx

This statement is quite similar to the keyword INPUT used in BASIC. Upon reading this statement, program execution is suspended and a prompt message is displayed on the console saying that an input from the operator is required to carry on further processing. xxxxxx represents a variable into which the data entered from the console will be saved. The data entered by the operator will be left-justified.

Example:

ACCEPT CHE-OUT.

where xxxxxx is again a variable name and yyyyy is a mnemonic representing a hardware device, or it is one of the three words DATE, DAY or TIME. In case it is a mnemonic representing a hardware device, data is taken in from the hardware device and stored in xxxxxx. In case it is one of the three specified words, the relevant data is taken from them and stored in xxxxxx.

Example;

ACCEPT PRESENT-TIME FROM TIME.

Here, the time is taken from the operating system clock and stored in the variable PRESENT-TIME.

The Display Statement

The DISPLAY statement serves a purpose like the WRITE statement, i.e., it outputs data. However, it is usually meant for outputting low-volume data onto the console, so as to send a message to the operator. It may also be used to send data to any other hardware device. It can be said to be the opposite of the ACCEPT statement. The general format is as follows:

DISPLAY xxxxxx

xxxxxx may be a variable or a record or even a literal. The value represented by xxxxx is displayed on the console. Multiple variables or literals or a mixture of both may be outputted with a single DISPLAY statement. The different variables and literals should be separated by commas. In case a literal is being output, it should be enclosed within quotes.

Example:

DISPLAY "THE ANSWER IS", RESULT.

Two data items are being displayed, One is the literal "THE ANSWER IS" and the second is the value held in the variable RESULT.

The second format of the DISPLAY statement is the use of the word UPON and a mnemonic name following the variables or literals to be displayed. In case the word UPON is used, data will be sent to the hardware device specified by the mnemonic rather than to the console.

Now that we have completed a study of the preliminary and most commonly used COBOL verbs, we can go ahead and write a complete COBOL program. The problem and the flowchart and program are clearly explained in the following example.

Sequence Control and Conditional Statements

Usually, a COBOL program is executed sequentially, i.e. the program statements are executed one after another in a serial manner. However, many a times, it is required that the program execution deviate from the serial execution. Certain steps may have to be repeated or certain steps may have to be skipped. To alter this sequence, the sequence control verbs are used. We saw in the previous chapter, the program for processing of a payroll. The verb

GO TO was used in two places to transfer program execution to a remote point specified by the procedure name given along with the GO TO verb. Hence, we can easily deduce that GO TO is a sequence control verb.

This transfer of control or execution of a program to a remove point is also known as branching. The program is said to branch off to a remote location. Branching can be divided into two types, namely,

1. Unconditional Branching and
2. Conditional Branching.

Unconditional branching is that form of branching whereby the branching takes place irrespective of any condition being satisfied or not. When the program reaches the branching statement, it always branches off to the point specified by the statement.

Conditional branching, on the other hand, takes place only when a certain specified condition is satisfied. A condition is an entity, which, at a time can have only one of the two values, i.e. True False. Conditional branching statements are usually carried out with the IF statement. There are a varied class of conditions which can be tested out with the IF statement. We shall study these classes of statements along with the IF statement.

THE GO TO STATEMENT

This verb is used to form the unconditional branching statement in COBOL. Control is transferred over, irrespective of anything, when this statement is encountered. This simplest form of the GOTO statement is as given below:

```
GO TO xxxxxxx
```

When xxxxxxx represents a procedure name. As a result of execution of this statement, control is transferred to the procedure name given following the word GO TO.

Example:

```
GO TO READ-FILE-PROC.
```

This command has been used in our previous programming example. It simply transfers control to READ-FILE-PROC procedure. The GO TO statement can optionally have a DEPENDING ON clause. This clause is useful when it is required that the program branch to different locations depending upon the value of a variable or literal, supplied after the Depending On clause. The general form of this statement is as follows:

```
GO TO xxxxx, yyyyyy, zzzzzz DEPENDING ON aaaa
```

where xxxxx, yyyyy and zzzzz are various procedure names, and aaaa is a numeric variable or a literal. The maximum value aaaa can have depends upon the number of procedures given before DEPENDING ON. If the procedures are 5 in number, aaaa should have a value between 1 and 5; if it is 3 then aaaa should have a value between 1 and 3. Hence, to the respective procedure, i.e. if the value is 4, then second procedure. It is important that the value should not exceed the number of procedures given and should be an integer between 1 and the total number of procedures. There is no limitation to the number of procedures that can be mentioned before the DEPENDING ON clause.

It is important to note that besides being used as a separate statement, the GO TO verb is also used along with other verbs to form complex statements which have GO TO as a part of themselves.

Example:

GO TO READ-FILE, MODI-FILE, CREAT-FILE

DEPENDING ON TEST.

THE STOP RUN STATEMENT

The STOP and the STOP RUN statements are relatively simple statements. The STOP RUN statements is used to cause termination of execution of the program. Upon encountering this statement, the program terminates and returns to the operating system level. The general form of this statement is very simple.

Stop Run

Besides being use like this, it also has one modification, Only the word STOP can be used to temporarily half the program and then statement is as follows:

STOP xxxxxx

where xxxxxx is a literal. If the literal is alphabetic or alphanumeric, it should be within quotes. This statement causes the program to halt and a message consisting of the literal output on the console or the printer. The program can then be re-started by manual intervention of the operator from the console.

Example:

STOP "THIS IS A SHORT BREAK".

THE IF STATEMENT

As previously mentioned this is a conditional branching statement and can be used for testing a variety of conditions. Before we go on to learn the different conditions that can be tested, let us learn the general form of the IF statement.

If xxxxxxx yyyyyy

where xxxxxx denotes a certain condition, and yyyyyy is the statement which should be carried out if the condition is found to be true. In case the condition is false program execution takes place in the normal fashion, i.e. the next statement is executed. The end of the IF statement is denoted by a period. The statement yyyy can be a multiple statement also. All the statements are executed till a period is encountered. In case the condition is false, control is transferred to the first statement after the period.

Another optional feature may be added to the IF statement. This is the ELSE or OTHERWISE clause. Either of the two words ELSE or OTHERWISE may follow the first statement and another statement will follow the clause. The general form is as follows:

If xxxxxx yyyyy OTHERWISE qqqqq

where qqqqq is another statement. This may also be represented as:

If xxxxxx yyyyy ELSE qqqqq

The difference here is that, if the condition is found to be false, control is transferred to the qqqqq statement. One important point to be noted here is that the end of the IF statement is denoted by a period at the end of the statement following the word OTHERWISE, i.e. qqqqq, which in turn may be multiple statement. In case there is no specific job to be done on the condition not being satisfied, then it is recommended that we write the reserved words NEXT SENTENCE after using ELSE in place of qqqq. The syntax would be as follows:

IF xxxxxxx pppppp ELSE NEXT SENTENCE.

6

The 'C' Language

A brief introduction to different types of software was made in previous chapter. Among the various kinds of software was a particular kind of software called a programming language with which other software programs can be written. These languages also fall under various classes, "C" is a languagc which is somewhere midway between a high level and a low level language. A large component of the C syntax follows the form and style of some high level languages and at the same time allows the programmer the latitute to meddle with the registers in the microprocessor and allow the built in DOS functions (known as interrupts) as well as the function hardwired into the microprocessor.

A complete understanding of C would take more than a book to write. In this chapter we shall be limited to the briefest of introduction to the C language and just get a feel of how does a C program look like perform.

Data Handling in C

Just like any other programming language, C also handles data. Data can be broadly classified into two types i.e. Constant and Variable Data. Constant data is that which does not change its value and represents itself. Constant data handling does not require very special methods or rules in C. On the other hand variable data is one whose value may change at any given time in the life of the program. Such variable data has to be represented by some particular name. Once a variable has been created by giving it a name it can be given any particular data value which may change as many times as required. The actual value is obtained by using the assigned variable name.

Variables

Variable data in C can have various types. Type means a certain form of data for e.g. character data or numeric data which allows calculations to be performed. The "C" language has different variable types. Some of these are listed below:

Character
Integer-Short
Integer-Long

Floating Point

Array

Character Variables types essentially store ASCII text, character by character. The variable can store in entire string which essentially is basically multiple characters stored together. This is done by using a character type Array.

The integer Variables types, both the Short and the Long, and the Floating point are essentially numeric variables. The Long format reserves four bytes to represent the number while the Short format uses two bytes to represent a number. The floating point is used to represent wither very small or very large numbers. The floating point variable standardly is represented in four bytes. A floating point variable is defined by using the word "float" at time of variable decleration.

The "C" language requires the type of all variables to be defined when creating the variable. The type of the variable has to be defined and then the variable being created. An initial value can be optionally assigned to the variable at this point. In case no value is assigned, the variable will hold a null value.

The last type i.e. Array is not really a variable type but rather is a different format of storing a large number of values to a single variable. A variable may be defined as an array. In case a variable is designated as an array, it also requires a type from those defined previously. An array can hold as many elements as defined in the size of the array. However all elements of the array have to be of the same type. A variable is defined as an array by following the variable name with the square brackets. The brackets should enclose a numeric value. This value represents the size of the array. It will have as many elements as the size of the array. Please note that the first element of the array in "C" is not the element represented by 1 but rather starts at 0. Hence the first element is the 0th element and not the 1st element. A few examples of array decleration:

```
chr x1[4]
x1[0] = 'A'
x1[1] = 'B'
x1[2] = 'C'
x1[3] = 'D'
x1[4] = 'E'
x1[5] = 'F'
int i[3] = [34, 123, 11,24]
int j[4]
```

Local & Static Variables

Other than having a variety of type of variables the behaviour of the "C" language variables depend upon another property of the variable. This is the class to which the variable belongs. The different classes of variables are generally known in the "C" language as Local & Static variables. The Local variables are also optionally known as automatic variables. By default all variables defined in the manner specified above are local/automatic variables. The class of a variable in essence defines the scope and lifetime of a variable.

Further on it will be evident that any "C" program is actually a collection of functions with one main calling function. A local/automatic variable is only available and exists for usage within the function that it has been created. Once the program flow returns from the defined function, the variable does not exist any more. Memory space is allocated for these variables dynamically i.e. at the time of variable creation. This memory space becomes free and available when control is returned from the function.

On the other hand static variable require that the term static precede the variable declaration and assignment, for eg.

```
static int i = 6
```

The above sentence will cause the variable i to be created as an integer type, but as a static variable. Defining the class of the variable as Static, changes the scope of the variable. Though the variable is not available in functions other than the one in which it was created, it still exists and retains the value that is had when control is passed on from the function in which it was created. When control is returned to the function a fresh copy of this variable is not made i.e. a new memory allocation is not done for this variable, but rather the last set value is picked up from the existing memory space.

Besides the local and static class of variable there exists another class of variable called the "global" variable. This kind of variable exists for the lifetime of the program. Memory is allocated for this variable before execution of the program starts, and is available in the entire lifetime of the program.

Operators in "C"

The "C" language has a plethora of operators for various tasks. These are the assignment operators, the arithmetic operators, compound, logical, relational and conditional operators. All these operators will now be studied in greater detail

The Assignment Operator

The "=" is the assignment operator and is used in the "C" language to assign a value to a variable. This operator may be used while creating the variable or at a latter stage. It is important to note that the value being assigned to a variable should be of the same type as that of the variable or else a type mismatch error will occur. Some examples of the use of the assignment operator are given below

```
int i = 33
int i
```

```
i = 21
chr x1 = "A"
chr x1
x1 = "A"
```

The "C" language allows a flexibility to be built into the assignment operator. This is known as the compound assignment operator. In this form the regular assignment operator "=" is combined with one of the mathematical operators to generate a value which is in turn assigned to the designated variable. An example is given below.

```
int i
i = 33
i = 1
i* = 2
```

In the above example i first gets a value of 33. This value is then decreased by one in the next assignment. The value is now set to 32. The next statement multiplies it by 2 and hence the value is now 64.

The Arithmetic Operators

The five basic arithmetic operators to be studied in C are as follows,+, -, *, / and %.

As is very evident multiplication and division. The fifth operator is for getting the modulus of any given number. The usage of these operators is very easy. The operators are used in the simple form for any kind of calculation and can be used in conjunction with the assignment operator as explained in the previous paragraph. In case these operators are used in combination then the "*" operator has the maximum precedence followed by "/", "+" and then the "-" operator. Examples of the operators are given below

```
i = 3*5
i = 3233/21
i = 4 + 4
i = 45-7
Combination Examples
i = 2*3+4
```

In this example 2 will be first multiplied by 3 and then the result will be added to 4. Hence the value being assigned to i will be 10 and not 24. The reason is that the "*" operator gets precedence over the "+" operator.

```
i =  4+8/2
```

In this example 8 is first divided by 2 and then added to 4 giving the result as 8. This is because the "/" operator gets precedence over the "+" operator.

However in case parantheses are used in a complex equation then the data in the parantheses is evaluated first within which the regular rules of operator precedence apply and then the result is evaluated with the rest of the formula. The previous example would evaluate differently with parantheses as follows

```
i = 2*(3+4)
```

In this example the result will be 14 since 4 is first added to 3 and then multiplied by 2.

The "%" operator generates the modulus value of any number. An example of this operator is

```
x = -12
i = %x
```

The value assigned to i will be 12 which is the modulus value of x.

The Increment/Decrement Operators

Besides being used as they are the "+" and the "-" operators are also used in a slightly different form to represent increment or decrement operators. The "+" operator when entered twice as follows, "++" represents an increment of the value of the associated variable by 1. Similarly a double "—" will decrement the value of the associated variable by 1. The general syntax of using these operators is as follows

```
int i = 10
i++
```

The above statement will increase the value of the variable "i" by 1. It is set to a value of 10 prior to the incrementing statement.

```
int i = 10
i—
```

The above statement will decrease the value of the variable "i" by one. Both these statements could also have been written in the following form

```
-i
++i
```

The above is also true. It does not matter whether the incrementing/decrementing operators appear before or after the variable which is being operated upon.

The Logical Operators

Logical operators are available in the "C" language to build up complex conditions and to create negative conditions. The three standardly used logical operators are "and", "or" and "not". As is very evident from the names, the "and" operator is used to add to a complex condition. If more then one logic has to be evaluated the multiple logics can be combined with the "and" operator and processing is initiated only if all the conditions built up with the "and" operator are satisfied.

The "or" operator is quite similar, except that it is used to create an either/or condition which very evident from the name itself. If conditions are built up with this operator then processing will be carried out even if any single condition is satisfied.

The "not" operator is basically used to test the negative of the condition as is very evident. Examples of these three operators are presented in the explanation of the "if" statement.

The Relational Operators

The relational operator are also used in evaluating conditions. These operators are "<", ">", ">=", "<=". These are actually two operators to test greater than or lesser than conditions and the following two are combination operators for greater than and equal to & lesser than and equal to. These can be used for comparison of numeric as well as character/ string values.

The Conditional Operator

The "?" Symbol is a conditional operator in the "C" language. This operator allows writing of very compact code, with an inherent disadvantage of poor readibility, especially for the newcomer to programming. However, it is a very useful operator in various instances while programming. This operator will always be used in a function and most commonly is used for assigning one of two values to a variable. The general syntax while using this operator is as follows

```
i = (cond ? exp1 exp2)
```

The entire logic is built into a single function enclosed by parantheses "cond" represents the condition being evaluated. This condition may be a simple or a complex condition. If the condition evaluates to be true, the variable i will get the value of "exp1" or else it will get the value of "exp2". "exp1" and "exp2" are either constant values or expressions returning a value or are functions returning the required value. Examples of the use of this operator will be made in the programs in the following pages.

The Structure of a "C" language program

Before proceeding and learning various "C" language commands and function, it is important to note the structure that any "C" program follows. A "C" language program is made up of C statements and C functions. The "C" language functions can be one of the predefined "C" functions available in a library along with the language or it can be user created function. The"C" language relies heavily on functions and even simple jobs like displaying on screen or printing is executed via a library function.

All "C" language programs start with a main calling function called main. A function encloses all statement within braces. The "main" function encloses open and close brackets. It is followed by all the required statements within curly brackets. In fact the simplest "C" program is given below. This program will actually do nothing, but is a complete program.

```
main()
{}
```

The curly braces include all the commands, functions etc required for the program being written. Almost always control passes on to other functions which are called from within the curly braces. All user created functions follow the same sequence. The function name is followed by the regular brackets and then the curly braces include all the required commands of the function. The regular brackets can optionally contain parameters being passed to the function.

Besides the above, almost all "C" language programs have include statements in the beginning of the program. These include statements appear before the main function. The general syntax of the include statement is as follows

```
#include < header file name>

#include <header file name>
```

The header file is a prewritten set of "C" code which should be included in the current program. In this fashion a lot of standard, routine purpose "C" code can be written and stored in header files. This code can be utilised in any other program by including the code with the include statement. Header files should have the extension set as "h". An example of the "include" statement is as follows

```
#include <head 1.h>
```

The "#" prior to the "include" statement indicates that this statement is what is knows as a pre-processor statement. There are other statements also which are formulated with the "#" symbol. Pre-processor means that statements are processed prior to compile time.

Having studied the structure of a "C" program, the basic "C" statements will be covered after which a few of the most common commands will be studied. The commands, statements can be divided into conditional statements, branching statements and looping statements.

Conditional Statements

These statements will test for a certain condition as specified and an either or action is carried out, depending upon if the condition was found to be true or false. The conditional statements to be studied are "if and "if-else".

"if" statement

This is the primary conditional statement. The general syntax of this statement is as follows

```
if(condition)
{
logic to be executed
}
```

In the above form the "if" word is followed by the condition enclosed in parantheses. As mentioned earlier the general format of this statement is very similar to the "main" function of the "C" language. The statements enclosed in the curly brackets will be executed if the condition is found to be true. If not the logic will bypass the curly brackets and continue onwards to the next available command.

The condition can be created with the conditional operators and is usually a comparision between a variable and a constant or some other variable for eg.

```
if(i = 45)
{
logic statements to be executed
}
```

In the above the condition being tested is the value of the variable "i". If this variable is equal to the value of 45 the logic in the curly brackets will be executed. In case "i" is not 45 then the logic is bypassed. A condition can also be created with string ie. character variables for eg.

```
if(x> 'A')
{
logic statements to be executed
}
```

In the above condition all values of X which start with an alphabet greater then "A" ie. falling after "A" in the alphabet will evaluate to true Complex conditions can be built up on a similar fashion, for eg.

```
if(x>'A' and x<'P')
{
logic statements to be executed
}
```

The complex condition has been made by using the logical operator "and". The logic of the above condition is self evident.

The "if" condition can be extended to include the "else" clause. If the "else" clause is used then two sets of program logic have to be created. If the condition evaluates to true the first set of statement is executed and if not then the second set of statements is executed The general syntax is as follows

```
if(condition)
{
first  statement set-will be executed if condition is true
}
else
{
second statement set-will be executed  if condition is false
}
```

Actual live examples of such conditions will be observed in the sample programs written in the past part of this chapter.

Branching Statements

Branching statements essentially alter the sequential flow of program and pass control to some remote location within the entire program. A few of the branching statements of the "C" language are "goto", "Switch", "case".

"goto" Statement

The "goto" statement is the simplest of the branching statements of the "C" language. This is an unconditional branching statement and is always executed and program control transferred to some other indicative point in the program. The general syntax of this statement is as follows

```
goto label
```

In the above example the word "label" represents any particular label name created by the user and in use within the program. Label names are very simply put, just some name given to an entry point in the program. The programmer may have as many have as many labels as desired in any program. However each label name should be unique. Label names have to be followed by a full colon i.e. "." The general form of entering a label is as follows

```
NAME1:
logic statements
```

In the above example the word "NAME1" is an user created label name. Applying the general form of the "goto" statement, the following example is created

goto NAME1

Even though this command is very simple and easy to use, it is not a much used command. The reason is that it becomes very difficult to trace the flow of logic if a lot of "goto" statements are used. Excellent program logics are those which do not make use of any "goto" statements or if necessary very minimal usage is made.

"switch" statement

The "switch" statement is utilised to carry out multiple branches. A single value is evaluated and depending of the different results different sets of statement are executed or else the program logic branches of to different functions. The "switch" statement is used in combination with the "case" statement to achieve this multiple branching. The general syntax of the "switch" statement is as follows

```
switch(var)
{ case var = val1
first set of logic
case var = val2
second set of logic
case var = val3
third set of logic}
```

In the above example var represents any particular variable which has been previously created and has a certain value. The "switch" statement followed by parantheses containing the variable to be evaluated initiates the process. The curly brackets enclose the "case" statements. Each case statement compares the variable obtained via the "switch" statement with a certain value. If the condition is true then the logic following the case statement is evaluated. In case it is not true then the next case statement is evaluated in the same manner and the process repeated till all the case statements have been evaluated.

Looping Statements

Looping statements are those which allow the programmer to repeat a set of logic repeatedly for either a preset number of times or till a certain logical condition is met. The looping statements available in the "C" language are "for", "while" & "do". These statements are used in a combination to create a loop. The general structure of a loop in any language is a combination of a head, a body and an end of loop marker. The loop also has an interator i.e. a counter or a condition test for ending the loop. The logic of the body of the loop will be repeated till the loop ends. The same applies to the "C" language looping syntax also. The "C" language has three forms of loops and depending upon the usage either one of them can be used. These three kinds of loops are the "for" loop, the "while" loop and the "do while" loop.

The "for" loop

This is the most common of the "C" language loops and also the simplest form. The general syntax of this loop is as follows

```
for(exp1, exp2, exp3)
{
logic statement forming the body of type loop
}
```

As is very evident, this statement also takes the general form of all "C" language statement i.e. the basic statement with parantheses followed by a pair of curly brackets enclosing the required statements. In this example, the "for" statement requires three expressions to be set in the parantheses. Each expression represents a specific task.

The first expression is generally known as the "initialisation expression". The second is called the "condition expression" and the third is known as the "end of loop expression". These three are essentially used in a combination to set up the iterator/counter and the condition for processing the loop. The logic within the curly brackets is repeated till the conditions in the expression are satisfied. The working will be more easily understood with the following example

```
for(i = 1, i<20, i++)
{
Logic to be processed
}
```

In this example the first expression establishes the value of the loop counter. In this case it is a int variable called i and has been set an initial value of 1. The second expressions is the condition, that is tested before the loop will be executed i.e. the loop will be processed if the value of i is less then 20. The third expression is evaluated at the end of each loop i.e. after the logic has been processed the third expression is evaluated. the third expression uses the "+" operator to increase the value of the variable "i" by one. This expression is evaluated once for each time the loop is processed. But at the end of the process. Hence, this example will execute the logic embedded in the body of the loop 20 times.

The "While" 1

This is the second most common form of a loop in the "C" language. The only difference between the "for" loop and the while loop is the method of writing the loop. In fact both these types of loops are interchangeable. The general syntax of this loop is as follows

```
while(condition)
{
logic to be processed
}
```

The conditional expression is processed before every process of the loop. If the condition fails the first time itself, the loop will never be executed. The change of data status to alter the status of the condition has to be built into the body of the loop. Even the initialisation has to be done prior to the "while" statement. The "while" loop as in the previous example will be as follows,

```
while(i<20)
{
logic to be processed
}
```

In the above example, the body of the loop will be continuously processed till the value of the variable "i" becomes more than or equal to 20. It is important to note that the changing of the value of the variable "i" has to be done withing the body of the loop. If this is not done then the loop will become an endless loop i.e. it will repeat itself infinite number of times.

The "Do While" Loop

This is the third form of creating a loop in the "C" language. This loop tests the condition after executing the body of the loop. Hence in this form, the loop will always execute at least once. The general syntax of this form of the loop is as follows

```
do
{
logic to be processed
}
while(condition)
```

The "while" statement with its condition has to be written at the end of the body of the loop. The start of the lop is set by the "do" statement. This type of loop functions exactly like the "while" loop in all other respects. The essential difference between this loop and the previous two loop is that this loop will always execute at lest once, while the previous two will not executed even once in case the condition expression evaluates to false.

The "Break" Statement

This statement will transfer control from within the body of a loop to outside the loop. It is a means of providing a direct exit point from any kind of loop without any conditional processing required. It is usually used to jump out of loops in exceptional conditions. The syntax of the "break" statement is very simple. It is as follows,

Break

This statement is only to be used within the body of the loop to have a proper effect.

The "continue" statement

This is another statement which affects program flow within a loop. This statement is to be always placed within the body of the loop. "continue" will transfer control to the beginning of the loop and start a fresh iteration of the loop without the previous iteration having being completed. The counters etc. are incremented as if the loop has been completed. The syntax of this statement is as follows

Continue

The "continue" statement will essentially skip the balance of the loop and start a fresh iteration of the loop However, the skipped iteration is counted as completed one for conditional testing.

The above statements cover the basic formative commands required for programming. However, one of the most important tasks of programming i.e. Input and Output of data has not been covered under these statements. The reason is that the "C" language uses specialised functions for even the most basic jobs like inputs and output of data. The following paragraphs will cover the various Input/Output functions of the "C" language.

The Output Functions

A few of the output functions in the "C" language are "printf" "putchar", "putc", "puts". These four are the most basic of the "C" language output functions. These functions are used to output data either to the screen/printer or file. These functions not only put data on the screen/printer/file but also allow the programmer to format the data and control how it will appear on the screen or the printer.

The "Printf"Function

This function will output string/character data or numbers to the screen. The general format of this function is as follows.

printf(data to be output)

As seen in the syntax this function does not have any curly brackets and data enclosed within the curly brackets. The data to be output is to be directly enclosed in the regular parantheses. This data is known as the parameters supplied to he "printf" function. An example of this function is as follows.

print f ("Hi!!1 This is a Computer Book!!!")

In the above example, the data being output is a constant string data. Such constant string data has to be enclosed in quotes. The function can output variable data as well.

Variable names are not enclosed within quotes. The "printf" function can take a variable number of parameters depending upon the job to be done.

There are two special characters which are not considered as constants but rather alter the data being output. These two characters are "\" and "%". The " | " character is used to represent an escape sequence. An escape sequence is used to alter the output style in some or the other fashion. The " | " character is followed by one of a set of prefixed characters. Each character represents one or the escape sequences. Certain escape sequences along with their actions are listed below

\n - The balance output starts from a new line

\b - Movement is one backspace

\r - This represents a carriage return

\f - A formfeed is issued

\t - A tab is inserted in the text

\\ - This will print the "\" character

\' - This will print the single quote character

\" - This will print the double quote character

The "%" sign on the other hand tells the "printf" function to insert a variable value in its place within the string. The variable data is to be supplied along with the "printf" function. the "%" sign is followed by one other character to specify the type of the variable value to be printed. The following are a few of the possible "%" signs which can be used.

%d - To print a signed integer value

%s - To print any other matching string value

%c - To print any other single string character

%u - To print an unsigned integer value

If more than one piece of data has to be output via the "printf" function the data has to be separated by commas. An example is one in which a character string has to be printed with a numeric value.

```
i = 10
printf("The value of i is %d points", i)
```

In this example, the working of the "%" sign is very clearly understood. The "%d" essentially acts as a template and replaces itself in the string being printed with the value held by the variable "i" which in this case happens to be 10. The next example is one in which the "\" is also used in the "printf" function.

```
i = 10
printf("The value of i is \t %d \n points", i)
```

In the above example, the "\t" will generate a tab and the cursor will move ahead by a tab space and then the "%d" will be replaced by the value of the variable "i", which in this case happens to be 10 and lastly the "/n" will move the cursor to the beginning of the next line and then the balance of the string "points" will be printed on the next line.

Even multiple variable values can be printed in one "printf" function by using as many "%" operators. The values are substituted from the variable list sequentially.

The "Putchar" function

This function is a simpler version of the "printf" function. This function allows the programmer to output one character of data at a given time. Please not that it can only print single characters at a time. In case any control characters have to be printed, they have to be enclosed within quotes with separate "putchar" function calls. The general syntax of this function is as follows

```
putchar(x)
```

In the above example, x represents the character which has to be printed. This function requires only a single parameter, and this parameter is what is printed on the output device. In case an escape character is to be printed as in the "printf" function it is done as follows

```
putchar("\n")
```

The "putchar" function may seem a bit superfluous at this stage since the same job can be as well done with the "printf" function. However, in case only single characters have to be printed, the "putchar" function *** One last point to note is that the "%" operator does not hold for the "putchar" function.

The "Puts" and the "Putc" Function

These two functions are essentially functions for putting a string of characters or a single character onto the output device. They are very commonly used for generating output to files. The "puts" function will output a string of data and add it to the current output file while the "putc" function does the same job, but with only a single character of data. The general syntax of these functions are as follows

```
putc(x)
puts(x)
```

The functions are followed by parantheses which encloses the data to be output. The data has to be either a string of data or a single character of data.

The Input Functions

Some of the standard input functions of the "C" language are "scanf", "gets" & "getchar". All these functions can be used to get input from the user within a program.

The "Scanf" Function

This is the most standard function utilised for input in the "C" language. This takes input from the standard input i.e. the keyboard. The data is echoed to the screen as it is keyed in. The general syntax of this function is as follows

scan f(string exp, var1)

As can be observed in the above example, the "scanf" function requires two parameters to passed to it. The first parameter is a sting in which the "%" operator is used to define the kind of input that will be accepted by this function. The second parameter defines the variable into which this input will be stored. Please note that the second parameter, i.e. the variable name has to be preceeded by an ampersand. An example of the "scanf" function is as follows

scanf("%d", &i)

In the above example, the expected input is to be integer data and the value obtained from the keyboard will be stored in the variable "i".

Some important features of the "scanf" function to be noted are that it ignores any leading and trailing spaces as the user enters data from the keyboard. The input begins only when a character which is blank come in and the input terminates the moment a blank is keyed in. This function does not return any value. In case the value being entered is a string and it has to be stored in an array then the "&" operator is not used to precede the variable name. An example would be as follows

scanf ("%s", str 1)

In this example str 1 is a string array which has been predefined. As just mentioned, the "scanf" function does not accept any white spaces and the input is considered to be terminated as soon as any blank space is keyed in. In case it is necessary to have blank space in the input, and this is more often the case than not, the problem is usually bypassed b using the "gets" input function.

The "Gets" Function

This is an input function to get a string of character data. This function will take all input till the enter key is pressed to signify the end of the input. It can take blank characters and all in its input. The general syntax of this function is as follows

gets(var 1)

This function just requires one parameter. This is the string variable to which the data being input will be stored. This function also echoes the characters to the screen as they are keyed in. The input is considered to be complete when the user hits the Enter key. the value entered is stored to the variable "var1" which has been previously defined. It is assumed that the variable "var1" is a character array.

The "Getchar" Function

This is another of the input functions. This function does not take any parameters and just returns the value of the key pressed. This function will cause the processor to wait for a key to be pressed and when any key is pressed, the processing is continued and the value of the key pressed is returned by the function. the general syntax of this function is as follows

```
x = getchar()
```

In the above example the program will pause and wait for keyboard input. As soon as any key is pressed the value of that keyboard character will be stored in the variable "x".

The "Return" Statement

This statement is standardly utilised in user defined program to return a value from a called function. The "return" statement causes termination of processing in the current function. Control is immediately transferred to the calling program on encountering a "return" statement. the return value has to be passed as a parameter along with the "return" statement. The general syntax of the "return" statement is as follows

```
return(val 1)
```

The value to be returned has to be enclosed in parantheses as a return value. In case no value is passed the return statement will still function, but a NULL value will be assigned to the variable receiving the return value.

1. Write a Program to Find the G.C.D of Two Numbers?

```
# include <stdio.h>
main()
{
int a;
int b;
int g;
int i;
int a1;
int b1
float b2;
float a2;
printf("Enter the First Number");
scanf("%d", &a);
printf("Enter the Second Number");
scanf("%d" &b);
```

```
if(b>a);
{
i = b;
}
else
{
i = a;
}
endif;
while(i>=1);
{
b1 = b/i;
a1 = a/i;
b2 = b/i;
a2 = a/i;
if(b1 = b2 and a1 = a2);
{
g = i;
break;
}
i—;
}
printf("The G.C.D of the two numbers is %d", g);
}
return;
```

2. Write a Program to Sort a Group of Numbers?

```
# include <stdio.h>
main();
{
int a[6];
int i;
int j;
int t;
printf("Enter the First Number");
scanf("%d", &a[0]);
```

```
printf("Enter the Second Number");
scanf("%d", &a[1]);
printf("Enter the Third Number");
scanf("%d", &a[2]);
printf("Enter the Fourth Number");
scanf("%d" &a[3]);
printf("Enter the Fifth Number");
scanf("%d", &a[4]);
print("Enter the Sixth Number");
for (i = 0, i<6, i++);
{
for(j=1, j<6, j++);
{
if(a[i]>a[j]);
{
t = a[i];
a[i] = a[j];
a[j] = t;
}
}
}
printf("The Sorted List of Numbers is"
for (i=1, i<6,i++)
{
printf("/n%d", a[i])
}
}
return:
```

3. Find the Mean and Standard Deviation of Five Numbers?

```
# include <stdio.h>
main()
{
int a;
int b;
```

```
int c;
int d;
int e;
int f;
int mn1;
int mtot1;
int mtot2;
int std;
printf("Input Value of "A")
scan("%d", &a);
printf("Input Value of B");
scanf("%d", &b);
printf("Input Value of C");
scanf("%d", &c);
printf("Input Value of E");
scanf("%d", &d);
printf("Input Value of F");
scanf("%d", &e);
printf("Input Value of F")'
scanf("%d",&f);
mn1 = (a+b+c+d+e+f)/6;
mtot1 = a+b+c+d+e+f;
mtot2 = a^2+b^2+c^2+d^2+e^2+f^2;
std = sqrt(mtot2-(mtot1^2/2));
printf("The mean of the Six Numbers is %d", mn1);
Printf("The Standard Deviation is %d", std);
}
return;
```

4. Find the Solution of a Quadratic Equation?

```
#include <stdio.h>;
main();
{
int a:
```

```
int b:
int c:
float sv;
int res1;
int res2;
printf("Input Value of A");
scanf("%d", &a);
printf("Input Value of B");
scanf("%d", &b);
print("Input Value of C");
scanf("%d", &c);
sv = sqrt(b*b-4*a*c);
res1 = (b+sv)/2*a;
res2 = (b-sv)/2*a;
printf("The Solutions of the Quadratic Equation are %d %d", res1, res2);
}
return;
```

5. Count the Number of Days between Two Dates?

It is assumed in this program that the number of days in a year are 365 and the number of days in a month are 30.

```
#include <stdio.h>
main();
{
int y1 = 0;
int m1 = 0;
int d1 = 0;
int y2 = 0;
int m2 = 0;
int d2 = 0;
int td1 = 0;
int td2 = 0;
int tdif = 0;
printf("Enter the Year, Month & Days of First Date");
```

```
scanf("%d, %d, %d",&y1,&m1,&d1);
printf("Enter the Year, Month & Days of Second Date");
scanf("%d, %d, %d", &y2, &m2, &d2);
td1 = 364*(y1-1) + 30*(m1-1)+d1;
td2 = 365*(y2-1)+30*(m2-1)+d2;
tdif = td2-td1;
printf("The days between the two dates are %d',tdif);
}
return;
```

6. Find the Simple and Compound Interest by the Interactive Method

It is assumed in this program that the interest is compounded annualy

```
# include <stdio.h>
main();
{
int princ = 0;
int irate = 18;
int ny = 0;
int si = 0;
int cv = 0;
int ci = 0;
int i = 0;
printf("Enter the principal amount");
scanf("%d", &princ);
printf("Enter the Annual Rate of Interest");
scanf("%d", &irate);
printf("Enter the Period in Years");
scanf("%d", &ny);
si = princ + princ*irate*ny/100;
cv = princ;
for(i = 1, i<=ny, i++);
{
ci = cv*irate/100;
cv = cv + ci;
}
printf('Principal Amount is = %d', princ);
printf('Rate of Interest = %d',irate);
printf('Period in Days = %d', ny);
printf('Simple Interest Value = %d', si);
printf('Compounded Value = %d', cv);
}
return;
```

7

Database and dBASE—Why, What and How?

Why dBASE?

When computers were first invented in 1948, man was struggling with the machine languages to communicate his problems to the machine. Man was making efforts for finding a more comfortable language for communicating with the machine. This resulted in the development of the so called High Level Languages (HLLs) like FORTRAN, COBOL, BASIC, PASCAL etc. These HLLs were almost English-like and so man was more comfortable with them. Apart from this, these languages are really wonderful, in that they are machine independent. By machine independence, we mean that one can learn these language just like any other spoken languages and write instructions to the machine without knowing anything about the anatomy of the machine. Man was really thrilled by these languages, since they liberated him from machine dependence.

In data processing environment, man works with two things, namely, the program and the data. The program has to tell three things to the machine about the data, namely, where the data are stored, how the data are stored and how the data are to be processed. This means that man must know not only about the data processing methods, but also about the data organisation inside the computer system. In fact, he has to describe the data organisation or the data description as it is called very elaborately in his program. We know that in a COBOL program one complete division (namely, The DATA DIVISION) is devoted to data description. This means that when the data organisation is changed to suit the problem situation, the data description has to be changed and hence the program has to be changed. This sort of data dependence puts severe strain on the data processing personnel and prevents him from concentrating on the data processing logic. Naturally man was looking for somebody or rather some other language which will liberate him from data dependence. So dBASE was born to the joy and delight of humans to give them the long awaited data independence. Of course man could not be relieved from problem independence as well, because the machines cannot understand the human problems. If the HLLs were discovered to relieve the man from machine dependence, dBASE was discovered to relieve the man from data dependence. We can call dBASE as a VERY HIGH LEVEL LANGUAGE or simply a VHLL. Now we will see the schematics of dBASE LOGIC.

We know that a program works with a data file. In the so called high level languages (HLLs), we have to describe the data file in our program. In other words, the program has to contain not only the data processing logic, but also the data organisation logic as shown in the Fig. 1. In dBASE, the data description logic is made part of the data file or data storage and so the program contains only the processing logic somewhat as shown in the Fig. 2. We see that, in dBASE there is a distinct advantage to the man, in that he is freed from data description in his program. This is what we call as data independence. Man has more freedom to concentrate in program logic without bothering about the data description. Thus dBASE came to be developed to liberate man from data dependence and make his life in the data processing world more comfortable. Now we have seen the answer for WHY dBASE.

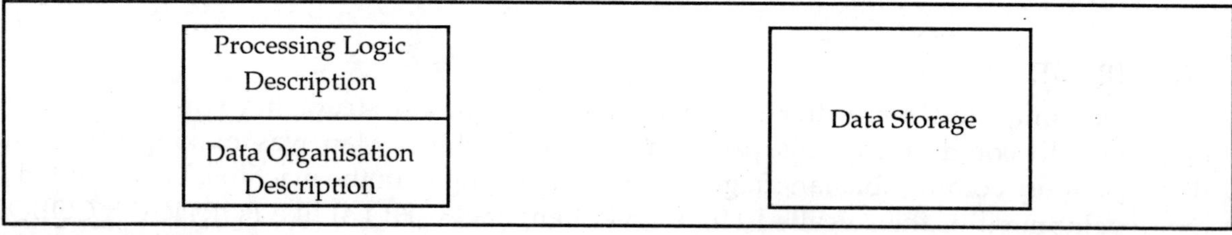

Fig. 1.

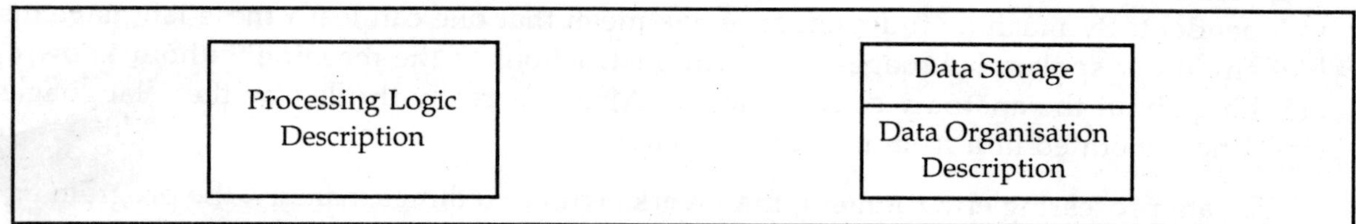

Fig. 2.

What is dBASE?

A computer system works with two things namely,

1. A program and
2. A set of data (stored in files)

We may have different sets or groups of data in an organisation, each set being used for extracting some information. For example, we can have a file containing the pay data of all the employees and this file will be used whenever we want to find the net pay payable to each of the employee in the organisation. Again we can have another file called the Finance File containing the financial data of the organisation and this file will be used to prepare the financial reports like Profit & Loss Account, Balance Sheet etc. We can have another file called the personnel File containing the personnel data of all the employes and this will be used to get any personal information such as the retirement age, earned leave available etc., about each of the employees. In the conventional data processing method, we keep each

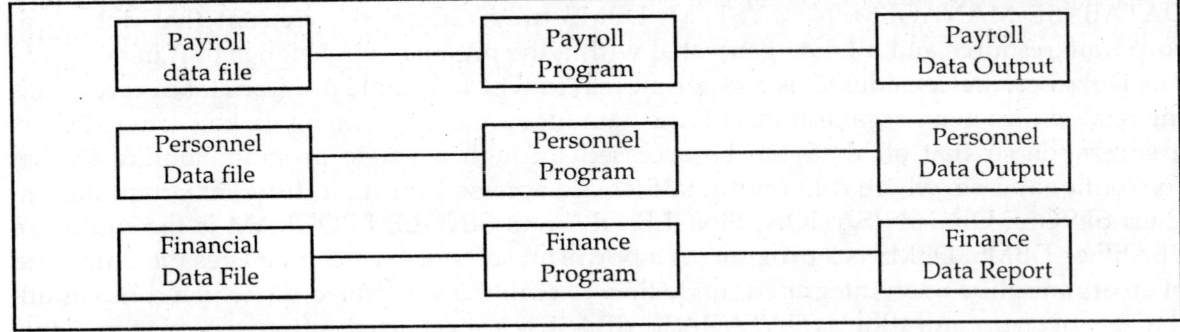

Fig. 3.

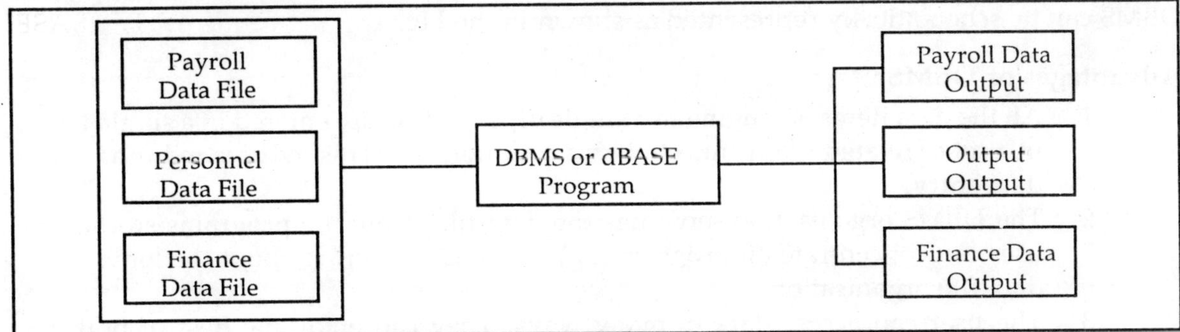

Fig. 4.

group of data in separate files and process each group separately using separate programs for producing the different reports. The process can be schematically represented as shown in the Fig. 3. In such an organisation, we will find that the same data items occur in different files. For example, some items like Basic Pay, allowances etc., relating to pay data of an employee will be present in both the payroll file as well as the finance data file. If such data items are changed, we have to be careful to see that they are changed in all the files, where they occur. This requires careful monitoring of all the files. Again if the data description changes, the program has to be changed. For example, if the data file is changed from sequential to indexed sequential or direct, both the data description and the program have to be changed. Thus we see that each program is tied down to a particular data organisation or data description and so it is, we say that the language is data dependent.

This type of data organisation is separate files results in redundancies. Keying the same data in different files results not only in wastage of memory space, but also large human interaction with data. The more the human interaction with data the more are the chances for keying wrong data. It is a wise strategy to keep human interaction with data a minimum. Again this type of data organisation does not reflect the concept, that any organisation is a single entity and all the data generated in the organisation belongs to it as a whole or that data is a global resource or a corporate resource and must not be the property of a particular functional unit. Again this organisation fails to impress the interdependence of the data files in an organisation. These drawbacks are sought to be overcome in dBASE, which is a

DATABASE MANAGEMENT SYSTEM. DBMS fully reflects the concept that data is a corporate resource and all data generated within the organisation belongs to it in entirety. The DBMS can be considered as a single system in which a single program takes care of all the related files in an organisation. All the data files are either suitably linked or written as a single file so that all data can be accessed through a single program, unlike in the conventional case, where different data files are accessed through different programs. In short SINGLE ORGANISATION, SINGLE FILE and SINGLE PROGRAM is the motto of dBASE or DBMS. DBMS is a program or a powerful software which manages the data files of an organisation as an integrated single file. We call this integrated file which contains all the data of an organisation as DATA BASE. dBASE is a specialised software used to manage a database or we say, dBASE is a powerful DATABASE MANAGEMENT SYSTEM. The DBMS can be schematically represented as shown in the Fig. 4.

Advantages of DBMS

1. All the data items belonging to a single organisation are entered in a single file or in a set of related files connected by a common key. This reduces redundancy of data entry.
2. The DBMS organisation separates the data files from the programs so that the user can concentrate on program logic without bothering about the logic of the data file organisation.
3. The user can access data in many ways. They can enjoy the best of both the worlds. That is, they can access data sequentially or directly depending on the specific request.
4. The data validation facilities, the data processing facilities and the data reporting facilities are far more comfortable than in the compiler languages like FORTRAN, BASIC, COBOL or PASCAL.

How will a DATABASE look like?

We will try to find the answer to the above question in a practical way by actually creating a DATABASE. Suppose I give you a slip of paper and each one of you to write down the factual details or the data as they are called for some of your attributes as shown in the Fig. 5.

1. NAME:
2. AGE:
3. QUALIFICATIONS:
4. COMMUNITY (BC/FC/SC):
5. SEX:
6. STREET:
7. CITY:
8. PIN:

Fig. 5.

I now have some slips giving the biodata of every individual somewhat as shown in the Fig. 6. I have now a collection of biodata particulars about all the individuals in this group. Let us now consider some of the features of this data collection.

1.	NAME:	B. S. Jauhari
2.	AGE:	59
3.	QUALIFICATIONS:	M.Sc., AICWA
4.	COMMUNITY (BC/FC/SC):	FC
5.	SEX:	M
6.	STREET:	Veera Desai Road,
7.	CITY:	Andheri, Bombay
8.	PIN:	400 058

Fig. 6.

Each slip contains eight particulars or attributes or facts or data pertaining to each individual. We have now a collection of data for the same eight attributes for all the persons in this group. Suppose we rearrange the personnel particulars of all the individual in what is called row-column format as shown in the Fig. 7. We call this collection of data arranged in a row-column as DATABASE or more strictly as RELATIONAL DATABASE. This is called relational database, because a row column relationship has been established among the data items. What exactly is the row column relationship? It is noticed that all data items along the same row denote the different attributes of the same entity (in this case it is the name of the person) and all the data items along a column denote the same attributes of the different entities. There are also other types of databases like hierarchical and network, but presently we will deal only with relational databases. We would like to give a name to this database, say BIODATA. I am sure you will agree that this name is meaningful. We would

Record No.	*Name*	*Age*	*Quali-fication*	*Commu-nity*	*Sex*	*Street*	*City*	*Pin*
1.	...	...	...	...	...	...	...	...
2.	...	...	...	...	...	...	...	...
3.	...	...	...	...	...	...	...	...
4.	...	...	...	...	...	...	...	...
5.	...	...	...	...	...	...	...	...
6.	...	...	...	...	...	...	...	...
7.	...	...	...	...	...	...	...	...

Fig. 7.

like to call the collection of eight data items pertaining to each individual as meaningful, a RECORD. Every RECORD gives particulars or data pertaining to eight attributes of a single entity. We would like to call these attributes as the STRUCTURE of the RECORD. In this example, the structure has only eight attributes. In general one can have a large number of attributes in a structure. I could have asked for more attributes like father's name, his occupation, his salary, his nativity etc. It is only for the sake of simplicity, I have restricted myself to collecting data for eight attributes. We call the collection of similarly structured records arranged in rows as the STRUCTURE of the DATABASE itself. In summary, we can define a DATABASE as a collection of all data of an organisation arranged or grouped in a row-column structure as shown in the Fig. 7. Now one would like to ask the question, what is the use of this DATABASE?

What is the use of the DATABASE?

We have now created a DATABASE called BIODATA as shown in the Fig. 7. We can make use of this particular DATABASE for preparing the following reports : To

1. Prepare the address labels for all the individuals.
2. Classify the individuals according to sex.
3. Classify the individuals according to age.
4. Classify the individuals according to the community.
5. Classify the individuals according to the qualification.
6. Sort the names of all individuals in the alphabetical order.
7. Sort all the individuals in the order of their age.

Possibly we can make use of this particular database for preparing some more such reports. I hope all of you will agree with me, when I say that these reports will be useful for many purposes in real life situations.

Will a Database Remain Constant?

Today we have created a database for preparing some more reports. Will the particulars in this database remain constant for ever? Certainly not. Some of the items like address, age, qualification etc., may change. A particular individual may leave the organisation. This means that his record must be removed from the database. A particular individual may join the organisation. This means that his record has to be inserted in the database. So any database must be amenable for quick updation so as to keep it always current.

Why not Create and Manipulate the DATABASE Manually?

All of you will agree that the creation of the DATABASE and preparation of the different reports can be done manually if the volume is small. In real life problems, data are really voluminous. In such cases, the manual method will be highly tedious, time consuming and also error prone. So it is, we would like to computerise the database creation and manipulation.

Examples of DATABASE in Real Life

You have a collection of data pertaining to the marks obtained by the students of a class in different subjects organised in a database. You would like to prepare a pass list, rank list etc.

You have a collection of data or database pertaining to the pay, allowances, deductions and other particulars about all the employees in an organisation. You would like to prepare different reports like payslips, salary statement, deduction statement etc.

Thus we see that preparing the different reports we have to first start from a DATABASE. We will now see the ways and means of creating and manipulating databases.

dBASE and DATABASE Re-visited

Thanks to the development of a very powerful software program called the dBASE, life has been made very comfortable for the users of DATABASE. The only requisite for using this powerful software is that one must know all details of data that are generated in the organisation and also the way in which they have to be manipulated for producing the relevant reports. In short he must have a thorough knowledge of the problem. dBASE software provides commands to do the following:

1. Create a Central DATABASE
2. Display a DATABASE
3. Sort a DATABASE
4. Modify a DATABASE
5. Write Programs to get tailored reports

One can say that the above facilities almost satisfy the major portion of data processing requirements. The key problem is to get at the relationship between the data items of an organisation to fit in with the row-column structure. Once you get the row-column relationship among the data items, you become the monarch in the data processing world, because you can generate whatever report you want with the help of dBASE. In fact you cannot ask for anything more than what dBASE gives you as far as data processing is concerned.

Evolution of dBASE

In the early eighties, Ashton-Tate introduced their first version of DBMS for 8 bit computer systems under the name dBASE II. With the advent of 16 bit systems and IBM PC compatibles, they made improvements to the old version and evolved dBASE III. Additional features have been added to this and the name is changed in dBASE III Plus. Adding new features is an ever-going process and already dBASE IV version has come out. Thank God, the essential logic of dBASE and DATABASE is still intact and so we can hope to keep ourselves abreast of times with the study of dBASE III Plus. In the following lessons we will see the salient features of dBASE III Plus.

We said that dBASE works only with a database file. So our next task is to create a database file from scratch. We must first plan the record structure and describe this structure to dBASE. Then we have to enter the data items when dBASE asks us to enter, by prompt messages. Once we enter the data values for all the records, the data items will go and sit in the file structure forming the database file. Before giving any dBASE commands, check up and see that the dot prompt appears on the screen. Type the word CREATE and press the Carriage Return key <CR>.

dBASE responds by asking you to enter the file name. File names are coined by combining alphabets and numbers to a maximum length of 8 characters.

Enter the Name of the New File

You key the word BIODATA and press the Carriage Return key (CR). dBASE will give the name of the file as BIODATA.DBF adding the extension DBF to the file name you have entered. As soon a you enter the file name and press the CR key, the screen prompt appears as shown in the Fig. 8. This is called the Structure Creation Screen.

Cursor	←	→	Insert			Delete			Up a field	:	↑
Char	←	→	Char	:	Ins	Char	:	Del	Down a field	:	↓ →
Word	Home	End	Field	:	∧N	Word	:	∧Y	Exit/Save	:	∧ end
Pan	∧←	∧→	Help	:	F1	Field	:	∧U	Abort	:	Esc

Field name	type	Width	Dec	Field Name	Type	Width	Dec
1	Character						

Create	A:	Biodata	Field: 1/1				

Fig. 8.

At this point, dBASE wants you to give the name of each field, the type of the field, the length of the field, and the number of decimal places, if the field is a numeric one. the Field names, the types, the lengths etc. are keyed one by one for all the fields. The keyed information will look as shown in the Fig. 9

1	NAME	Character	5
2	AGE	Numeric	2
3	QUALIFY	Character	5
4	COMMUNITY	Character	2
5	SEX	Character	1
6	STREET	Character	10
7	CITY	Character	10
8	PIN	Numeric	6
9		Character	

Fig. 9.

Suppose you have only 8 fields in your database. When the prompt for entering the 9th field occurs, press the CR key without typing any field names. Now the structure is saved. The prompt appears on the screen as below:

INPUT DATA RECORDS NOW? (Y/N)

For the present type N. You are returned to the dot prompt. Now we would like to see the structure that is saved by dBASE. Key the following:

.USE BIODATA (CR)
.LIST STRUCTURE (CR)

Before you start giving any command, you must tell the name of the file which you want to operate. This information is given to dBASE by typing USE BIODATA. The USE command is similar to OPEN FILE statement in the conventional High Level Languages. Then the command, LIST STRUCTURE will cause the display of the structure as shown in the Fig. 10

.USE BIODATA
.LIST STRUCTURE

Structure for database: B: biodata:dbf
Number of data records 0
Date of last update : 01/01/80

Field	Field Name	Type	Width	Dec
1	NAME	Character	5	
2	AGE	Numeric	2	
3	QUALIFY	Character	5	
4	COMMUNITY	Character	2	
5	SEX	Character	1	
6	STREET	Character	10	
7	CITY	Character	10	
8	PIN	Numeric	6	
Total			42	

Fig. 10.

You will find that total length of the field given the dBASE is greater than the actual length by 1. dBASE has reserved this extra character length for future use. You will see later that when you give a delete command for deleting a record it will add a * mark in the first of the record that is marked or deletion. dBASE will use this extra space for putting this * mark.

How to Correct Typographical Errors?

The four arrow keys can be freely used to bring the cursor to any desired location and any desired character can be typed on the cursor location. This will overwrite on the character which is already there. New fields can be inserted by keying ^N. The various editing operations that can be done during the structure creation process is displayed on the screen at the to as shown in the Fig. 11. Suppose you want to edit the structure after it has been saved. Give the following commands:

.USE BIODATA

.MODIFY STRUCTURE

Immediately the CREATE screen as in the Fig. 12 appears on the screen and the editing can be done as per the instructions given at the top of the screen. The CREATE screen is practically a full screen editor. Press ^ End to exit from MODIFY structure and save any changes.

How to Enter Data?

To get the screen for data entry, the command APPEND is given. Type the commands

.USE BIODATA

.APPEND

					Up	Down						
Cursor	←	→	Field	:		↓	Delete			Insert Mode	:	Ins
Char	←	→			↑		Char	:	Del	Exit/Save	:	^End
Word	Home	End	Page	:	PgUp	PgDN	Field	:	^Y	Abor	:	Esc
			Help	:	F1		Record	:	^U	Memo	:	^Home

NAME

AGE

QUALITY

COMMUNITY

SEX

STREET

CITY

PIN

Fig. 11.

Record No. 1

Cursor ← →	Field : Up ↓ Down ↑	Delete	Interest mode : Ins
Char ← →		Char : Del	Exit/Save : ^End
Word Home End	Page : PgUp PgDN	Field : ^Y	Abort : Esc
	Help : F1	Record : ^U	Memo : ^Home

NAME	bala
AGE	40
QUALITY	be
COMMUNITY	fc
SEX	m
STREET	int st.
CITY	bombay
PIN	400 001

Fig. 12.

Immediately dBASE displays a full screen form for entering data in the first record. The screen form looks as shown in the Fig. 11.

You notice that the range of every field is highlighted by reverse video. Now you can start filling up the data items in the different fields one by one. If the data occupies the entire length of the field, the cursor automatically goes to the next field, otherwise press the CR key to go to the next field. If there is no data in a field, simply press CR key when the cursor is in the first position of the field. After filling the data items for the first record, the screen will look as shown in the Fig. 12.

After filling the data of the last field, if you press the CR key, the structure display appears on the screen for the second record. Fill in the required data in the different fields and then go to the third record and son on. If you make any typographical errors use the control keys to position the cursor in any desired position and overtype the correct character. Whenever in doubt, refer to the cursor control menu which appear at the top of the screen. Suppose you want to stop with the seventh record. That is, you want to come out of the APPEND mode after saving the data items you have keyed in the first seven records. When you press the CR key at the end of the 7th record, the screen displays the structure for the 8th record. Without entering any data in the 8th record, simply press the CR key. Now you are returned to the dot prompt. You have entered data items for seven records and you would like to see how they have been arranged in the database. To see your database file, give the following commands;

.USE BIODATA

. LIST

The database file appears on the screen as shown in the Fig. 13

Record #	*NAME*	*AGE*	*QUALIFY*	*COMMUNITY*	*SEX*	*STREET*	*CITY*	*PIN*
1	bala	40	be	fc	m	mint st.	bombay	400001
2	raji	25	me	bc	f	mount road	madras	600002
3	gayi	30	msc	sc	f	rr street	tiruchi	620001
4	raman	60	mphil	bc	m	ram street	karakudi	624001
5	krish	50	dsc	bc	m	p.h. road	madurai	625006
6	murug	45	bsc	fc	m	mp street	pasumalai	585001
7	latha	37	msc	sc	f	grant road	delhi	110001

Fig. 13.

Now you see the database in the famous row column format. There are seven rows and nine column in the above database. The first column which gives the record number has been added by dBASE for your convenience. You gave only 8 fields in the structure, but now 9 fields appear. The record number field is not a data field since you cannot manipulate its value. You can manipulate the data in the remaining 8 fields. Again remember that it is the dBASE that has organised your bunch of data in this row column format. You simply entered the data as per the prompt given by the dBASE. It is dBASE that has arranged the data in the above format.

A Database Created

Now you have done a fine job of creating a database from scratch. Let us now recapitulate what has been done. First we decided about the attributes or the data items that have to be entered in the data-base. Then we coined some meaningful names for the data items. Then we decided about the length to be given for each data item and also the type that must be given, whether numeric or character or logical or memo. We call this above information as the structure of the record. We gave this information as the structure of the record to dBASE. Then we entered the data items in each record in the data entry screen presented by dBASE. We entered data only for seven records for the sake of simplicity. Then we came out of the data entry mode after saving the data items that have been entered. Then we gave the command to view the database file organised by dBASE. The database file looked exactly as per our definition. Please remember that we have defined a database as a collection of data arranged in what is called the row-column structure. Though we did not enter the record number, dBASE itself entered the number sequentially for the seven records typed by us, by adding one more column. Now we have safely stored the database file under the name BIODATA.DBF in the disk. We must now see how we can make use of the dBASE commands to manipulate this data-base file and produce different meaningful reports.

How to Enter Memo Data

Let us now start from the CREATE screen. Suppose our record structure consists of only two fields, the first one being a Character field and the second one being a Memo field. The first data name is NAME and is of 10 characters width. Let the second data be BIODATA. As soon as you type the Character M below the Type column, the width column is automatically filled up as 10 and the cursor moves to the next field. We can now come out of the CREATE screen by pressing the CR key, when the cursor is in the beginning of the third field. The CREATE screen will look as shown in the Fig. 14. The number 10 does not indicate the width of the Memo field, but is used for giving some information to dBASE about which we need not worry now.

Cursor <——> Char <——> Word Home End Pan ^<— ^—>	Insert : Char Ins Field : ^N Help : F1	Delete Char : Del Field : ^Y Field : ^U	Up a field : ↑ Down a field : ↓ Exit/Save : ^End Abort : Esc

	Field name	type	Width	Dec	Field Name	Type	Width	Dec
1	Name	Character	10					
2	Biodata	Memo	10					
3	[ ]	[Character]	[ ]		[ ]	[ ]		

Create A: RR Field: 3/3

Fig. 14.

We have now created a record structure with a Memo field. Let us now see how we can enter data in the Memo field of each record. We enter the APPEND mode by giving the APPEND command. We enter the value for the first field NAME as KRISH. The data for the second field which is the Memo field cannot be entered in this screen. We have to invoke the Memo data entry screen by press ^Home. We will get another screen for entering Memo data. The APPEND screen and the Memo screen will look as shown in the Fig. 15 and 16 respectively.

Cursor <——> Char <——> Word Home End	Up Down : ↓ ↑ Page : PgUp PgDN Help : F1	Delete Char : Del Field : ^Y Record : ^U	Interest mode : Ins Exit/Save : ^End Abort : Esc Memo : ^Home

Name	krish
Biodata	Memo

Fig. 15.

				Up	Down						
Cursor	<——>	Field	:			Delete			Interest mode	:	Ins
Char	<——>			*	*	Char	:	Del	Inser Line	:	^N
Word	Home End	Page	:	PgUp	PgDN	Field	:	^T	Save		^End Abort Esc
Line	^<— ^—>	Find	:	^KF		Line	:	^Y	Read file	:	^KR
		Refind		^KL					Write file	:	^KW

Fig. 16.

krish has obtained his master degree in computer science from Madurai Kamaraj Unversity in the year 1988. He is currently working on dbms.

A cursor control menu appears at the top of the screen. The memo information is keyed just like any text matter. After completing the entry press ^End or ^W. You are now returned to the screen shown in the Fig. 15. To enter data in the second record press the CR key. After entering the data for two fields in the second record, come to the third record. Suppose we want to stop with only two records, press the CR key. You are returned to the dot prompt. It must be noticed that the memo information in the DBF file RR.DBR is not stored in the DBF file, but it is stored in any file with an extension DBT. The memo information is stored in the file RR.DBT. Suppose you go the commands

```
.USE RR
.List
```

The detabase looks as shown in the Fig. 17.

Record #	Name	Biodata
1	krish	Memo
2	ramu	Memo

Fig. 17.

In order to view the contents of the Memo information in the two records, you have to give the command

.LIST BIODATA

The information stored in the file RR.DBT appears on the screen as shown in the Fig. 18.

Record	#	BIODATA
	1	krish has obtained his masters degree in computer science from Madurai Kamaraj University in the year 1988. He is currently working on dbms.
	2	ramu has obtained doctors degree in computer science from madras university. he is currently doing research in artificial intelligence.

Fig. 18.

It must be noted that the memo field can be entered only from the dBASE full-screen data entry commands: APPEND, INSERT, CHANGE or EDIT. The memo field cannot be entered from the full-screen command BROWSE. When an entry or editing of a memo field is completed, you will be returned to the data-entry screen that was used to enter the field. You may notice that the cursor control commands of the memo screen has a number of word-processing commands. An external disk file can be read into a memo field using the ^KR command. The contents of a memo field can be copied to an external file with ^KW. A memo field which is stored in the structure is used to store some pointers which link the DB1 file.

Size and Number of Fields and Records in a dBASE File

dBASE III Plus allows as many as 128 fields in a record subject to a maximum of 4000 characters of field widths. Character field can be as long as 254, numeric can be as long as 19, date will be 8, logical will be 1 and memo will be 10. Though the memo field requires only 10 bytes, the actual memo field information is stored separately in another file. In a dbf file the memo field occupies only 10 bytes. The number of fields in a record will be limited if the total field length reaches 4000 first. The number of records can be as high as 1 billion (1,000,000,000). Of course no pc will support an auxiliary memory of that mush size as to hold so many records. Possibly one can keep up to 1 million records on line with pc's having a hard disk of capacity of about 160 MB.

In the next lesson we will see how we can view the database in different ways.

dBASE COMMANDS (II)

So far we have seen how we can create a database using the CREATE: and APPEND commands. We also saw how we can view the database by using the LIST command. A database can be viewed selectively by making use of the LIST and DISPLAY commands with appropriate qualifying attributes. Let us use the same dBASE file BIODATA. DBF which we created earlier.

Suppose you want to view the database without the record number. Give the commands as

.USE BIODATA
.LIST FOR
dBASE responds as shown in the Fig. 19

NAME	*AGE*	*QUALIFY*	*COMMUNITY*	*SEX*	*STREET*	*CITY*	*PIN*
bala	40	be	fc	m	min st.	bombay	400001
raji	25	me	bc	f	mount.road	madras	600002
gayi	30	msc	sc	f	rr street	tiruchi	620001
raman	60	mphil	bc	m	ram street	karaikudi	624001
krish	50	dsc	bc	m	p.h.road	madurai	625006
murug	45	bsc	fc	m	mp street	pasumalai	585001
latha	37	msc	sc	f	grant road	delhi	110001

Fig. 19.

Suppose you want to view the database for which pin is 625006. Give the command as

.USE BIODATA
.LIST FOR COMMUNITY

dBASE responds as shown in the Fig. 20

Record #	*NAME*	*AGE*	*QUALIFY*	*COMMUNITY*	*SEX*	*STREET*	*CITY*	*PIN*
5	krish	50	dsc	be	m	p.h. road	madurai	625006

Fig. 20.

Suppose you want to view the database which satisfy two conditions, say community 'fc' and age > 40. Give the commands

.USE BIODATA
.LIST FOR COMMUNITY 'FC' AND AGE > 40

dBASE responds as shown in the Fig. 21

Record #	*NAME*	*AGE*	*QUALIFY*	*COMMUNITY*	*SEX*	*STREET*	*CITY*	*PIN*
6	murug	45	bsc	fc	m	mp street	Pasumalai	585001

Fig. 21.

Suppose you want to view the database with only the NAME and AGE fields. Give the commands

.USE BIODATA
.LIST NAME, AGE

dBASE responds as shown in the Fig. 22.

Record #	*NAME*	*AGE*
1	bala	40
2	raji	25
3	gayi	30
4	raman	60
5	krish	50
6	murug	45
7	latha	37

Fig. 22.

You can also display the fields in any order by listing it in the command as

```
. USE BIODATA
.LIST AGE, NAME
```

In this case the age field will come first and the name field net as shown in the Fig. 23.

RECORD #	*AGE*	*NAME*
1	40	bala
2	25	raji
3	30	gayi
4	60	raman
5	50	krish
6	45	murug
7	37	latha

Fig. 23.

Suppose you give the commands

```
. USE BIODATA
.LIST AGE, NAME "BACA"
```

dBASE simply types the header without typing any data. It is because there is no record in which the NAME field matches with the data "BALA." In the database file, the NAME is given in small letters, whereas in the query, you have given the data in capital letters. So dBASE returns to the dot prompt immediately after typing the header. There must be perfect match between the data in the query command and the data in the database file. Then only dBASE can find the required record.

Suppose you give the commands as

```
. USE BIODATA
.LIST FOR COMMUNITY = "6"
```

When you give single letter for the value, it does not mean equality but all values which begin with b. In this case all records for which the community is be will be output.

The General Form of the LIST Command

The general form of the LIST command is

```
.LIST [OFF] [(scope] [(expression list)] [FOR/WHILE(condition)] [TO PRINT]
```

In giving the general forms of commands, square brackets are used to denote optional clauses and curly brackets are used to denote to be given by the user and words with small case letters to denote programmer supplied items and words with capital letters to denote command words provided by the language. In the above case all clauses excepting the LIST clause are optional. The clause "TO PRINT" is used to get the output on the printer. For getting the output on the printer you give the following commands also:

.set print on

.list

.set print off

The command set print on will activate the printer. Once the printing is over the printer is deactivated by the command set print off.

The DISPLAY Command

The DISPLAY command is used to position a particular record which is to be display. Suppose you give the command

```
.USE BIODATA
.DISPLAY
```

dBASE will display only the first record along with the header.

Suppose you give the command

```
.USE BIODATA
.GOTO BOTTOM
.DISPLAY
```

dBASE will display the last record in the file along with the header.

Suppose you give the command

```
.USE BIODATA
.GOTO 4
.DISPLAY
```

dBASE will display the 4th record in the file along with the header.

We way that a record pointer is moved by the GOTO command and it positions itself at the particular record given by the GOTO command. The simple DISPLAY command displays only the record against which the record pointer is positioned. To find the record number towards which the record pointer is positioned, give the command

```
.DISPLAY RECNO()
```

dBASE will respond somewhat as shown below:

Record #	recno 0
5	5

Suppose you give the command

.Display Record 4

dBASE will display the 4th record along with the header. The Record Printer can also be moved by SKIP command. The general form of the SKIP command is

.SKIP n (n is the number of records to be skipped from the current position)

Suppose you give the command

. Use BIODATA

.DISPLAY RECORD 4

When the database file BIODATA is opened, the record pointer is positioned against the first record. The command SKIP 5 moves down the record pointer to the 6th record. dBASE responds to the above command by displaying

Record No. 6 (This means that the record pointer is against the 6th record)

If you give the 'DISPLAY' command, the record number 6 will be displayed.

Suppose you give the command

.USE BIODATA

.DISPLAY ALL

All the records in the BIODATA file will be displayed. Though this command is similar to the LIST command, there is a small difference. The DISPLAY ALL command will display only 19 records at a time on the screen and then dBASE will wait for the user to press any key, at which point it will display the next 19 records and so on. The LIST command will not stop at the end of every 19 records, but will display the entire database on the screen in a rapid scroll mode.

The general form of the DISPLAY command is the same as the general form of the LIST command and can be given as follows:

.DISPLAY [OFF] [(scope)] [(expression list)] [FOR/WHILE(condition)] [TO PRINT]

You may notice that all clauses excepting the DISPLAY clause are optional.

The following are the possible ways of giving the DISPLAY Commands.

1. DISPLAY—Displays record number and contents of current record.
2. DISPLAY OFF—Displays contents of current record omitting the record number display.

3. DISPLAY RECORD n—Displays record number and contents of record number n.
4. DISPLAY NEXT n—Displays record number and contents of next n records.
5. DISPLAY ALL—Displays all records pausing after every 15 records.
6. DISPLAY ALL TO PRINT—Displays all records to the screen and printer.
7. DISPLAY RECNO ()—Displays current record number.
8. DISPLAY field1, field2,..—Displays contents of specified fields.
9. DISPLAY FOR expressions(s)-Displays records matching expression(s).
10. DISPLAY fieldname(s)For expression(s) Off—Combines 8 & 9 above.
11. DISPLAY 'expression'$fieldname—Displays record numbers that have strings within the specified field that match the string in the expression.
12. DISPLAY WHILE—expression—Displays records while the expression is true.
13. DISPLAY STRUCTURE—Displays database structure.
14. DISPLAY HISTORY—Displays last ten commands in the order entered.
15. DISPLAY MEMORY—Displays active Memory variables.
16. DISPLAY FILES—Displays all database files in the logged drive.
17. DISPLAY STATUS—Displays active database filename(s), the status of the SET commands, and the commands issued by four computer's function keys.

Displaying Some Numeric Values Regarding the Contents of a Database.

The commands COUNT, SUM and AVERAGE are used to do the corresponding arithmetic for the records which meet a specified criteria. Suppose you give the following commands.

.USE BIODATA

.COUNT FOR AGE >40

You will get the response as

(3 Records)

Suppose you give the following commands:

.USE BIODATA

.SUM AGE FOR AGE > 40

You will get the response as

(3 records summed)

AGE
155

Suppose you give the following commands:

.USE BIODATA

.AVERAGE AGE FOR AGE > 40

You will get the response as

(3 records averaged)

AGE

52

In all the above cases you can store the sum or the count or the average by adding the clause 'TO variable-name' to respective commands.

For example you can give commands as

.COUNT for age> 40 to x

Then the memory variable x will store the value counted by dBASE. Similar commands can be given for the SUM and AVERAGE commands.

Thus you are able to view the database according to different criteria, either arithmetical or relational. We say that dBASE responds to different types of queries by the user or in other words dBASE is a query language. The conventional languages like Basic or Cobol also will respond to queries, but you have to tell not only what you want but also how to get it. In dBASE, you only tell what you want and the system figures out how to get the answer.

The LOCATE Command

The LOCATE command is used to find the records in a database which satisfy certain conditions. The general form of the LOCATE command is

.LOCATE [(scope)] FOR (condition)

Suppose you give the command

.USE BIODATA

.LOCATE FOR PIN = 110001

dBASE will respond as

(Record = 7)

For displaying that particular record give the command 'DISPLAY.' If you want to continue the search give the command

.CONTINUE

If there is another record which satisfies the condition, it will display the record number, otherwise it will display

End of LOCATE Scope

The scope clause can be given as below:

.USE BIODATA

.LOCATE NEXT 5 FOR PIN = 110001

In this case the search will be restricted only to the next 5 records, but if the scope is not specified, the search will be made in the entire database.

In this lesson we have seen the different ways of viewing the database and also finding specific records based on some criteria. In the next lesson we will see some dBASE Commands used for editing the database.

dBASE COMMANDS (III)

So far we have seen the following Major Commands

1. CREATE for creating the structure as well as entering data in the records.
2. LIST for viewing the structure of the record and the database.
3. DISPLAY for viewing the structure of the record and the database.
4. LOCATE for locating a record which meets certain specified criteria.

In this lesson we will study the following commands:

1. APPEND for adding records to a database.
2. INSERT inserting records in a database.
3. DELETE for deleting records in a database.
4. EDIT for changing the contents of a particular record.
5. BROWSE for changing the contents of a number of records.
6. CHANGE & REPLACE for making global changes.
7. MODIFY STRUCTURE for changing the structure of the record in the given database.

The APPEND Command

The APPEND command is used to start entering data for the first time or entering additional data on subsequent occasions. Suppose we want to add some more records to the BIODATA file which we have already created. Give the following commands:

.USE BIODATA

.APPEND

Immediately dBASE displays a full screen form for entering data in the eighth record, since we have already entered data for the first seven records. The screen form looks as shown in the Fig. 24.

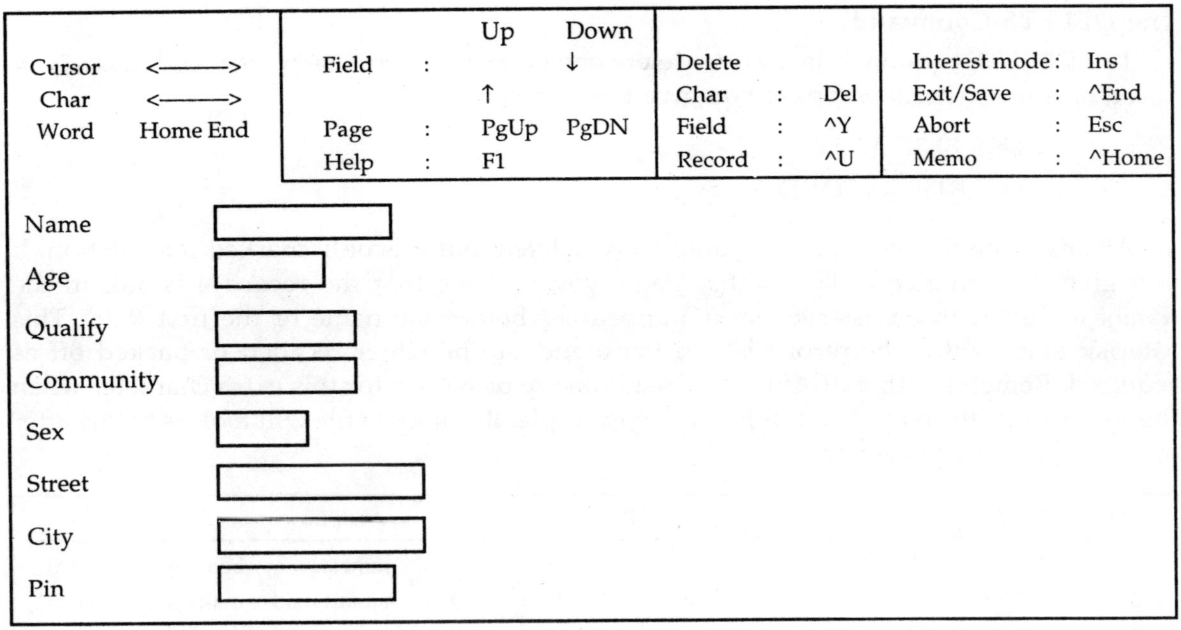

Cursor	<———>	Field :	Up ↓	Down ↑	Delete		Interest mode :	Ins
Char	<———>				Char :	Del	Exit/Save :	^End
Word	Home End	Page :	PgUp	PgDN	Field :	^Y	Abort :	Esc
		Help :	F1		Record :	^U	Memo :	^Home

Name
Age
Qualify
Community
Sex
Street
City
Pin

Fig. 24.

Now you can start entering data field by field. After entering the data for the last field, when you press the CR key, the structure display appears on the screen for the 9th record. If you want, you can continue or exit from the APPEND mode after saving the 8th record by simply pressing the CR key. It must be noted that by using the APPEND command one can only add records at the end of the file.

The INSERT Command

Suppose you want to insert a new record at the 7th position. Give the command as follows:

```
.USE BIODATA
.GOTO 7
.INSERT BEFORE
```

Immediately dBASE displays a full screen form for entering data in the 7th record. The data which were originally present in 7 are pushed to record 8 and the record 8 to record 9 and so on. After entering the data in the record 7, press Ctrl-W or Ctrl-End for saving the newly entered record. It may be noted that by suing the INSERT without adding the word BEFORE, the full screen form for entering data in the 8th record appears on the screen. The succeeding records will have their numbers changed accordingly. In all cases the data entry form will be the same as shown in the Fig. 24.

The DELETE Command

The DELETE command is used to delete one or more records either unconditionally or based on some criteria. Suppose you give the command:

.USE BIODATA

.DELETE RECORD 4

At this state the record is not completely deleted, but it is only marked for deletion. If you give the command LIST at this stage, you will see that the record 4 is still in the database, but with an asterik mark(*) appearing before the name of the first field. This asterisk tells us that the record is still there and can be either recalled or packed off as required. Remember that dBASE has already made provision for this extra character when the structure of the record was defined. For example, the biodata file will look as below after executing the above command.

Record #	*NAME*	*AGE*	*QUALIFY*	*COMMUNITY*	*SEX*	*TELE*	*STREET*	*CITY*	*PIN*
1	bala	40	be	fc	m	0	mint st.	bombay	400001
2	raji	25	me	bc	f	0	mount road	madras	600002
3	gayi	30	me	sc	f	0	rr street	tiruchi	620001
4	*raman	60	mphil	bc	m	0	ram street	karaikudi	624001
5	krishnan	50	dsc	bc	m	0	p.h.road	madurai	625006
6	murugan	45	bsc	fc	m	0	mp street	pasumalai	585001
7	latha	37	msc	sc	f	0	grant road	delhi	110001

Suppose you give the command

.RECALL RECORD 4

This command simply unmarks the asterisk placed by he DELETE command. If you give the LIST command now, you will find that the asterisk mark at the beginning of the first data field has disappeared. Suppose you give the following command immediately after the DELETE Command

.PACK

This command will remove all the marked records from the database file. If you give the LIST command now, the record 4 is no longer there and the remaining records have been renumbered accordingly. Now there is no way of getting back the record 4 which has been packed. Deletion command can also be given with FOR condition as follows:

.DELETE FOR expression.

For deleting an entire file you give the command as

.DELETE emp. dbf

You cannot delete a file which is opened by the USE command. You can delete files which are not opened. Once deleted, there is now way of recalling the file as in the case of a record. Remember that delete record command can be given only for the file in USE.

The EDIT Command

The EDIT command is used to edit the data values in any one record at a time. When you give the command

```
.EDIT  RECORD 5
```

dBASE displays the same screen for as APPEND or INSERT as shown in the Fig. 24. One can change the values in any or all fields and at the press Ctrl-W or Ctrl-End for saving the corrections made to that particular record. It must be noted that in the EDIT mode only one record can be edited at a time.

The BROWSE Command

The BROWSE command is used to edit values in one screenful of records which are displayed in the same way as the data file. Suppose you give the commands as follows:

```
.USE BIODATA
.BROWSE
```

Immediately dBASE displays a screenful of records as shown in the Fig. 25. The currently selected record is highlighted. After making the corrections in that record you can move the highlighting to another record by pressing the up or the down arrow as required.

				Up	Down						
Cursor	<———>	Field	:		↓	Delete			Interest mode	:	Ins
Char	<———>			↑		Char	:	Del	Exit/Save	:	^End
Word	Home End	Page	:	PgUp	PgDN	Field	:	^Y	Abort	:	Esc
		Help	:	F1		Record	:	^U	Memo	:	^Home

NAME	*AGE*	*QUALIFY*	*COMMUNITY*	*SEX*	*STREET*	*CITY*	*PIN*
bala	40	be	fc	m	min st.	bombay	400001
raji	25	me	bc	f	mount.road	madras	600002
gayi	30	msc	sc	f	rr street	tiruchi	620001
raman	60	mphil	bc	m	ram street	karaikudi	624001
krishnan	50	dsc	bc	m	p.h.road	madurai	625006
murugan	45	bsc	fc	m	mp street	pasumalai	585001
latha	37	msc	sc	f	grant road	delhi	110001

Fig. 25.

The following additional controls may be used with the BROWSE command:

1. Pressing the CR key will make the cursor go forward field by field in the horizontal direction.
2. Within a field, the Ctrl-V option can be used for the Insert feature.
3. Within a field, the Ctrl-C option can be used to delete the character under the cursor.
4. Within a field the Backspace key can be used to delete the character to the left of the cursor.
5. To leave the BROWSE mode after saving the changes press Ctrl-End. In case of doubt refer to the cursor control panel which appears at the top of the display.

The REPLACE Command

The REPLACE command is used to change the values of any number of fields in any number of records at the same time. Suppose you give the command.

```
.USE BIODATA
.REPLACE  ALL  AGE  WITH AGE + 10
.LIST
```

In the current listing of the database you will find that the ages of all the persons have been increased by 10. In the above example, we have changed the contents of only AGE field in all records. You specify any number of fields. Again REPLACE command can be given for specified records using the FOR condition.

The CHANGE Command

The CHANGE command is to change the contents of a specified field within the current record with whatever you type. Suppose you give the command

```
.USE  BIODATA
.CHANGE  FIELD AGE
dBASE responds as below:
Record No.    1
AGE           40
```

You simply change the age to 50 and press the CR key. If you display the record 1, you will see that the change has been incorporated.

The MODIFY STRUCTURE Command

Sometimes you would like to modify the structure of the record itself by either adding one or two fields or by deleting one or two fields in the record structure. The MODIFY STRUCTURE command is used to modify the structure is stated above. Suppose you give the command.

```
.USE BIODATA
.MODIFY STURCTURE
```

Immediately dBASE displays a screen which is identical to the CREATE screen as shown in the Fig. 26.

Cursor	<———>	Insert	:		Delete			Up a field	: ↑
Char	<———>	Char		Ins	Char	:	Del	Down a field :	↓
Word	Home End	Field	:	^N	Word	:	^Y	Exit/Save	: ^End
Pan	^<— ^—>	Help	:	F1	Field	:	^U	Abort	: Esc

Field	name	type	Width	Dec	Field Name	Type	Width	Dec
1	Name	Character	5					
2	Age	Numeric	2					
3	Qualify	Character	5					
4	Community	Character	5					
5	Sex	Character	1					
6	Street	Character	10					
7	City	Character	10					
8	Pin	Numeric	8					
9		Character						

Fig. 26.

In modifying the structure, you have three options. You can add fields at the end. You can insert fields in the middle. You can delete one more fields. For adding fields at the and type the field name, type and width at the 9th field position. Press Ctrl-W for saving the new structure. For inserting a field between 5 and 6, bring the cursor to the beginning of the 6th field and press Ctrl-N. The 6th field will now become blank. You can enter the new name, type and width. Suppose you want to enter telephone number field. Enter TELE for the name, Numeric for type and 4 for width. Store the new structure by pressing Ctrl-W. For deleting a field, bring the cursor to that field position and press Ctrl-U. Finally leave the MODIFY mode by pressing Ctrl-W for saving the modifications made. Now list the structure. The new structure will look as shown in the Fig. 27. List the database. You will find the new listing as shown in the Fig. 28. You will find that there is no data in the telephone field. You can enter the required data using the BROWSE edit command.

```
Scructure for detabase       :   A:biodata.dbf
Number of data records       :   7
Date of last update          :   01/13/89
```

Field	Field Name	Type	Width	Dec
1	Name	Character	10	
2	Age	Numeric	2	
3	Qualify	Character	5	
4	Community	Character	2	
5	Sex	Character	1	
6	Tele	Numeric	4	
7	Street	Character	10	
8	City	Character	10	
9	Pin	Numeric	6	
Total			51	

Fig. 27.

Record #	NAME	AGE	QUALIFY	COMMUNITY	SEX	TELE	STREET	CITY	PIN
1	bala	40	be	fc	m	0	mint st.	bombay	400001
2	raji	25	me	bc	f	0	mount road	madras	600002
3	gayi	30	me	sc	f	0	rr street	tiruchi	620001
4	raman	60	mphil	bc	m	0	ram street	karaikudi	624001
5	krishnan	50	dsc	bc	m	0	p.h.road	madurai	625006
6	murugan	45	bsc	fc	m	0	mp street	pasumalai	585001
7	latha	37	msc	sc	f	0	grant road	delhi	110001

Fig. 28.

Thus we have seen the different ways of editing and changing the structure of the database. In the next page we will see how the database can be organised and searched.

dBASE COMMANDS (IV)

In this lesson we will study the following commands:

1. SORT
2. INDEX
3. FIND & SEEK

We would like to place the data records in some sequence either alphabetical or numeric or chronological order according to one or more fields. Let us now consider a database by name BIODATA, whose structure is shown in the Fig. 28 and whose contents is shown in the Fig. 29.

Structure for database : A biodata dbf
Number of data records : 7
Date of last update : 01/13/89

Field	*Field Name*	*Type*	*Width*	*Dec*
1	Slno	Numeric	2	
2	Name	Character	10	
3	Sex	Character	1	
4	Birthday	Date	8	
5	Age	Numeric	2	
	Total		24	

Fig. 29.

Record #	*Sl. No*	*Name*	*Sex*	*Birthday*	*Age*
1	1	bala	m	01/15/48	40
2	2	raji	f	02/12/63	25
3	3	gayi	f	03/16/58	30
4	4	ramani	f	04/10/28	60
5	5	krishnan	m	01/23/38	50
6	6	murugan	m	03/29/43	45
7	7	latha	f	02/09/51	37

Fig. 30.

Suppose you want to sort the records according to the increasing order of the AGE field. You give the command as

SORT ON AGE TO TEMP

TEMP is the name of a file in which the sorted records are written. Of course the original datafile BIODATA also will be present when this sorted file is created. dBASE will give the message as follows:

100% sorted 7 Records sorted

To see the contents of the sorted file give the following commands:

.USE TEMP

.LIST

The sorted file TEMP.DBF looks as shown in the Fig. 29. Since TEMP.DBF is a new file you find that the record numbers given by dBASE is in the usual ascending order. But the field SLNO given by us is not in sequence. You find that the AGE field is in sequence:

Record #	*Sl. No*	*Name*	*Sex*	*Birthday*	*Age*
1	1	raji	f	00/12/63	25
2	2	gayi	f	03/16/58	30
3	3	latha	f	02/09/51	37
4	7	bala	m	04/15/48	40
5	5	murugan	m	01/29/43	45
6	6	krishnan	m	03/25/38	50
7	4	ramani	f	02/10/28	60

Fig. 31.

Suppose you want to sort the records according to the alphabetical order of the names. Give the following commands:

.SORT ON NAME TO TEMP 1

The above command will alphabetise the names and write all the records in a file called TEMP1.DBF. If you list the file TEMP 1, you will see that the records are re-arranged in the field SLNO in the order 1,3,5,7,6 & 4. You will see that this sequence puts the names in the alphabetical order.

Suppose you give the command

SORT ON SEX/D TO TEMP2

The above command will arrange the records sex-wise with the males listed first and females listed next. The symbol/D after SEX stands for descending order. The SLNO field will be in the order 1,5,6,2,3,4 & 7.

Suppose you want to sort the records sex-wise and within the sex field, you want to sort age wise, that is, sort within sort, you give the command as follows:

.SORT ON SEX/D, AGE TO TEMP

The above command will re-arrange the records with the SLNO field in the order 1,6,5,2,3,7 & 4. This arrangement will put the ages of the males and females in the ascending order.

Indexing

dBASE provides another alternative to sorting and this is called indexing. In indexing a separate indexed file is not created, but the same file is read in a different order using what is called an Index file. Suppose you give the command

.Index on Birthday to Birthndx

dBASE creates an Index file by name BIRTHNDX.NDX in which the key field BIRTHDAY is accessed by an index somewhat similar to the Index in a book. In Indexing the record numbers of the original file are not changed but they seem to be arranged in a different order which reflects the type of sorting that is required. If you give the LIST command, you will see that the database file looks as shown in the Fig. 32.

Record #	*Sl. No*	*Name*	*Sex*	*Birthday*	*Age*
4	4	ramani	f	04/12/28	60
5	5	krishnan	m	01/16/38	50
6	6	murugan	m	03/09/43	45
1	1	bala	m	01/15/48	40
7	7	latha	f	02/29/51	37
3	3	gayi	f	03/25/58	30
2	2	raji	f	02/10/28	25

Fig. 32.

Index files can be created for every field separately and such files can be used for accessing any record according to the field which is indexed. For viewing the above indexed file you give the command as

```
.USE BIODATA INDEX BIRTHNDX
.LIST
```

Advantages of Indexing

1. The first advantage is that the indexes that are currently active against a given file are automatically updated if that indexed file is in any way changed or altered in the key field values. Suppose you edit the key field of the record 2 as 02/12/23. You will see that after this edit operation record 2 is logically positioned before the record 4. You can see the listing by giving the command

```
.USE BIODATA INDEX BIRTHNDX
.LIST
```

You will find that the record numbers appear in the order 2,4,5,6,1,7 &3. In the sorting method the sorted file is not automatically updated. You have to once again do sorting after updating the given file. You will find indexing very useful in applications where the files have to be updated in on-line mode.

2. The second advantage of the index feature is that you can ask dBASE whips in a few seconds to position itself at the record you want. This instant access is done through the use

of a FIND and SEEK commands. The restriction with the FIND and the SEEK commands is that they can be used only with numeric and character fields and not with logical and fields.

The FIND Command

We have seen that the LOCATE commands can be used either with the sorted file or the unsorted file. The FIND command can be used only with an indexed file. Suppose you want to find the record whose age field has a value 37. First of all index the field on age. The following set of commands will find the desired record and display the same on the screen:

```
.USE BIODATA
.INDEX ON AGE TO AGENDX
.USE BIODATA INDEX AGENDX
.FIND 37
.DISPLAY
```

The FIND command will move the record pointer to the first record which matches with the FIND query and the display command will display it on the screen. In a similar fashion one can index on any character field, say NAME and use it to find the record which matches with any desired name. The general form of the FIND command is

FIND<character string>

This means that the FIND command will work only with characters either numeric or character. In the case of character strings the string need not be delimited by quotes. FIND will not work with variables. For example one cannot write

```
.store 37 image
.Index on age to agendx
.FIND image
```

One cannot use numeric variables with the 'FIND' command. Can we use string variables with 'FIND'? String variables also cannot be used with the 'FIND' command. But one can use a macro which is a substitution or a replacement for the string. For example, let us assume that the file is indexed on name and you want to find whether the name 'ramani' is in the file. One can use the commands as below:

```
.store "ramani" to mname
.find & mname
```

& mname is called a macro which simply replaces the string "ramani" It must be noted that "ramani" is not the value of & mname, but the macro is a replacement for the string "&mname." Macros can be used only with string variables and not with numeric variables. This means employee number field cannot be found with a macro substitution. One has to simply use the `find' command with the actual value. For finding string values one can write the value without quotes or use the macro substitution command. For example, for finding the employee name "ramani", one must write as

```
.find ramani
```

The value ramani must not be enclosed within quotes.

The SEEK Command

Just as the FIND command the SEEK command also works only with an indexed file. When you use SEEK command with strings, you must use delimiters. For example, to SEEK the NAME ramani, you must give the commands as follows:

```
.USE BIODATA INDEX NAMENDX
.SEEK `ramani'
.DISPLAY
```

The SEEK command also acts like the FIND command, in that both of them find the first match within a database. There is some difference in their general forms. The general form of the SEEK command is

```
.SEEK expression
```

This means that SEEK command is used with a value and not a string as the FIND command. So one can use either a variable or a value with the SEEK command. One can write the SEEK commands as below:

```
.SEEK mage or SEEK 37
```

where mage is a variable which stores the value 37.

The character strings must be enclosed with quotes when the SEEK command is used. For example for seeking the name ramani, one must give the command as

```
SEEK "ramani"
```

SEEK command will not work with macros. In general SEEK command is used with numeric fields as FIND command is used with string fields. Of course you can use the SEEK command for both numeric and string fields. This means that the FIND command is used only when use of macros becomes inevitable.

INDEXING on Multiple Fields

Suppose you want to index on the SEX field and within that field you want to index on NAME, you give the commands as follows:

```
.USE BIODATA
.INDEX ON SEX + STR (ACE, 2) TO AGENDX
```

INDEXING IN DESCENDING Order

The indexing feature in dBASE does not support the parameter /D, for descending as the SORT command does. But one can write like this:

```
.USE  BIODATA
.INDEX  ON 999-AGE TO  AGENDX
```

The expression 999 - AGE will be ascending in the indexed file whereas the AGE will be descending.

TOTAL Command for Getting Subtotals

Suppose you have a sorted file shopping as shown in the Fig. 33.

```
.use shopping
.list
```

Record #	*DEPT*	*QUANTITY*	*COST*
1	electrical	200	8000.00
2	electrical	500	625.00
3	electrical	300	150.00
4	fruits	600	450.00
5	fruits	400	1100.00
6	fruits	1000	600.00
7	fruits	1200	2100.00
8	hardware	700	175.00
9	hardware	200	500.00
10.	hardware	900	1350.00

Fig. 33.

If you want to find the subtotals departmentwise, give the total command as follows. The subtotals are output in another database file shopping 1 as shown in the Fig. 34.

```
total on dept to shopping 1
10    Record(s) totalled
3     Records generated
use shopping1
list
```

Record #	*DEPT*	*QUANTITY*	*COST*
1	electrical	1000	8775.00
2	fruits	3200	4250.00
3	hardware	1800	2025.00

Fig. 34.

The general form of the TOTAL command is

TOTAL ON <key field> TO <file-name> [<scopes>] [FIELDS<field-lidt>] [FOR/WHILE <conditions>]

Unless otherwise specified by the scope or the FOR/WHILE clause all records will be totalled. All numeric field will be totalled unless the field lists are specified in the FIELDS clause. All records with the same value in the specified key field becomes a single record in the target database. All numeric fields appearing in the FIELDS list will contain totals. All other fields will contain the data from the first record in the key field set. Before using the TOTAL command the database must either be sorted on the key field or indexed.

In Data Processing Applications, Sorting and Indexing are used very often and the readers must carefully study these important commands.

MULTIPLE FILE HANDLING

What is Multiple File Handling?

We have seen so far, how we can give commands to manipulate data retrieved from a single database file. Sometimes, we may have to get data from different database files for purpose of manipulation and reporting. dBASE has facility to keep up to 10 database files open at the same time and access data from them. This is called Multiple File Handling.

Operations Involved in Multiple File Handling

Let us take only two database files at a time for the sake of simplicity for doing multiple file operations. Later on, we can extend the operations to more number of files, up to the maximum permitted by dBASE. We may have to do the following operations with the two files:

1. We may have to access data from one or more database files at the same time.
2. We may require to create a database file which contains either all the fields in the records of the two files or only the selected fields from the records of the two files. Again, we may like to have only certain specified records in the new file. In short, we may have to crate a database file from the two given files, based on certain selection criteria for the fields or records or both.
3. We may require to update one or more fields in a file called the master file taking the data from another file called the transaction file.

Some Characteristics of Multiple Files

Suppose we have two database files. In general, we may find the following three features between them.

1. The two files will have the same number of records, but may have different number of fields and also different types of fields.

dBASE PROGRAMMING (I)

We are now familiar with using the different dBASE commands at the dot prompt, interactively one by one. Of course one can solve all problems by commanding dBASE interactively. But this method is laborious and time consuming especially when a large number of commands are required for solving a problem. This is because we can give a second command only after the first is executed. We cannot club together all the commands and wait for execution. In the programming mode it is possible to club together any number of commands and write them in a single file, with a name. Then a single command for executing this file is given. This single command will cause the execution of all the dBASE commands contained in that file without any human intervention at any stage of operation. This will quicken the execution of the program. Further there are more commands in the programming mode than in the interactive mode. For example, in the interactive mode we cannot command to execute a set of commands repetitively a specified number of times. Again we cannot command the computer to branch off to another command based on some specific comparison test. The programming mode is made more powerful by removing these limitations.

Important Commands Used in the Programming Mode

1. Control Commands or Control Statements
2. Input Commands or Input Statements and
3. Output Commands or Output Statements are some of the important commands used in dBASE in the Programming mode in addition to all the dot prompt commands we have seen earlier.

The Control Statements available in dBASE are

(1) do while
(2) if else endif
(3) do case

We will now consider the general forms of these commands.

Do While Command or Statement

This statement is used when a particular segment of commands have to be executed repeatedly a specified number of times. This is also called the looping logic. The general form of this statement is

```
DO WHILE logical expression
_____________________________
_____________________________
_____________________________
_____________________________
ENDDO
```

The logical expression is first tested. If it is true the statements in the loop body (statements bracketed between DO WHILE and ENDDO) will be executed once. Again the control goes to the top and tests the logical expression. If it is again true the loop body will be again executed, otherwise the loop body will be skipped and the control passes on to the statement immediately following the ENDDO statement. The loop body will be repeatedly executed so long as the logical expression is true. If the logical expression is false even in the first instance the loop is not executed even once. The following program segment illustrates the use of DO WHILE logic.

```
s = 0
n = 1
do while n<101
s = s + n
n = n + 1
enddo
```

The above program segment sums the natural numbers from 1 to 100 as is seen from the do while logic.

The Exit Statement

Sometimes the loop may have to be terminated based on certain condition. In that case exit statement can be used as shown below:

```
do while n< 101
s = s + 1
n = n + 1
if n = 20
exit
endif
enddo
```

The exit statement completely exits the control from the loop when n = 20 and brings it to the statement immediately following the enddo statement.

The Loop Statement

Sometimes it may be required to stop executing some of the statements at the lower end of the loop body and transfer the control to the beginning of the loop. In that case the loop statement is used as shown below:

```
do while logical expression
____________
____________
```

```
if condition
loop
endif
__________
enddo
```

The above loop statement means that if the condition is true the control is to be transferred to the beginning, otherwise the control is to go through the normal route for ending the loop, i.e. via the enddo statement.

The IF and the DO CASE commands

The IF and the DO CASE Commands are used or branching purposes. The IF command can be written in two forms, namely, with and without ELSE option as follows:

```
1. If expression
   ........
   ........
   ........
   ENDIF
2. If expression
   ........
   ........
   ........
   ELSE
   ........
   ........
   ........
   ENDIF
```

In the first, form the expression after the word IF is tested for true or false value. If the expression is true, then all the commands up to ENDIF are executed. If the expression is false, then the control skips all the commands up to ENDIF statement and passes on to the command immediately following the ENDIF statement. In the second from, if the expression is true, all the commands up to ELSE are executed, but the commands after ELSE and upto ENDIF are skipped. If the expression is false, all the commands up to ELSE are skipped, but the commands after ELSE and upto ENDIF are executed.

The IF command is used to make a selection between two given alternatives. If one has to make a selection from more than two alternatives the DO CASE command is used.

The general form of DO CASE Command is

```
DO CASE
    ........
    ........
    ........
    CASE expression
    ........
    ........
    ........
    CASE expression
    ........
    ........
    ........
    CASE expression
    ........
    ........
    ........
ENDCASE
```

When the control encounters the DO CASE command, it will check the true or false value of expression entered after the word CASE starting from the first CASE. If the expression is true it will execute all the commands up to the next CASE and then go to the ENDCASE statement. If more than one CASE is true, only the first one will be executed. If the OTHERWISE clause is present and one of the CASE's are true, then the alternative in the OTHERWISE clause will be executed. If there is no OTHERWISE clause and none of the CASE's are true, then the entire DO CASE will be skipped.

Inputting Commands in dBASE

The following input Commands are used in dBASE to get data into the program.

1. INPUT
2. ACCEPT
3. @ SAY

The general form of the INPUT command is

INPUT <prompt-string> TO <memory-variable>

The INPUT command is used to get numeric data for a memory variable. Suppose you write INPUT "enter value for the principal" To principal

The computer will display the prompt string on the screen and will wait until the user keys the value for the variable principal.

The general form of the ACCEPT command is

ACCEPT <prompt-string> TO <memory-variable>

The ACCEPT command is used to get string or character data for a memory variable. Suppose you write

ACCEPT "enter the value of the employee name" TO empname.

The computer will display the prompt string on the screen and will wait until the user keys the value for the variable empname. The file variables cannot be keyed in or accessed through the above commands. We make use of @SAY command for this purpose.

The general form of the @ SAY command is

@ROW, COL SAY <prompt-string> GET (file-variable) (memory-variable)
[PICTURE, template>]
[RANGE <value>, value>]
READ

For purpose of display the computer screen is divided into 24 rows and 80 columns and numbered from 0 to 23 and 0 to 79 respectively. The above form is used to get both memory variables and file variables either numeric or string. If values are to be obtained for memory variables they must have been initialised in the beginning. The numeric variables are initialised to zero and memory variables are initialised to space. File variables don't need initialisation since they have already been defined in the database. The prompt string will appeal at the specified row and column. The location for entering the variable will appear in reverse video and its length is fixed by the specification in the PICTURE template clause. Suppose you write

```
empno = 0
empname = space(10)
@2,4 say "enter value for the employee number"
GET empno PICTURE "9999" RANGE 1,4000
@ 3,4 say "enter value for the  employee name"
GET empname PICTURE "xxxxxxxx"
READ
```

The prompt stings will appear in the 2nd and 3rd rows and their corresponding PICTURE templates will appear by their side in reverse video as shown below:

enter value for the employee number [ ]

enter value for the employee name [ ]

The initial values of the variables will appear in the respective locations. The edit cursor will be located in the position where data have to be entered. After entering the values for the two variables, the enter key is pressed. Now the new values have been assigned to the variables. One facility available with this input form is that you can specify the range of numeric values. If you try to enter values outside the specified range the control will give a message reminding the user about the range and asking the user to press space to make the correct entry. The template simply consists of some characters which will replace each digit or character in the actual data. For example, the template "9999" tells that only numeric data with a maximum of 4 digits can be entered. Similarly the template "xxxxxx" tells that only string data with a maximum of 10 characters. The READ command at the end enables the data entered in the reverse video portion to be edited. The GET clause also can be given locations by specifying the rows and columns. For example, one can write as

```
empno = 0
empname = space(10)
@ 2,4 say "enter value for the employee number"
@ 2,40 GET empno PICTURE "9999" RANGE 1,4000
@ 3,4 say "enter value for the employee name"
@ 3,40 GET empname PICTURE "xxxxxxx"
READ
```

One can highlight the data entry region by asking dBASE to enclose the region by a double lined rectangular box, by giving the command

```
@ 1,2 to 5,45 double
```

The above command will draw a rectangular box with 1,2 and 5,45 as the coordinates of the diagonally opposite corners. The @SAY command is very widely used in custom designed screens for data entry. We will see more about this command later.

Outputting Commands in dBASE

There are only two outputting commands in dDBASE. They are

1. ? variables-list
2. @ ROW, COL SAY expression [PICTURE CLAUSE]

Suppose you have three variables x, y and z whose values are 234 567, 5678.9807 and -12345.5678 respectively. Suppose you give the command

? x, y, z

The output will lock as below:

234.567 5678.9807 -12345.5678

In order to make the output more meaningful and give the values rounded off to two decimal places one has to give the format and write as

```
? "x=", transform(x, "###.##"), space(5), "y =", transform (y, "###.##"), space(5),
"z =", transform (z, "######.##")
```

The output will look as below:

x = 234.57   y = 5678.98   z = -12345.57

The numbers are rounded off to two decimal places.

Suppose you use the SAY command and write

```
@5, 2 say str(x,7,3) + str(y, 9,4) + str(z,11,4)
```

The output will appear in the 5th row and 2nd column as

234.5675678.9807-12345.5678

It must be remembered that you cannot write the statement as

```
@5,2 say x,y,z
```

Since you have to write an expression, x, y and z must be converted to strings and then concatenated by the + operator. If you want to output only one value in a line you can write

```
@ 5,2 say x
@ 6,2 say y
@ 7,2 say z
```

In order to output all the three values in a meaningful way one can write as

```
@ 5,2 say "x =" + str(x,7,2) + space(5) + "y =" + str(y, 9,4) + space(5) + "z =" +
str(z,9,2)
```

The output will appear as

x = 234.57 y = 5678.98 z = -12345.57

The number are rounded off to two decimal places. One can also write the output statements as below:

```
@ 2,2 say "x ="
@ 2,7 say x picture "999.99"
@ 2,25 say "y ="
@ 2,15 say "y ="
@ 2,20 say y picture "9999.99"
@ 2,30 say "z ="
@ 2,37 say z
```

The above statements also will print all the three values in the same line. You have to correctly calculate the coordinates where each item should appear in the screen.

How to Get the Outputs in the PRINTER or the FILE?

The simple? command will output the result on the screen. In order to direct the output in the printer the following commands are given in the beginning and in the end of the program as shown below:

```
set print on
. . . . . . .
. . . . . . .
. . . . . . .
set print off
return
```

In order to direct the output to the file the following commands are given in the beginning and in the end as shown below:

```
set alternate to rr.txt
set alternate on
. . . . . . .
. . . . . . .
. . . . . . .
. . . . . . .
set alternate off
set alternate to
```

The output will be written in the file named rr.txt. The name of the file is programmer coined, but the extension is system defined. If you don't give the txt extension dBASE will give it.

The simple @SAY command will output the result in the screen. In order to direct the output on the printer, the following commands are given in the beginning and in the end as shown below:

```
set device to print
. . . . . . .
. . . . . . .
. . . . . . .
. . . . . . .
set device to screen
```

The outputs produced by the @SAY command on the screen cannot be written on a file. There is no directing command to the file in the case of @SAY command. If one wants the output in a file one must use only the? command.

Editing & Executing a dBASE Program

The dBASE program is entered by invoking the dBASE Editor using the following form of command:

.MODIFY COMMAND filename

The filename is user coined. One can give a name say 'pg1.' As soon as you give the above command with the filename and press the CR key, dBASE displays its Editor Mode Screen as shown in the Fig. 34.

Edit: A:PG1.PRG

					Up	Down						
Cursor	:	← →	Field	:			Delete			Interest mode :		Ins
Char	:	← →		↑	↓		Char :	Del		Inser Line	:	^N
Word	:	Home End	Page	:	PgUp	PgDN	Field	:	^T	Save ^W		Abort: Esc
Line	:	^← ^→	Find	:	^KF		Line	:	^Y	Read file	:	^KR
Reformat:		^KB	Refind		^KL					Write file	:	^KW

Fig. 35.

The word 'Edit' and the name of the program 'pgl.prg' appears at the left hand top corner of the screen. The cursor control menu for full screen editing appears in the next 5 lines. The remaining space is empty for the user to enter the program. There is no dot prompt. The editing screen is like the WORDSTAR screen (non-document mode). The user can type the commands one by one. The command list is terminated by 'RETURN.' After entering all the commands, the command file or the dBASE program is saved in the file using the command^W. For executing this program give the following command from the dot prompt.

.DO program-name

All the commands in the command file will be executed one by one and finally dBASE returns to the dot prompt.

General Rules for writing a dBASE Program

A dBASE program can be entered either through the dBASE Editor or through the WORDSTAR Editor (non-document mode). When WORDSTAR Editor is used the program file name must be given the extension .PRC. A dBASE program is simply a text file and so it can be typed outside the dBASE mode. A dBASE program can be executed only inside the dBASE mode at the dot prompt.

Only one command statement can be written in one physical line. A physical line is normally 254 characters wide.

A command statement can be continued in the next line after breaking it in between words and putting a semicolon mark at the end of the first line. There must be one space between the last word of the line and the semicolon mark.

An asterisk mark (*) at the start of a line indicates to dBASE that the line is to be treated as a comment and not as a command. If you want to add a comment after a command, start the command by entering two ampersand symbols (&&).

Start writing a program after entering the CLEAR command, which will clear the screen.

At the end press ^W for saving the program file in the disk. If you want to abandon the program typed so far, press ^Q or Esc.

The words CREATE COMMAND or MODIFY COMMAND can be used or invoking the dBASE Editor.

dBASE programs are similar to the programs in the conventional high level languages like basic, cobol, pascal, fortran etc. We use the same three types of logic, namely, the sequenctly the looping and the decision for implementing the algorithms. Commands on dBASE are analogous to statements in the hll's. A dBASE program is merely a collection of logically organised commands for implementing a particular problem logic. We will consider examples of dbase programs where data are accessed through console and database files. Remember that dBASE is essentially a file processing language and so all data are stored only in files. All the same dBASE allows 256 independent or memory variables to be used in a program. Values for memory variables cannot be read from files, but can be read either through the console or assigned in the program.

In the first instance we will consider some programs which use only the unstructured variables or the memory variables. These programs are intended to understand the logic of the different control statements and other programming commands. Then we will learn to write programs using file variables or databases.

This is a program for finding the simple interest and compound interest for one set of values of p, r & n.

```
*1 program for simple and compound interest
set talk off
input "enter the value of principal         "to p
input "enter the value of rate percent      "to r
input "enter the value of number of years "to n
si = p*n* r/100
ci = p *(1 +r/100) ^n - p
?
? "principal is ",p
```

```
? "rate percent is ",r
? "number of years is ", n
? "simple interest is ",si
? "compound interest is", ci
return
```

Explanation

The first statement is a comment statement intended for the users to know what the program is about. The second line instructs the computer not to output any dbase dialogue such as '100% sorted' etc. The other lines are simply dot prompt commands, for of course written without dots. The last line is return statement, which causes the control to return to the dot prompt after executing the program.

The output looks as below:

```
enter the value of principal            100
enter the value of rate per cent          5
enter the value of number of years        5
principal is                            100
rate per cent is                          5
number of years is                        5
simple interest is                        25.00
compound interest is                      27.63
```

From the above output we find that the figures at the output are not aligned properly with appropriate decimal points. Proper alignment can be made by formatting using the transform function as shown in the next program. For getting the output on the printer introduce the command'set print on' in the beginning of the ? command and the statement 'set print off' at the end of the ? command.

```
*2 program for simple and compound interest using the transform function
set talk off
input "enter the value of principal     "to p
input "enter the value of rate per cent " to r
input "enter the value of number of years "to n
si = p* n* r/100
ci = p* (1 + r/100)^ n - p
?
? "principal is          "transform (p, "####.##")
? "rate per cent is         ",transfer(r, "####.##")
```

```
? "number of years is ",transform(n, "####.##")
? "simple interest is ",transform (si, "####.##")
? "compound interest is ",transform (ci, "####.##")
return
```

The following is the output:

```
enter the value of principal              100
enter the value of rate per cent            5
enter the value of number of years          5

principal is                           100.00
rate per cent is                         5.00
number of years is                       5.00
simple interest is                      25.00
compound interest is                    27.63
```

We see from the output that the figures are properly aligned. If you want to find the simple interest and compound interest for more set of values you must introduce looping statement. The program shown below uses the DO-WHILE statement for looping:

```
*3 program for simple and compound interest using DO-WHILE logic
set talk off
choice = 1
do while choice <2
input "enter the value of principal          "to p
input "enter the value of rate per cent      "to r
input "enter the value of number of years "to n
si = p* n* r/100
ci = p* (1 +r/100) ^n - p
?
? "principal is "transform     (p, "####.##")
? "rate per cent is            "transform(r, "####.##")
? "number of years is          ",transform (n, "####.##")
? simple interest is           ",transform (si, "####.##")
? "compound interest is        ",transform (ci, "####.##")
input "any more trials: enter 1 for yes & 2 for no " to choice
enddo
return
```

The output will be similar to the output in the program 2. The simple? command will print the output on the screen. For printing the information on paper, give the command "set print in the beginning of the ? command and at the end of all the? command, give the command `set print off." The command `set print on' will activate the printer and the command `set print off" deactivate the printer.

The interest program is now written using @ say command for inputting and outputting the data.

```
*4 programme for finding simple and compound interest using @ say commands
set talk off
k=1
p=0
n=0
r=0
do while k<2
clear
@ 2,4 say "enter value for principal            "get p pict "9999.99"
@ 3,4 say "enter value for rate per cent        "get r pict "99.99"
@ 4,4 say "enter value for number of years      "get n pict "99"
read
si=p*n*r/100
ci=p*(1+r/100)^n-p
set device to print
@ 6,4 say "principal is"
@ 6, 30 say p pict "99999.99"
@ 7,4 say "rate per cent is"
@ 7, 30 say r pict "99999.99"
@ 8, 4 say "number of years is"
@ 8,30 say n pict "99999.99"
@ 9,4 say "simple interest is"
@ 9,30 say si pict "99999.99"
@ 10,4 say "compound interest is"
@ 10,30 say ci pict "99999.99"
@ 11,2 say " "
set device to screen
@ 14, 4 say "enter 1 for more trials and 2 for stopping" get k
```

```
red
enddo
return
```

The output will look as below:

```
enter value for principal              [          ]

enter value for rate per cent             [     ]

enter value for number of years            [    ]

principal is                          350.00
rate per cent is                        6.50
number of years is                      7.00
simple interest is                    159.25
compound interest is                  193.89
enter 1 for more trials and 2 for stopping
```

Summary

In this lesson we have seen the INPUT, OUTPUT and the CONTROL statements available in dBASE for writing programs or command files. We have also given a few examples of programs which use only unstructured or memory variables. In the next lesson we will consider some more programs using unstructured variables and then take to programs which use structured variables or file variables.

dBASE PROGRAMMING (II)

In this lesson we will consider some more programs which use unstructured variables only

1. This is a simple program for finding the sum of natural numbers from 1 to 100. Do-while logic is used for looping in this program.

```
*program for finding the sum of natural numbers
set talk off
s = 0
n = 1
do while n < 101
s = s + n
n = n + 1
enddo
```

```
? "sum of natural numbers up to 100 is", s
return
```

The output will look as below:

sum of natural numbers up to 100 is   5050

2. This is a program for reversing a string using do-while logic.

```
*program for reversing a string
set talk off
accept "enter a string of character:" to x
? " given string is," x
c = less (x)
? "length of the string is",
? "the string in the reverse order is"
choice = 1
do while choice <=c
?? left (right (x, choice), 1)
choice = choice + 1
enddo
return
```

The following is a typical output:

enter a string of characters abcdefgh
given string is abcdefgh
length of the string is   8
the string in the reverse order is hgfedcba

3. The following is a program for finding the square root of a number using what is called the successive approximation method. The relation between two successive guesses S(i+1) and S(i) is given by the relation S(i+1) = (S(i) + a/S(i)/2, where a is the given number. We start with an initial guess of a/2 and apply the above algorithm repeatedly until the absolute difference between S(i + 1) and S(i) is less than or equal to some small quantity depending on the accuracy required for the result. In this program the result is found correct to three decimal places.

```
.type sroot.prg
* program for finding square root of a number
set talk off
set decimals to 4
```

```
trial = 1
do while trial < 2
input "enter the number "to a
s1 = a/2
choice = 1
x = 1
do while choice < 10
s2 = (s1 + a/s1)/2
if abs(s1-s2) <= .0001
? "square root is", s1
choice = 10
loop
else
? "s1 is", s1, " s2 is", s2
s1 = s2
choice = choice + 1
x = x + 1
endif
enddo
if x = 10
? "solution does not converge"
endif
input "any more trials (1 for yes and 2 for no)" to trial
enddo
return
```

-The following are some typical outputs:

```
 do sroot
enter the number 345
s1   is          172.5000       s2   is         87.2500
s1   is           87.2500       s2   is         45.6021
s1   is           45.6021       s2   is         26.5838
s1   is           26.5838       s2   is         19.7808
s1   is           19.7808       s2   is         18.6110
s1   is           18.6110       s2   is         18.5742
```

```
square root is    18.5742
any more trials (1 for yes and 2 for no) 1
enter the number 345678
    s1  is      172839.0000     s2  is   86420.5000
    s1  is       86420.5000     s2  is   43212.2500
    s1  is       43212.2500     s2  is   21610.1248
    s1  is       21610.1248     s2  is   10813.0604
    s1  is       10813.0604     s2  is    5422.5145
    s1  is        5422.5145     s2  is    2743.1316
    s1  is        2743.1316     s2  is    1434.5737
    s1  is        1434.5737     s2  is     837.7679
    s1  is         837.7679     s2  is     625.1929
solution does not converge
any more trials (1 for yes and 2 for no) 1
enter the number 25
    s1  is          12.5000     s2  is       7.2500
    s1  is           7.2500     s2  is       5.3491
    s1  is           5.3491     s2  is       5.0114
    s1  is           5.0114     s2  is       5.0000
square root is                  5.0000
    any more trials (i for yes and 2 for no) 2
```

4. The following is a program for finding the hcf and lcm of two integers. The program uses Euclid's algorithm, which is given as follows:

```
hcf(x,y)     =     hcf(x, x-y) if x is greater than y
hcf(x,Y)     =     hcf(y-x, y) if y is greater than x
hcf(x, y)    =     x or y if x is equal to y
* program for finding hcf & lcm of two given integers
set talk off
set decimals to 0
trial = 1
do while trial <2
input "enter the first integer number:" to x
input "enter the second integer number:" to y
```

```
x1 = x
y1 = y
p = .t.
do while p
if x > y
x = x - y
loop
endif
if x < y
y = y - x
loop
endif
p = .f.
enddo
lcm = x1 *(y1/x)
? "hcf of the two given numbers", x1 "and", y1 "is", x
? "lcm of the two given numbers", x1, "and", y1, "is" , lcm
input "any more trials (enter 1 for yes and 2 for no)" to trial
enddo
return
```

The following is a typical output:

```
enter the first integer number: 34
enter the second integer number: 46
hcf of the two given numbers      34 and     46 is     2
lcm of the two given numbers      34 and     46 is     782
any more trials (enter 1 for yes and 2 for no) 2
```

5. The following program is intended for printing address labels:

```
*program for printing address labels
set talk off
trial = 1
do while trial < 2
accept "enter your name (give 15 characters including blanks)" to n
accept "enter street(give 15 characters including blanks)" to s
```

```
accept "enter city(give 15 characters including blanks)" to c
accept "enter pincode(give 15 characters including blanks)" to pin
choice = 1
do while choice < 10
?
? n. space(5), n
? n, space(5), s
? c, space(5), c
? pin, space(5), pin
?
choice = choice + 1
enddo
input "any more trials (enter 1 for yes and 2 for no)" to trial
enddo
```

The following is a typical output:

```
enter your name(give 15 characters including blanks)xxxxxxxxxxxxxxx enter
street(give 15 characters including blanks) yyyyyyyyyyyyyyy enter city(give 15
characters including blanks) zzzzzzzzzzzzzzz enter pincode(give 15 characters
including blanks) 600001

xxxxxxxxxxxxxxxx     xxxxxxxxxxxxxxx
yyyyyyyyyyyyyyy      yyyyyyyyyyyyyyy
 zzzzzzzzzzzzzzz      zzzzzzzzzzzzzzz
          600001               600001
 xxxxxxxxxxxxxxx      xxxxxxxxxxxxxxx
yyyyyyyyyyyyyyy       yyyyyyyyyyyyyy
 zzzzzzzzzzzzzzz       zzzzzzzzzzzzzz
          600001               600001

any more trials(enter 1 for yes and 2 for no) 2
```

6. The following program is intended for solving a quadratic equation:

```
*program for solving quadratic equations
set talk off
set decimals to 4
trial = 1
```

```
do while trial < 2
input "enter the coefficient a" to a
input "enter the coefficient b" to b
input "enter the coefficient c" to c
d = b*b - 4* a* c
do case
case d > 0
? "root are real and unequal"
x1 = (-b + sqrt(d)/(2*a)
x2 = (-b - sqrt(d)/ (2*a)
? "root 1 is ",x1
? "root 2 is ",x2
case d = 0
? "roots are real and equal"
x1 = -b/*2*a)
? "root is", x1
case d < 0
? "roots are imaginary"
endcase
input "any more trials (enter 1 for yes and 2 for no)" to trial
enddo
return
```

The following are some typical outputs:

```
enter the coefficient a 1
enter the coefficient b 2
enter the coefficient c 4
roots and imaginary
any more trials (enter 1 for yes and 2 for no) 1
enter the coefficient a 1
enter the coefficient b 4
enter the coefficient c 4
roots are real and equal
root is          -2.0000
any more trials (enter 1 for yes and 2 for no)1
enter the coefficient a 1
```

```
enter the coefficient b -7
enter the coefficient c 12
roots are real and unequal
root 1 is          4.0000
root 2 is          3.0000
any more trials (enter 1 for yes and 2 for no)2
```

7. The following is a program for finding the factorial of numbers:

```
*program for finding factorial of numbers
set talk off
fact = 1
num = 1
do while num < 10
fact = fct* num
? "factorial of the number ",num, "is", fact
num = num + 1
enddo
return
factorial of the number        1   is        1
factorial of the number        2   is        2
factorial of the number        3   is        6
factorial of the number        4   is       24
factorial of the number        5   is      120
factorial of the number        6   is      720
factorial of the number        7   is     5040
factorial of the number        8   is    40320
factorial of the number        9   is   362880
```

8. The following is a program for printing payslips:

```
*program for printing payslip
trial = 1
do while trial < 2
input "enter employee number" to empno
accept "enter employee name" to empname
input "enter deductions "to deds
```

```
?
alls = basic *0.1
gpay = basic + alls
netpay = gpay - deds
? "employee number", space(5),      transform(empno, "####")
? "employee name", space(5),        empname
? "basic pay    ",space(5),         transform(basic,"#####.##")
? "allowances   ",space(5),         transform(alls, "#####.##")
? "gross pay    ",space(5),         transform(gpay, "#####.##")
? "deductions   ",space(5),         transform(deds, "#####.##")
? "netpay       ",space(5),         transform(netpay, "#####.##")
?
? "date.........                              signature"
?
input "any more trials(enter 1 for yes and 2 for no)" to trial
enddo
return
```

The following is a typical output:

```
enter employee number 34
enter employee name xxxxxxxx
enter basic pay 500.85
enter deductions 45.65
employee number                  34
employee name              xxxxxxxx
basic pay                    500.85
allowances                    50.08
gross pay                    550.93
deductions                    45.65
netpay                       505.28
date......                signature
any more trials (enter 1 for yes and 2 for no)2
```

9. The following program is intended for finding prime numbers:

```
*program for finding prime numbers in the range 1 to 100
set talk off
```

```
? "prime numbers are 1 2 3"
?
k1 = 0
k2 = 0
x = 5
do while x < 100
y = 3
do while y < = x - 2
if int(x/y <> x/y
y = y + 2
k1 = 2
loop
else
y = x - 2
k2 = 1
endif
enddo
if k1 = 1 .and. k2 = 0
?? x
k1 = 0
k2 = 0
x = x + 2
else
k1 = 0
k2 = 0
x = x + 2
endif
enddo
return
```

The following is a typical output:

```
prime numbers are 1 2 3
        5       7       11      13      17      19      23
29      31      37      41      43      47      53      59
61      67      71      73      79      83      89      97
```

10. The following is a program intended for finding the sum of the digits in the given number:

```
*Program for finding the sum of the digits in a number
set talk off
trial = 1
do while trial < 2
input "enter the number up to a maximum of 5 digits:" to x
y = str(x, 5)
l = len(y)
s = 0
i = 1
do while i < l + 1
s = s + val(left(right(y, i), 1))
i = i + 1
enddo
? "sum of the digits of the number", x, "is", s
input "any more trials(enter 1 for yes and 2 for no)" to trial
enddo
return
```

The following is a typical output:

```
enter the number up to a maximum of 5 digits: 56789
sum of the digits of the number 56789 is 35.0000
any more trials(enter 1 for yes and 2 for no) 2
```

11. The following is a program for finding the day of a date:

```
*program for finding day of date
set talk off
trial = 1
do while trial < 2
accept "enter date in the form mm/dd/yy: " to d
da = cdow(ctod(d))
? "the date", d, "is", da
input "enter 1 for more trials and 2 for stopping" to trial
enddo
```

```
return
```

The following is a typical output:

```
enter date in the form mm/dd/yy: 12/18/89
the date 12/18/89 is Monday
enter 1 for more trials and 2 for stopping : 2
```

12. This program is intended to find the number of days elapsed between two dates:

```
*program for finding the number of days elapsed between two dates
trial = 1
do while trial < 2
accept "enter the value of first date in the form mm/dd/yy" to d1
accept "enter the value of the 2nd date in the form mm/dd/yy" to d2
d = ctod(d1) - ctod(d2)
? "number of days elapsed between ",d1" and ",d2," is ",d
input "any more trials(enter 1 for yes and 2 for no: "to trial
enddo
return
```

The following is a typical output:

```
enter the value of first date in the form mm/dd/yy12/19/89
enter the value of the 2nd date in the form mm/dd/yy12/19/88
number of days elapsed between 12/19/89 and 12/19/88 is 365
```

13. This is a program for printing the calendar for any month of any year in the 20th century.

```
.type calendar.prg
*program for printing the calendar for any month
set talk off
choice = 1
do while choice < 2
accept "enter first date in mm/dd/yy format: " to y
input "enter the number of days in the month: " to m
d = ctod(y)
dw = dow(d)
n = 1
```

```
x = 1
?" calendar for", cmonth(d), year(d)
?" sun mon tue wed thu fri sat"
? " "
dw = dw - 1
do while x <= dw
?? "  "
x = x + 1
enddo
do while dw <= 7 .and . n<=m
?? transform(n, "###"), space(2)
n = n + 1
dw = dw + 1
if dw > = 7
dw = 0
? " "
endif
enddo
input "for more trials enter 1 & for stopping enter 2:" to  choice
enddo
return
.do calendar
enter first date in mm/dd/yy format          : 01/01/90
enter the number of days in the month        :     31
calendar for January 1990
```

sun	mon	tue	wed	thu	fri	sat
	1	2	3	4	5	6
7	8	9	10	11	12	13
14	15	16	17	18	19	20
21	22	23	24	25	26	27
28	29	30	31			

for more trials enter 1 & for stopping enter 2 :1

enter first date in mm/dd/yy format: 12/01/90
enter the number of days in the month: 31
calendar for December 1990

sun	mon	tue	wed	thu	fri	sat
						1
2	3	4	5	6	7	8
9	10	11	12	13	14	15
16	17	18	19	20	21	22
23	24	25	26	27	28	29
30	31					

14. This is a program for amortising a loan in equal monthly instalments.

```
*program for amortisation
set talk off.
input "enter the loan amount:" to bal
input "enter the number of monthly instalments:" to n
input "enter the yearly interest rate percent:" to r
r = .05/12
instal = (r*(1 + r)^n/(((l + r)^-1))*bal
i = 1
? "schedule of payments"
? "month interest principal instalment balance"
do while i<=n
dint = bal*r
prin = instal - dint
bal = bal - prin
? transform(i, "#####"), transform (dint, "#######.##"),,
transform(prin, "######.##"), transform(instal, "#######.##"),,
transform(bal, "#######.##")
i = i + 1
enddo
return
.do inst
```

enter the loan amount : 5000
enter the number of monthly instalments : 30
enter the yearly interest rate per cent 5

Schedule of Payments

month	interest	principal	instalment	balance
1	20.83	156.81	177.65	4843.19
2	20.18	157.47	177.65	4685.72
3	19.52	158.12	177.65	4527.60
4	18.86	158.78	177.65	4368.81
5	18.20	159.44	177.65	4209.37
6	17.54	160.11	177.65	4049.26
7	16.87	160.77	177.65	3888.49
8	16.20	161.44	177.65	3727.04
9	15.53	162.12	177.65	3564.93
10	14.85	162.79	177.65	3402.13
11	14.18	163.47	177.65	3238.66
12	13.49	164.15	177.65	3074.51
13	12.81	164.84	177.65	2909.67
14	12.12	165.52	177.65	2744.15
15	11.43	166.21	177.65	2577.94
16	10.74	166.91	177.65	2411.03
17	10.05	167.60	177.65	2243.43
18	9.35	168.30	177.65	2075.13
19	8.65	169.00	177.65	1906.13
20	7.94	169.70	177.65	1736.43
21	7.24	170.41	177.65	1566.02
22	6.53	171.12	177.65	1394.89
23	5.81	171.83	177.65	1223.06
24	5.10	172.55	177.65	1050.51
25	4.38	173.27	177.65	877.24
26	3.66	173.99	177.65	703.25
27	2.93	174.72	177.65	528.53
28	2.20	175.44	177.65	353.09
29	1.47	176.18	177.65	176.91
30	0.74	176.91	177.65	0.00

15. This is a program for finding the check digit for a number using modulo 11 method. The digit are multiplied by the respective weights, starting with a weight of 1 from the left end. The weighted sum is added and modulo 11 is obtained, Modulo11 means the remainder obtained by dividing the number by 11. If the remainder is 0 or 10, the check digit is 0 else the check digit is 11 - the modulo.

```
.type chkdigit.prg
* program for finding check digit using modulo 11
set talk off
set decimals to 0
choice = 1
do while choice < 2
accept "enter the number whose check digit is required:" to n
kk = 0
a = len(n)
i = 1
do while i <=a
k = val(substr(n , i, l))
k = k*i
kk = kk + k
i = i + 1
enddo
r = kk -int(kk/11)*11
if r = 0 .or. r = 10
check = 0
else
check = 11 - r
endif
numb = val(n)*10 + check
? "The check digit of", n, "is", check
? "The number with the check digit is ", numb
input "any more trials? enter 1 for yes and 2 for no:" to choice
enddo
return
.do chkdigit
```

```
enter the number whose check digit is required: 3456
The check digit of 3456 is 5
The number with the check digit is 34565
any more trials? enter 1 for yes and 2 for no: 1
enter the number whose check digit is required: 387678
The check digit of 387678 is 7
The number with the check digit is 3876787
any more trials? enter 1 for  yes and 2 for no:2
```

16. This is a program for generating the sides of a right angled triangle using the pythagorous theorem.

```
.type pytho.prg
*program for generating the sides of a right angled triangle
set talk off
? "the sides of a right angle are"
i = 1
do while i <= 10
j = i + 1
do while j < = 100
k = i*i + j*j
y = sqrt(k)
if y = int(y)
?transform(i, "######"), transform (j, "######"),,
transform(y, "######")
endif
j = j + 1
enddo
i = i + 1
enddo
return
do pytho
the sides of right angled triangle are
   3           4           5
   5          12          13
   6           8          10
```

7	24	25
8	15	17
9	12	15
9	40	41
10	24	26

17. This is a program for finding armstrong numbers. Armstrong number is one whose sum of the cubes of the digits of the number is equal to the number itself. For example, 153 = 1^3 + 5^3 + 3^3. Hence 153 is an armstrong number.

```
* program for finding armstrong numbers
set talk off
i = 1
? "the armstrong numbers are"
do while i < 10
s = i^3
if i = s
? i
endif
i = i + 1
enddo
do while i>= 10 .and. i < 100
d1 = int(i/10)
d2 = i - d1*10
s = d1^3 + d2^3
if i = s
? i
endif
i = i + 1
enddo
do while i >= 100 .and. i <= 500
d1 = int(i/100)
d2 = int(i - dl*100)/10)
d3 = i -int(i/10)*10
s = d1^3 + d2^3 + d3^3
if i = s
```

```
?i
endif
i = i + 1
enddo
return
.do armstron
the armstrong numbers are
    1
  153
  370
  371
  407
```

18. This is a program for generating random numbers. The algorithm used is modulo algorithm. x(n) = mod(c*x(n-1,y). c is taken as 291. The initial seed x(0) is taken as 19879. The divisor y is taken as 100000.. x(n) is are successively generated.

```
type random.prg
*program for generating random numbers
set talk off
seed = 19879
i = 1
do while i <= 100
rand = seed*291
seed = rand/100000
seed = rand - (int(seed)* 100000)
?? seed
i = i + 1
enddo
return
do random
```

84789	73599	17309	36919	43429
37839	11149	44359	8469	64479
63389	46199	43909	77519	58029
86439	53749	40959	19069	49079

81989	58799	10509	58119	12629
75039	36349	77559	69669	73679
40589	11399	17109	78719	7229
3639	58949	54159	60269	38279
39189	3999	63709	39319	41829
72239	21549	70759	90869	42879
77789	36599	50309	39919	16429
80839	24149	27359	61469	87479
56389	9199	76909	80519	31029
29439	66749	23959	72069	72079
74989	21799	43509	61119	85629
18039	49349	60559	22669	96679
33589	74399	50109	81719	80229
46639	71949	37159	13269	61279
32189	66999	96709	42319	14829
15239	34549	53759	43869	65879

The readers should carefully go through the programs given in this lesson and fully understand how the different logics are implemented. They should also see whether better algorithms can be devised for doing these problems.

dBASE PROGRAMMING (III)

1. Let us now see how we can write a program using database files. The following program simply prints the database BIODATA and its structure:

```
*program for listing a database and its structure
set talk off
set echo on
use biodata
list structure
wait
use biodata
list
set echo off
return
```

The output will look as shown below:

```
use biodata
```

list structure
Structure for database C : biodata.dbf
Number of data records : 7
Date of last update : 05/27/89

Field	*Field Name*	*Type*	*Width*	*Dec*
1	Name	Character	5	
2	Age	Numeric	2	
3	Qualify	Character	5	
4	Community	Character	2	
5	Sex	Character	1	
6	Street	Character	10	
7	City	Character	10	
8	Pin	Numeric	6	
**Total""			42	

Press any key to continue...
use biodata
list

Record #	*NAME*	*AGE*	*QUALIFY*	*COMMUNITY*	*SEX*	*STREET*	*CITY*	*PIN*
1	bala	40	be	fc	m	mint.st.	bombay	400001
2	raji	25	me	bc	f	mount road	madras	600002
3	gayi	30	msc	sc	f	rr street	tiruchi	624001
4	raman	20	mphil	bc	m	ram street	karaikudi	624001
5	krish	19	dsc	bc	m	p.h. road	madurai	625001
6	murug	45	bsc	fc	m	mp street	pasumalai	585001
7	latha	37	msc	sc	f	grant road	delhi	110001

Before using any database it is advisable to view its structure and also its listing. The echo on command causes the printing of the actual command in the output. The echo off command deactivates the above facility. The wait command causes the computer to halt until any key is pressed. This command is used whenever you want a particular screen output to stay on as long as is required. If this command is not given the output will run through the screen and we will not be able to examine the output carefully.

2. This is a program intended to view the database selectively. We start with a database

file by name db1.dbf and view the same through different filters as they can be called.

```
*program for viewing the database selectively
set talk off
set echo on
use db1
list
wait
list off
wait
list empname, desig, basic
wait
list desig, dept, empname
wait
go top
disp
wait
go bottom
disp
wait
skip - 10
disp
wait
skip
disp
disp recno()
wait
list for desig = "prof"
wait
list for basic >= 2000 .and. basic <= 4000
wait
list for empname = "krish"
wait
goto 5
disp
wait
goto 10
```

```
disp
wait
locate for desig = "lect"
continue
disp
continue
disp
continue
disp
set echo off
return
```

The output for the above program will look as given below:

list

Record #	*EMPNO*	*EMPNAME*	*DEPT*	*DESIG*	*BASIC*	*DEDS*
1	18	arjun	civil	lect	1450.00	160.00
2	26	govind	mech	prof	2570.00	230.00
3	20	ragava	elect	lect	1560.00	185.00
4	30	raghu	phys	dir	6000.00	450.00
5	12	ganesa	elect	prof	2000.00	260.00
6	6	bala	engg	prof	5000.00	567.00
7	7	muruga	civil	lect	4000.00	543.00
8	25	aswin	mech	engr	7000.00	897.00
9	19	avinas	elect	prof	5000.00	656.00
10	10	krish	elect	prof	6785.00	345.00

Press any key to continue ....
list off

EMPNO	*EMPNAME*	*DEPT*	*DESIG*	*BASIC*	*DEDS*
18	arjun	civil	lect	1450.00	160.00
26	govind	mech	prof	2570.00	230.00
20	ragava	elect	lect	1560.00	185.00
30	raghu	phys	dir	6000.00	450.00
12	ganesa	elect	prof	2000.00	260.00
6	bala	engg	prof	5000.00	567.00
7	muruga	civil	lect	4000.00	543.00
25	aswin	mech	engr	7000.00	897.00
19	avinas	elect	prof	5000.00	656.00
10	krish	elect	prof	6785.00	345.00

Press any key to continue...
list empname, desig, basic

Record#	*empname*	*desig*	*basic*
1	arjun	lect	1450.00
2	govind	prof	2570.00
3	ragava	lect	1560.00
4	raghu	dir	6000.00
5	ganesa	prof	2000.00
6	bala	prof	5000.00
7	muruga	lect	4000.00
8	aswin	engr	7000.00
9	avinas	prof	5000.00
10	krish	prof	6785.00

Press any key to continue...
list desig, dept, empname

Record#	*desig*	*dept*	*empname*
1	lect	civil	arjun
2	prof	mech	govind
3	lect	elect	ragava
4	dir	phys	raghu
5	prof	lect	ganesa
6	prof	engg	bala
7	lect	civil	muruga
8	engr	mech	aswin
9	prof	elect	avinas
10	prof	elect	krish

Press any key to continue....
go top
disp

Record#	EMPNO	EMPNAME	DEPT	DESIG	BASIC	DEDS
1	18	arjun	civil	lect	1450.00	160.00

Press any key to continue...

go bottom

disp

Record#	EMPNO	EMPNAME	DEPT	DESIG	BASIC	DEDS
10	10	krish	elect	prof	6785.00	345.00

Press any key to continue...

skip-10

disp

Record#	EMPNO	EMPNAME	DEPT	DESIG	BASIC	DEDS
1	18	arjun	civil	lect	1450.00	160.00

Press any key to continue...

skip

disp

Record#	EMPNO	EMPNAME	DEPT	DESIG	BASIC	DEDS
2	26	govind	mech	prof	2570.00	230.00

disp recno()

Record#	recno()
2	2

Press any key to continue...

list for desig = 'prof'

Record#	EMPNO	EMPNAME	DEPT	DESIG	BASIC	DEDS
2	26	govind	mech	prof	2570.00	230.00
5	12	ganesa	elect	prof	2000.00	260.00
6	6	bala	engg	prof	5000.00	567.00
9	19	avinas	elect	prof	5000.00	656.00
10	10	krish	elect	prof	6785.00	345.00

Press any key to continue...

list for basic >= 2000 .and. basic <= 4000

Record#	EMPNO	EMPNAME	DEPT	DESIG	BASIC	DEDS
2	26	govind	mech	prof	2570.00	230.00
5	12	ganesa	elect	prof	2000.00	260.00
7	7	muruga	civil	lect	4000.00	543.00

Press any key to continue...
list for empname = 'krish'

Record#	EMPNO	EMPNAME	DEPT	DESIG	BASIC	DEDS
10	10	krish	elect	prof	6785.00	345.00

Press any key to continue...
goto 5
disp

Record#	EMPNO	EMPNAME	DEPT	DESIG	BASIC	DEDS
5	12	ganesa	elect	prof	2000.00	260.00

Press any key to continue...
goto 10
disp

Record#	EMPNO	EMPNAME	DEPT	DESIG	BASIC	DEDS
10	10	krish	elect	prof	6785.00	345.00

Press any key to continue...
locate for desig = 'lect'
continue
disp

Record #	EMPNO	EMPNAME	DEPT	DESIG	BASIC	DEDS
3	20	ragava	elect	lect	1560.00	185.00

continue
disp

Record#	EMPNO	EMPNAME	DEPT	DESIG	BASIC	DEDS
7	7	muruga	civil	lect	4000.00	543.00

continue
disp

Record#	EMPNO	EMPNAME	DEPT	DESIG	BASIC	DEDS

3. This is a program for sorting a database on a single field.

```
*program for sorting a database on a single field.
set talk off
```

```
use emp
list
sort on empno to temp2
use temp2
list
return
```

The output looks as below:

Record#	*EMPNO*	*EMPNAME*	*DEPT*	*DESIG*	*BASIC*	*DEDS*
1	23	ganes	elect	lect	500.00	45.00
2	12	raman	mech	lect	500.00	67.00
3	56	murug	mech	prof	700.00	35.00
4	23	ravi	civil	prof	645.00	78.00
5	42	bala	elect	prof	876.00	98.00
6	45	mani	civil	lect	345.00	32.00
7	26	aswin	elect	lect	666.00	76.00
8	10	sunil	mech	lect	444.00	46.00
9	5	raju	mech	lect	347.00	76.00
10	69	sundu	civil	prof	989.00	79.00

Record#	*EMPNO*	*EMPNAME*	*DEPT*	*DESIG*	*BASIC*	*DEDS*
1	5	raju	mech	lect	347.00	76.00
2	10	sunil	mech	lect	444.00	46.00
3	12	raman	mech	lect	500.00	67.00
4	23	ganes	elect	lect	500.00	45.00
5	25	ravi	civil	prof	645.00	78.00
6	26	aswin	elect	lect	666.00	76.00
7	42	bala	elect	prof	876.00	98.00
8	45	mani	civil	lect	345.00	32.00
9	56	murug	mech	prof	700.00	35.00
10	69	sundu	civil	prof	989.00	79.00

4. The following program is used to sort a database on two fields:

```
*program for sorting on two fields
set talk off
```

```
use emp
list
sort on dept, empno to temp3
use temp3
list
return
```

The following shows the output:

Record#	EMPNO	EMPNAME	DEPT	DESIG	BASIC	DEDS
1	23	ganes	elect	lect	500.00	45.00
2	12	raman	mech	lect	500.00	67.00
3	56	murug	mech	prof	700.00	35.00
4	25	ravi	civil	prof	645.00	78.00
5	42	bala	elect	prof	876.00	98.00
6	45	mani	civil	lect	345.00	32.00
7	26	aswin	elect	lect	666.00	76.00
8	10	sunil	mech	lect	444.00	46.00
9	5	raju	mech	lect	347.00	76.00
10	69	sundu	civil	prof	989.00	79.00

Record#	EMPNO	EMPNAME	DEPT	DESIG	BASIC	DEDS
1	25	ravi	civil	prof	645.00	78.00
2	45	mani	civil	lect	345.00	32.00
3	69	sundu	civil	prof	989.00	79.00
4	23	ganes	elect	lect	500.00	45.00
5	26	aswin	elect	lect	666.00	76.00
6	42	bala	elect	prof	876.00	98.00
7	5	raju	mech	lect	347.00	76.00
8	10	sunil	mech	lect	444.00	46.00
9	12	raman	mech	lect	500.00	67.00
10	56	murug	mech	prof	700.00	35.00

5. The following program is intended for indexing a database on a single field.

```
*program for indexing on a single field
set talk off
```

```
use emp
list
index on empno to empndx
use emp index empndx
list
return
```

The following gives the output:

Record#	*EMPNO*	*EMPNAME*	*DEPT*	*DESIG*	*BASIC*	*DEDS*
1	23	ganes	elect	lect	500.00	45.00
2	12	raman	mech	lect	500.00	67.00
3	56	murug	mech	prof	700.00	35.00
4	25	ravi	civil	prof	645.00	78.00
5	42	bala	elect	prof	876.00	98.00
6	45	mani	civil	lect	345.00	32.00
7	26	aswin	elect	lect	666.00	76.00
8	10	sunil	mech	lect	444.00	46.00
9	5	raju	mech	lect	347.00	76.00
10	69	sundu	civil	prof	989.00	79.00

Record#	EMPNO	EMPNAME	DEPT	DESIG	BASIC	DEDS
9	5	raju	mech	lect	347.00	76.00
8	10	sunil	mech	lect	444.00	46.00
2	12	raman	mech	lect	500.00	67.00
1	23	ganes	elect	lect	500.00	45.00
4	25	ravi	civil	prof	645.00	78.00
7	26	aswin	elect	lect	666.00	76.00
5	42	bala	elect	prof	876.00	98.00
6	45	mani	civil	lect	345.00	32.00
3	56	murug	mech	prof	700.00	35.00
10	69	sundu	civil	prof	989.00	79.00

6. The following program is intended to index on two fields:

```
*program for Indexing on two fields
set talk off
```

```
use emp.
list
index on dept + str(empno, 2) to emplndx
use emp index emplndx
list
return
```

The following shows the output

Record#	*EMPNO*	*EMPNAME*	*DEPT*	*DESIG*	*BASIC*	*DEDS*
1	23	ganes	elect	lect	500.00	45.00
2	12	raman	mech	lect	500.00	67.00
3	56	murug	mech	prof	700.00	35.00
4	25	ravi	civil	prof	645.00	78.00
5	42	bala	elect	prof	876.00	98.00
6	45	mani	civil	lect	345.00	32.00
7	26	aswin	elect	lect	666.00	76.00
8	10	sunil	mech	lect	444.00	46.00
9	3	raju	mech	lect	347.00	76.00
10	69	sundu	civil	prof	989.00	79.00

Record#	*EMPNO*	*EMPNAME*	*DEPT*	*DESIG*	*BASIC*	*DEDS*
4	25	ravi	civil	prof	645.00	78.00
6	45	mani	civil	lect	345.00	32.00
10	69	sundu	civil	prof	989.00	79.00
1	23	ganes	elect	lect	500.00	45.00
7	26	aswin	elect	lect	666.00	76.00
5	42	bala	elect	prof	876.00	98.00
9	5	raju	mech	prof	347.00	76.00
8	10	sunil	mech	lect	444.00	46.00
2	12	raman	mech	lect	500.00	67.00
3	56	murug	mech	prof	700.00	35.00

7. The following is a program for searching a record using the seek command:

```
*program for searching a record using seek command
set talk off
```

```
trial = 1
do while trial < 2
use emp index empndx
input "enter the value of empno of the seek record:" to n
seek n
if found ()
display
else
? "the record whose empno value is ", n," is not found"
endif
input "any more trials(enter 1 for yes and 2 for no): " to trial
enddo
return
```

The following shows the output :

enter the value of empno of the seek record: 5

Record#	EMPNO	EMPNAME	DEPT	DESIG	BASIC	DEDS
9	5	raju	mech	lect	347.00	76.00

any more trials(enter 1 for yes and 2 for no):1

enter the value of empno of the seek record:45

Record#	Empno	Empname	Dept	Desig	Basic	Deds
6	45	mani	civil	lect	345.00	32.00

any more trials(enter 1 for yes and 2 for no) : 1

enter the value of empno of the seek record : 46

the record whose empno value is 46 is not found

any more trials(enter 1 for yes and 2 for no) : 2

8. The following program is intended to find the record of an employee using the find command.

```
*program for finding a record with a particular employee code
set talk off
option = 1
use fl
list
wait
```

```
index on code to cndx
use fl index cndx
do while option = 1
accept "enter the employee code to find:" to mcode
find &mcode
if found()
display
else
? "the employee code", mcode, "is not found"
endif
wait
input "any more trial for find (1 for yes & 0 for no): " to option
enddo
return
```

The output looks as shown below:

Record#	Code	Name	Age	Basic	Desig	Dept
1	a2	rajagopan	45	567.00	prof	phy
2	b2	ravi	43	453.00	lect	chem
3	d7	bala	55	678.00	prog	comp
4	c4	raghu	24	500.00	peon	gen
5	15	murugan	34	1200.00	manag	pffic

Press any key to continue...

cndx.ndx already exists, overwrite it? (Y/N) Yes

enter the employee code to find: a2

Record#	CODE	NAME	AGE	BASIC	DESIG	DEPT
1	a2	rajagopan	45	567.00	prof	phy

Press any key to continue.....

any more trials for find (1 for yes & 0 for no): 1

enter the employee code to find a34

the employee code a34 is not found

Press any key to continue...

any more trials for find (1 for yes & 0 for no): 0

9. The following is an example of a menu driven program using the IF statement:

```
*example of a menu driven program
set talk off
choice = 1
do while choice < 4
*main menu
?
? 'main menu'
?
?'1. list the database'
?
? '2 sort the database agewise'
? '3. list name,street,city, pin'
?
? '4. exit'
input 'enter your choice:' to choice
if choice = 1
use biodata
list
?
wait
endif
if choice = 2
delete file temp.dbf
use biodata
sort on age to temp
use temp
list
?
wait
endif
if choice=3
use biodata
list name, street, city, pin
```

```
?
wait
endif
if choice = 4
return
endif
enddo
```

The output looks as below:

main menu

1. list the database
2. sort the database agewise
3. list name, street, city, pin
4. exit

enter your choice:1

Record#	*SLNO.*	*NAME*	*SEX*	*BIRTHDAY*	*AGE*	*STREET*	*CITY*	*PIN*
1	1	bala	m	01/15/48	40	mint.st.	bombay	400001
2	2	raji	f	02/12/23	65	mount road	madras	600002
3	3	gayi	f	03/16/58	30	rr street	tiruchi	620001
4	4	ramani	m	04/10/28	60	ram street	karakudi	624001
5	5	krishnan	m	01/25/38	50	p.h. road	madurai	625006
6	6	murugan	m	03/29/43	45	mp street	pasumalai	585001
7	7	latha	f	02/09/51	37	grant road	delhi	110001

Press any key to continue...

main menu

1. list the database
2. sort the database agewise
3. list name,street, city, pin
4. exit

enter your choice.2

Record#	*SLNO.*	*NAME*	*SEX*	*BIRTHDAY*	*AGE*	*STREET*	*CITY*	*PIN*
1	3	gayi	f	03/16/58	30	rr street	tiruchi	620001
2	7	latha	f	02/09/51	37	grant road	delhi	110001

3	1	bala	m	01/15/48	40	mint, st.	bombay	400001
4	6	murugan	m	03/29/43	45	mp street	pasumalai	585001
5	5	krishnan	m	01/25/38	50	p. h. road	madurai	625006
6	4	ramani	m	04/10/28	60	ram street	karakudi	624001
7	2	raji	f	02/12/23	65	mount road	madras	600002

Press any key to continue...

main menu

1. list the database
2. sort the database agewise
3. list name street,city,pin
4. exit

Record#	*name*	*street*	*city*	*pin*
1	bala	mint st.	bombay	400001
2	raji	mount road	madras	600002
3	gayi	rr street	tiruchi	620001
4	ramani	ram street	karakudi	624001
5	krishnan	p.h. road	madurai	625006
6	murugan	mp street	pasumalai	585001
7	latha	grant-road	delhi	110001

Press any key to continue...

main menu

1. list the database
2. sort the database agewise
3. list name,street, city,pin
4. exit

enter your choice:4

10. This is an example of a menu-driven program using the CASE command. For displaying the menu, we have used the TEXT-ENDTEXT statement. Any matter enclosed between the words TEXT and ENDTEXT will be printed as entered. The program and the output are given below:

```
*example of a menu driven program using case statement
set talk off
```

```
store ''to choice
do while .not. choice = '4'
*main menu
text
main menu
        1.  list the database
        2.  sort the database agewise
        3.  list name,street,city,pin
        4.  exit
endtext
?
accept 'enter your choice' to choice
?
do case
case choice = '1'
use biodata
list
?
wait
case choice='2'
delete file temp.dbf
use biodata
sort on age to temp
use temp
list
?
wait
case choice='3'
use biodata
list name,street,city,pin
?
wait
endcase
enddo
```

return

The output looks as below:

main menu

1. list the database
2. sort the database agewise
3. list name,street,city,pin
4. exit

enter your choice:1

Record#	*SLNO*	*NAME*	*SEX*	*BIRTHDAY*	*AGE*	*STREET*	*CITY*	*PIN*
1	1	bala	m	01/15/48	40	mint st.	bombay	400001
2	2	raji	f	02/12/23	65	mount road	madras	600002
3	3	gayi	f	03/16/58	30	rr street	tiruchi	620001
4	4	ramani	m	04/10/28	60	ram street	karaikudi	624001
5	5	krishnan	m	01/25/38	50	p.h.road	madurai	625006
6	6	murugan	m	03/29/43	45	mp street	pasumalai	585001
7	7	latha	f	02/09/51	37	grant road	delhi	110001

Press any key to continue...

1. list the database
2. sort the database agewise
3. list name,street, city, pin
4. exit

enter your choice:2

Record #	*SLNO*	*NAME*	*SEX*	*BIRTHDAY*	*AGE*	*STREET*	*CITY*	*PIN*
1	3	gayi	f	03/16/58	30	rr street	tiruchi	620001
2	7	latha	f	02/09/51	37	grant road	delhi	110001
3	1	bala	m	01/15/48	40	mint st.	bombay	400001
4	6	murugan	m	03/29/43	45	mp street	pasumalai	585001
5	5	krishnan	m	01/25/38	50	p.h.road	madurai	625006
6	4	ramani	m	04/10/28	60	ram street	karaikudi	624001
7	2	raji	f	02/12/23	65	mount road	madras	600002

Press any key to continue...

main menu

1. list the database
2. sort the database agewise
3. list name,street,city,pin
4. exit

enter your choice:3

Record#	*Name*	*Street*	*City*	*Pin*
1	bala	mint.st.	bombay	400001
2	raji	mount road	madras	600002
3	gayi	rr street	tiruchi	620001
4	ramani	ram street	karakudi	624001
5	krishnan	p.h.road	madurai	625006
6	murugan	mp street	pasumalai	585001
7	latha	grant road	delhi	110001

Press any key to continue...

main menu

1. list the database
2. sort the database agewise
3. list name,street,city, pin
4. exit

enter your choice:4

In this lesson we have used database files as a whole and have written programs to view them in different forms. We have not done anything with the data in the files. In the next lesson we will see how data can be accessed from files for purposes of manipulation and reporting.

dBASE PROGRAMMING (IV)

1. We will now start reading a database file and use the data for manipulation. The following program reads the database file biodata.dbf and prints the address labels of all the persons in three columns. The database file looks as below:

Record#	*NAME*	*AGE*	*QUALIFY*	*COMMUNITY*	*SEX*	*STREET*	*CITY*	*PIN*
1	bala	40	be	fc	m	mint st.	bombay	400001
2	raji	25	me	bc	f	mount road	madras	600002
3	gayi	30	msc	sc	f	rr street	tiruchi	624001
4	raman	20	mphil	bc	m	ram street	karaikudi	624001
5	krish	19	dsc	bc	m	p.h. road	madurai	625001
6	murug	45	bsc	fc	m	mp street	pasumalai	585001
7	latha	37	msc	sc	f	grant road	delhi	110001
8	aswin	35	msc	fc	m	rr street	madras	600001
9	avina	45	me	fc	m	ar street	bombay	400003

```
*program for printing address labels using ? command
set talk off
use biodata
do while .not. eof()
?name,space(10), name,space(10),name
?street,space(5),street, space(5),street
?city,space(5), city,space(5),city
?pin, space(9),pin,space(9),pin
?
skip
enddo
return
```

SET COMMANDS

Default SETTINGS of dBASE III PLUS

When dBase is initially installed it comes with certain default settings or status as they are called. Most of them relate to what are called SET values. To know the different default settings, give the following command at the dot prompt.

.DISPLAY STATUS

You get two screenfuls of information about the different default settings as given in the Fig. 36.

File search path:

Default disk drive: A:

Print destination: PRN:

Margin = 0

Current work area = 1;

ALTERNATE	-	OFF	DELETED	-	OFF	FIXED	-	OFF	SAFETY	-	ON
BELL	-	ON	DELIMITERS	-	OFF	HEADING	-	ON	SCOREBOARD	-	ON
CARRY	-	OFF	DEVICE	-	SCRN	HELP	-	ON	STATUS	-	OFF
CATALOG	-	OFF	DOHISTORY	-	OFF	HISTORY	-	ON	STEP	-	OFF
CENTURY	-	OFF	ECHO	-	OFF	INTENSITY	-	ON	TALK	-	ON
CONFIRM	-	OFF	ESCAPE	-	ON	MENU	-	ON	TITLE	-	ON
CONSOLE	-	ON	EXACT	-	OFF	PRINT	-	OFF	UNIQUE	-	OFF

Programmable function keys:

F2	-	assist;
F3	-	list;
F4	—	dir;
F5	—	display structure;
F6	—	display status;
F7	—	display memory;
F8	—	display;
F9	—	append;
F10	—	edit;

Fig. 36.

Let us now see what some of these settings mean.

1. The SET ALTERNATE command is used to store all your dialogue with dBASE using dot prompt commands only in a separate ASCII file with .TXT extension. Result of full-screen commands such as APPEND, EDIT etc., will not be recorded in the text file. This is one of the debugging device used in dBASE. You can check the data or the commands you have keyed and the response given by dBase by looking at the alternate file that has been created by this command. In the beginning you give the following commands at the dot prompt.

```
.SET ALTERNATE  TO data.txt
.SET ALTERNATE ON
```

Then you start interaction with dBASE. Every interaction is now stored in the ASCII file named data.txt. By receiving this file you will be able to find out any error that you have committed and also to find out any changes that have to be made. To stop storing the interaction and save what has been done so far, give the commands

```
.SET ALTERNATE OFF
.SET ALTERNATE TO
```

The command SET ALTERNATE TO without any argument closes the file data.txt which was opened in the beginning by the SET ALTERNATE TO data.txt command. The default setting is OFF as you see in the status display shown in the Fig. 36

Use of Alternate Files in the Programming Mode

In the programming mode the 'SET ALTERNATE' command is used to write the output generated by all the? mark commands in a text file. In fact this is the only command available in dBASE to write the output in an ASCII file. The output generated by the @SAY command cannot be directed to the file by this command. So if at all you want the output from a dBASE program to be written in a file you have to use the 'SET ALTERNATE' command along with the? mark output command.

2. SET BELL ON/OFF: In APPEND, EDIT and MODIFY commands, every time the cursor goes to the end of the field in which you are entering the data, the cursor goes to the next field after making a beep sound. The default is ON. In case you don't want this beep sound you can set if OFF by giving the command at the dot prompt as

```
.Set Bell off
```

The default is ON.

3. SET CARRY OFF/ON" In data entry there may be repetitions of some data in the fields of consecutive records. In such cases you can ask dBASE to type values by using the command SET CARRY ON at dot prompt. When you give the APPEND command the screen will display the data entered in the previous screen. You need modify or edit only those data values which are changed. The default is OFF.

4. SET CATALOG TO file-name command is used to create or open a CATALOG file. The command SET CATALOG ON/OFF command is used to activate or deactivate the CATALOG command. Normally the command is OFF. If you set the switch 'ON', you will get all the facilities of the CATALOG file. Refer to lesson 24 for further details.

5. SET CENTURY ON/OFF: When the switch is 'ON' the date is displayed in the form 07/05/1990. The 'OFF' setting displays the date in the form 07/05/90. The default is 'OFF'.

6. SET CONFIRM OFF/ON: Normally when the cursor reaches the end of a field. it drops down to the next field with a beep sound. When you give the command at the dot prompt as SET CONFIRM ON, the cursor will not go to the next field automatically, but will wait for you to press the CR key. In short you want to confirm that you have completed the entry in that particular field before going to the next field. The default is OFF.

7. The SET CONSOLE OFF/ON command is used to turn the screen display ON or OFF within a program. The default setting is ON. Printer output is not affected by this command. The OFF option will be also suppress the error messages on the screen.

8. The SET DEBUG ON/OFF command is used along with the SET ECHO command to direct the display of the commands processed to the printer. When the command 'SET ECHO ON' is given, it will interfere with the program's screen operations. So it is advisable to direct the ECHO to the printer. The following set of commands will direct the ECHO to the printer.

```
.SET ECHO ON
.SET DEBUG ON
```

The printed copy of the sequence of the commands carried out by the program can then be used or debugging purposes. The default settings are SET ECHO OFF and SET DEBUG OFF.

9. The SET DELETED ON/OFF command is used to ignore or not to ignore the records marked for deletion during FIND and SEEK operations. The default is OFF.

10. The SET DELIMITERS ON/OFF command is used to enclose the data entry or the editing fields with delimiters. With the command SET DELIMITERS ON, you set the delimiter by the command SET DELIMITER TO '/' the field boundaries will be marked by the '/' delimiter. The default is OFF.

11. The SET DEVICE TO SCREEN/PRINT is used along with the @SAY command to direct the output either to the screen or to the printer. You cannot direct the output both to the screen and the printer simultaneously. The default is SCREEN. This command will not work with ? mark command.

12. The SET DO HISTORY ON/OFF command is used along with the SET HISTORY ON/OFF command. If the SET HISTORY is ON and if the SET DO HISTORY is ON the commands from the program will be recorded in the HISTORY file. If the SET DO HISTORY is OFF, only the commands from dot prompt will be recorded in the HISTORY file. The HISTORY file can be seen by giving the command LIST/DISPLAY HISTORY. THIS is a debugging command. The default is OFF for the SET DO HISTORY command and ON for SET HISTORY command.

13. The SET ECHO ON/OFF command determines whether or not the commands from a program will be echoed on the screen or not. The default is OFF. If the s witch is ON all the commands that are executed in a program will be displayed on the screen. This is a debugging command.

14. The SET ESCAPE OFF/ON command is used to halt or not to halt a program execution. When the switch is ON, the program will be terminated in pressing the ESCAPE key. When the switch is OFF, the program will not be terminated when the ESCAPE key is

pressed. The default is ON.

15. The SET EXACT ON/OFF used during comparison of strings. When the switch is ON, only exact matchings will be true. When the switch is OFF partial matchings will suffice.

16. The SET FIELDS TO command is used to restrict database view to specific fields. The syntax is SET FIELDS TO < list of variables>. This option can be deactivated by the command SET FIELDS OFF and can be activated once again by the command SET FIELDS on.

17. The SET FIXED ON/OFF command determines whether the number of decimal places displayed are set to the default value of 2 places or set to the value 'n' given by the SET DECIMALS TO n command. The default is OFF. The number of decimal places can be specified from the SET menu option.

18. The SET HEADING ON/OFF determines as to whether the field names should appear at the top in the database file or not. The default is ON.

19. The SET HELP ON/OFF command controls the display of 'Do you want some help? (Y/N)' when you make some error in the entry. The default is ON.

20. The SET HISTORY ON/OFF command determines whether the commands that are given earlier can be recalled or not. SET HISTORY is normally ON. In this mode the last 20 commands typed earlier at the dot prompt can be recalled one by one by pressing the up arrow key. The recalled commands can be edited and executed again by pressing the enter key. The list can also be seen in entirety by giving the command LIST/DISP HISTORY at the top prompt. If you want more commands to be recalled or stored, you can initially give the command SET HISTORY TO 50. In this case the last 50 commands can be stored and recalled provided the switch SET HISTORY is on. 50 is the maximum number of commands that can be stored by this command.

21. The SET INTENSITY ON/OFF: command turns video on and off when @SAY-GET commands are used. The default is ON. The GET field will be in reverse video (dark letters in bright background).

22. SET MENU ON/OFF: In the full screen CREATE, EDIT and APPEND modes you will get a help screen at the top which tells the various editing features available and how the cursor movements can be controlled. If you want this Cursor Control Menu at the top of the screen, you give the command SET MENU OFF at the dot prompt. the default is ON.

23. The SET PRINT ON/OFF command is used to direct the text displayed by the ? mark command to the printer. The default is OFF.

24. The SET SAFETY ON/OFF command is used to provide some safety against overwriting on already existing files. The default is ON. When On, if we try to copy a file on an existing file, dBASE gives a warning message, 'file-name already exists overwrite it ? (Y/N).'

25. The SET SCOREBOARD ON/OFF command determines whether or not messages like CAPS, INS etc., are to be displayed on the status line or not. The default is ON.

26. The SET STATUS ON/OFF is used to toggle the status bar displayed at the row 22. When ON, the status line gives information about the current drive, file name, record pointer position etc. When OFF, this line will be suppressed. The default is ON.

27. The SET STEP ON/OFF command is used in conjunction with SET ECHO ON command to display the command as well as the result of execution of the command one by one. At the end of each command, the message' Press Space to step, S to suspend, or ESC to cance;. " will be displayed on the screen. This is debugging command. The default setting is OFF.

28. SET TALK ON/OFF: When dBASE executes the commands, it sends out confirmation messages to you. For example, if you ask dBASE to sort a file, it will tell you how many records sorted and sorting is over etc. If you want dBASE stop talking to you in this fashion, give the command SET TALK OFF. The default is ON.

29. The SET TITLE ON/OFF command is used along with SET CATALOG command to decide whether a file title description should be displayed or not. The default is ON. When ON, if a file from a catalog is selected, the file description title is automatically displayed at the bottom. In the OFF mode this title description will not be displayed.

30. The SET UNIQUE ON/OFF command is used with the INDEX command to develop an index that does not contain duplicates. The default is OFF. Suppose you give the commands as

```
.SET  UNIQUE  ON
.INDEX  ON age TO  agdx
125 records indexed
```

This means that there are 125 records with unique values for ages. If two or more persons have the same age those records will not be indexed.

31. SET FUNCTIONn TO expression command is used to reprogram the function key(n). The F1 key cannot be reprogrammed. The expression can have a maximum of 30 characters. The semicolon(;) is used to provide an automatic carriage return. For example one can write

```
.SET  FUNCTION 2 to "use  biodata; list"
```

After giving this command if you press F2, the commands within the quote marks will be executed.

Changing the DEFAULT SETTINGS

We have said that dBASE comes to you with different default settings and sometimes you would like to change them temporarily in a particular program or sometimes change them permanently in all your programs. This can be done in three ways:

1. By changing the default settings at the dot prompt.
2. By changing the default settings in the SET Menu obtained by giving the SET, Command and
3. By writing the commands for the new setting in a file called CONFIG.DB and forcing dBASE to read this file when it is booted in the system.

Options | Screen | Keys | Disk | Files | Margin | Decimals

Alternate	Off
Bell	On
Carry	Off
Catalog	
Century	Off
Confirm	Off
Deleted	Off
Delimiters	Off
Device	Screen
Dohistory	Off
Escape	On
Exact	Off
Fields	Off
Fixed	Off
Heading	On
Help	On
History	On
Intensity	On
Menu	On
Print	Off
Safety	On
Scoreboard	On
Status	Off
Talk	On
Title	On
Unique	Off

Set   A: Opt: 1/25   Caps

Position Selection bar ↓ ↑   Change < CR >   Leave Manu -><- Exit-Esc

Specify the dBase environment options

Fig. 7.37.

The Set Menu

Let us see how the default settings can be changed in the SET Menu. To get the SET Menu enter the command at the dot prompt as

.SET < CR>

The above command provides the list of seven basic menus at the top of the screen. Each menu may have further submenus. In the beginning the first item Options is highlighted by the reverse video. The submenu of the first item is displayed below it which gives the different default settings shown in the Figure 37.

The Options Menu

The Options Menu has 25 items under it and their default settings are given by their side. Any one can be selected by moving the cursor and entering the desired option against each them. Confirm by pressing the CR key before and after making the changes. The History File is as debugging device. If you want to save the commands you give during the course of your interaction, you can do so by starting with the command SET DOHISTORY ON at the dot prompt. After this setting all the commands that are executed will be saved in a HISTORY file. To display this HISTORY file give the command LIST HISTORY at the dot prompt. This will display the last 20 commands to enable you to go through the commands and look for any error. Normally the DOHISTORY is OFF, since the ON condition will slow down the execution. Only for debugging purposes it is set ON.

Options | Screen | Keys | Disk | Files | Margin | Decimals

Display Type	Colour
Standard Display	
Foreground:	White
Background:	Black
Itensity:	Dim
Blink:	No
Blank:	No
Enhanced Display	
Foreground:	Black
Background:	White
Itensity:	Dim
Blink:	No
Blank:	No
Border	
Colour:	Black
Itensity:	Dim

Set A: Opt: 1/13

Position selection ban ^ Change <CR> LEAVE MENU→ ← EXIT—ESC

Choose Foreground and background colour or intensity

Fig. 38.

The Keys Menu

The Keys men is shown in the Fig. 39. This figure shown the current settings of the Function Keys. Changes in the contents of the function key commands can be made if required by bringing the light bar over that function and entering the contents after pressing the CR key. The setting is confirmed by pressing the CR key at the end of typing.

```
Options    Screen    [Keys]    Disk    Files    Margin    Decimals

                     F2    assist;
                     F3    list;
                     F4    Dir;
                     F5    display structure;
                     F6    display status;
                     F7    display memory;
                     F8    display;
                     F9    append;
                     F10   edit;

Set               A:               Opt 1/7               Caps

Position Selection bar  ↑  ↓     Change <CR>     Leave Manu -> <- Exit-Esc

                        Define Function Keys
```

Fig. 39.

The Disk Menu

The Disk Menu is shown in the Fig. 40 and it shows the default disk drive. Any change in the drive or the drive search path can be entered if required.

```
Options    Screen    Keys    [Disk]    Files    Margin    Decimals

                             Default Disk Drive A:
                             Disk drive search path

Set               A:               Opt 1/7               Caps

Position selection bar  ↑  ↓     Change <CR>     Leave Manu -><-Exit-Esc

                     Change the default disk drive
```

Fig. 40.

The Files Menu

The Files Menu is shown in the Fig. 41 and gives the names of the Alternate, Format and Index files that are in use in the current work area.

Options Screen Keys Disk **Files** Margin Decimals

Alternate
Format
Index

Set A: Opt 1/3 Caps

Position selection bar ↑ ↓ Change <CR> Leave Manu -><-Exit-Esc

Enter a file name to use for alternate output

Fig. 41.

The Margins Menu

The Margins Menu is shown in the Fig. 42 and is used to set the margin for all printed outputs and the width of the memo field displays.

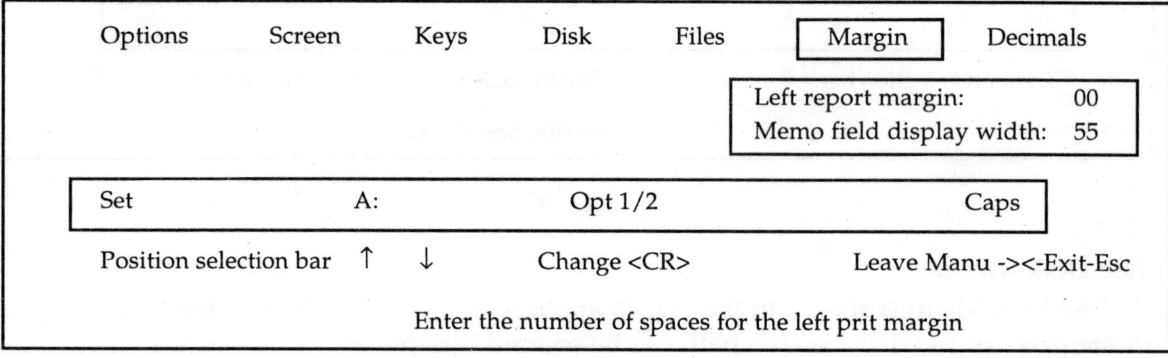

Fig. 42.

The Decimal Menu

The Decimal Menu is shown in the Fig. 43 and is used to set the number of decimal places that are to be displayed as a result of arithmetic computation.

Options Screen Keys Disk Files Margin Decimals

Decimal Places 02

Set A: Opt 1/2 Caps

Position selection bar ^ Change <CR> Leave manu -><- Exit-Esc

Entr the minimum number of decimals to be displayed

Fig. 43.

8

Applications Software

Applications software is software that is used to perform specific tasks or functions such as word processing, accounting, and filing. In this chapter, we look at some of the most common types of applications software such as word processors, electronic spreadsheets, data management, and graphics, and discuss how they work and how they are used.

APPLICATIONS SOFTWARE

Introduction

Application software or programs are those which do work for you, such as making payroll calculations and printing cheques. These programs can be quite complex and can be developed in-house or purchased from a software house (a firm which develops and sells computer programs), a computer equipment manufacturer or a computer retail store. Sometimes a consultant is hired to develop the required application programs; however, this alternative can at times be very expensive.

Developing computer programs is expensive because the programming must be done by humans, not computers and because little has been done in recent years to increase programming productivity. Applications programs may be developed by using third generation programming languages like BASIC, FORTRAN, COBOL, etc, or applications may be developed using available productivity software packages.

Micro Computer Software

Traditionally, computers were confined to a separate section of an organisation and were manned by a team of skilled analysis and programmers. With the arrival of low cost personal computers, a dramatic shift has taken place. Computers have moved towards the actual users. They are no more managed by specialists. The end user, a doctor, engineer or a manager is now making use of a computer directly without any major assistance from computer specialists. This has happened because computer software, thc man machine interface, has changed to a stage where a non-computer person can understand the language spoken by his personal computer.

As PC softtware is used by end users who are subject experts rather than computer experts, it has certain differences from other computer softwares in terms of:

1. User friendly interface
2. Menu driven
3. On-line help
4. Clear diagnostic messages
5. On-line tutorial
6. Supported by easy-to-read user mannuals(s)
7. Graphical outputs
8. Interactive in nature

Thousands of commercially available software packages run on microcomputers, but the most popular business software is the family of "productivity" software packages. These programs are the foundation of personal computing in the business world. Microcomputer productivity tools include:

1. **Word Processing**—Word processing software permits users to enter, store, manipulate and print text.

2. **Electronic Spreadsheet**—Electronic spreadsheet software permits users to work with the rows and columns of a matrix (or spreadsheet) of data. Several spreadsheets can be contained in a single worksheet.

3. **Data Management**—Data management or data base software permits users to create and maintain a data base and to extract information from the data base.

4. **Graphics**—Graphics software permits users to create charts and line drawings which graphically portray the data in an electronic spreadsheet or data base.

5. **Integrated Software**—An integrated software package incorporates a number of programs into one. Various component programs perform a variety of tasks, but they can exchange information among themselves. The first such integrated software package was Lotus 1-2-3, introduced in 1983.

6. **Idea Processors**—Idea processor software helps users organise and document their thoughts and ideas.

7. **Communications**—Communications software permits users to send and receive transmissions of data to/from remote computers, and to process and store the data as well.

These seven categories of software packages are now proven productivity tools in any field that requires people to work with text, numbers, graphics or ideas (and that list does not leave out many people!). These packages are often characterised as productivity tools because they help to relieve the tedium of many time-consuming manual tasks.

No more retyping—thanks to word processing software. Electronic spreadsheets permit us to perform certain arithmetic and logic operations without writing programs. With data management software, we can format and create a data base in minutes. Say goodbye to grid paper, plastic templates, and the manual plotting of data: graphics software prepares bar, pie, and line charts without our drawing a single line. An integrated package like Lotus 1-2-3 incorporates in a single program the functions of an electronic spreadsheet, a graphics program and a data base management program. Data generated by one program can be easily used as an input to another program. When brainstorming with idea processors, the result is a logical outline of conclusions, not indecipherable notes on a yellow pad. And communications software helps to minimise redundant data entry by permitting the transfer of files between computers.

In each productivity tool category, there are dozens of commercially available software packages from which to choose. The software packages in each category accomplish essentially the same functions. They differ primarily in the scope and variety of the special features they have to offer and in their "user-friendliness."

Interacting with the System

1. **User Friendly**—Software is said to be user friendly when someone with relatively little computer experience has little difficulty using the system. User-friendly systems communicate easily understood words and phrases to the end user, thus simplifying the user's interaction with the computer system. A central focus of the design of microcomputer productivity software is user friendliness.

There are, of course, degrees of user friendliness. At the first level, it is assumed that the user has little or no experience and that the user's interaction with the software will be tentative and deliberate. At this level, the system offers some welcome "hand holding." For example, some software packages use icons or pictographs, rather than words or phrases, to communicate with the end user.When you wish to issue a file handling command, for example, you position the cursor near the icon representing files (perhaps a file cabinet or a diskette). After selecting a particular icon, you arc presented with a menu of file handling choices. Your choices might be to save, retrieve, or delete a file.

The first level of user friendliness may be too friendly, even cumbersome, for the seasoned user. Too much hand holding forces experienced users to work more slowly than they would like. Microcomputer software, therefore, provides alternatives. As you become familiar with the software, you can learn and use techniques that offer more efficient interaction with the system.

A handy feature available on most software packages is the help command. When you find yourself in a comer, you can press the "help" key, and more explanation or instruction is displayed on the screen. When you finish reading the help information, the system returns you to your work at the same point that you left it.

2. **Input and Control**—A microcomputer's keyboard is normally the primary input and control device. You enter data and issue commands via the keyboard. It has, besides the standard typewriter keyboard, function keys, also called soft keys. When pressed, these function keys trigger the execution of software, thus the name 'soft' key. For example, pressing a particular function key might call up a menu of possible activities that can be performed. Another function key might rearrange the words in a paragraph for right and left justification. Some keyboards are equipped with a 10-key pad (numbers for rapid numeric data entry).

A keyboard also has cursor control keys. These 'arrow' keys allow you to move the cursor up, down, left and right. Pressing the HOME key results in different actions for different packages, but often, the cursor is moved to the beginning of a work area (e.g., the start of the document in word processing).

Other important keys common to most keyboards are the backspace (BKSP), escape (ESC), control (CTRL), and alternate (ALT) keys. Press the BKSP key to move the cursor one position to the left and delete the character in that position. The ESC key may have many functions, depending on the software package, but in most situations you can press the ESC key to negate the current command. The CTRL and ALT keys are used in conjunction with another key. You hold down a CTRL or ALT key to give another key new meaning. For example, on some word processing systems you press HOME to move the cursor to the top left comer of the screen. When you press CTRL and HOME together, the cursor is positioned at the beginning of the document.

Pointing devices are alternative to keyboard inputs for giving commands/data to the computer. Pointing device results in cursor movement on screen in response to mechanical movement of the device itself. These devices have the advantage of visual feedback. Some such devices are Mouse, Joy stick, Digitiser and Light pen.

The hand-held mouse, used for input and control, is connected to the computer by an electrical cable (the mouse's tail) and rolled over a desktop to move the cursor. Buttons on the mouse are activated to select a menu item or to perform certain tasks, such as moving blocks of data from one part of the screen to another.

3. **Menus**—When using these productivity tools, you issue commands and initiate operations by selecting activities to be performed from a hierarchy of menus. These hierarchies are sometimes called 'menu trees.' When you select an item in the main menu, you are normally presented with another menu of activities, and so on—thus the 'tree'. Depending on the items you select, you may progress through as many as eight levels of menus before processing is initiated. The menus appear in a control panel or a pull-down menu. The control panel is usually, but not always, located at the bottom or top of the screen. The pull-down menus are superimposed in a window over whatever is currently on the screen. You select a particular menu item by positioning the cursor over or next to the desired menu item with the cursor control keys or a mouse.

The main menu of a graphics software package might give you the choice of what type of chart you want produced: bar chart, pie chart, or line chart. If you select bar chart, then another menu gives you more choices: Do you wish to create a new one or revise an existing one? If you select create, then more menus ace presented that permit you to describe the appearance of the chart (e.g., labels) and to identify what data are to be charted.

At some point in the menu hierarchy, the user is asked to enter the specifications for data to be charted (graphics software) or the size of the output paper (word processing software), and so on. As a convenience to the user, many of the specification options (size of output paper) are already filled in to reflect common situations (e.g., document size is set at 8-1/2 by 11 inches). If the user is satisfied with these default options, no further specifications are required. The user can easily revise the default options to accommodate less common situations. For example, to print a document on legal size paper, the default paper length of 11 inches would need to be revised to 14 inches.

In conventional software, all commands were typed by the user resulting in the possibility of typing error. In menu driven software, the user is shown all possible commands on screen and he makes a selection either by typing a single character or by using a point and click device. Example of one of the menus in Library applications software is:

LIBRARY SOFTWARE

1. Search by Author
2. Search by Title
3. Search by Key word
4. Quit

Enter-Option__

4. **Operating System**—The nucleus of a microcomputer system is its operating system. All hardware and software, including microcomputer productivity software, are under the control of the operating system. It is to the advantage of the users of microcomputer software to learn something about the operating system for their particular microcomputer. Besides being the 'boss' program, the operating system enables users to run application programs such as word processing. It also provides users with a variety of file handling capabilities. Unfortunately, the logic, structure, and nomenclature of different operating systems vary considerably.

An IBM PC has a single user operating system called MS-DOS. It supports a tree structured filing system residing on multiple disks. It supports multiple programming languages and can handle various kinds of devices for input and output. Another operating system available on PC-AT is XENIX, which is a spin-off of UNIX and is a multiuser operating system. It is not as popular as MS-DOS. A new series of IBM personal computer PS/2 is coming with OS/2 which is a multitasking operating system with presentation manager and some data base handling capability.

Before you can use a microcomputer, you must 'boot the system.' The procedure for booting the system on most microcomputers is simply to load the operating system from disk storage into main memory. For most microcomputers, this is no more difficult than inserting an operating system diskette (floppy disk) in a disk, drive and flipping the "on" switch. On some systems all you have to do is turn the system on. A few seconds later, with the operating system in memory, you are ready to begin processing. Some operating systems give you the option to enter date and time data before displaying the system prompt.

The system prompt is the operating system's message to you, the user, that you can now enter a system command (e.g., to copy files from one diskette to another) or the name of the program (e.g., if you wish to run an applications program such as an electronic spreadsheet). The form of the system prompt varies among operating systems. A common prompt is the 'greater than' symbol prefaced by a disk drive specification (e.g., A> is the prompt when the disk drive 'A' is the active or default drive). Other common system prompts are the "$" (dollar sign) and the "J" (close bracket).

Once you have loaded the operating system to memory and the system prompt is displayed on the screen, you are ready to run a graphics package, a word processing package, or any other software package. To run a software package, you simply insert the diskette containing the software in the appropriate disk drive (if needed), then enter the name of the file that contains the applications software. For example, to run a particular word processing package on an MS-DOS based microcomputer, you would load the software diskette to drive A, then key in ' WS' (the name of the program file) after the system prompt. The command would look like this:

A>WS

The next thing you will see is the opening screen and eventually the main menu for the word processing package. Aμ microcomputer productivity tools are run in the

2. WORD PROCESSING

Introduction

Even though word processing has only blossomed during the last few years, it has already been accepted as a cornerstone of modern offices abroad. In the Indian context, where secretarial costs are generally lower and equipment cost considerably higher, the relevance of the word processor is naturally questioned. Word processors, besides improving typing productivity, offer a number of distinct advantages which may have greater relevance in the Indian context. For example, accuracy, quality and the speed of production of the final documentation may be more relevant from our view point.

Survey conducted in this area has revealed that:

1. Long documents, repetitive letters, memos and general correspondence are the most widely used applications for word processors.
2. The most significant advantage of word processors is increased productivity.

Word processing started as a simple piece of equipment designed to capture keystrokes of a somewhat limited amount of text for minor revisions and repetitive playback. It has evolved into a system designed to handle large amounts of text, sophisticated revisions of any size, creation of documents from stored segments and information processing. Essentially, word processing is an application of computer technology to the task of document preparation. The primary emphasis is in increasing the quality, the speed and the efficiency of document preparation. The resulting flexibility, just as in any computer application, is an added benefit.

What is Word Processing?

Word processing is a computer age term for typing and editing any kind of text— letters, memos, articles, reports, monographs, and books. Word processing involves typing into a computer, and more. Although the computer keyboard looks a lot like a typewriter keyboard, it has special keys that a typewriter does not.

With a typewriter, you see words on paper as you type. When you use a word processor, you see words on the computer terminal screen as you type. As you read your text on the screen, you can change it or rearrange it and when it looks just the way you want it to, you print a paper copy on your computer printer.

You can save text typed with a word processor and again use it later. Your text is saved electronically in a computer file on your floppy diskette, magnetic tape or hard disk. When you want to work with a file again, you simply ask for it by its name. You can then make any changes you wish, and print the new version.

Often, the full benefits and impact of such a technology application are not immediately obvious. The word processor is bound to have a revolutionising effect in offices, even in India. Initially, it is seen as yet another way of producing documents; a costly replacement of basic typewriters. Word processing systems yield benefits because they permit better quality document preparation with increased speed and reduced wastage, both in terms of time and material.

Word processing equipment is very adaptable to most paperwork tasks. It deals with character codes in the same objective way as a computer deals with number codes. Just as a computer can be adapted to handle almost any computational job, a word processor can be employed to handle almost any form of word communication. Unlike computers which require programming expertise on the part of the user, word processors come equipped with necessary 'programmes' to perform the desired jobs.

Whereas data processing (DP) is concerned with the processing of data, word processing

(WP) is concerned with the efficient processing of words or text. The technique is designed to provide a more efficient way of meeting the typing needs of a business and is typically used for the production of standard letters and for preparing reports and documents which are subject to change before they are finalised. As disk storage has become cheaper the word processor is being increasingly used for all correspondence originating in an office and copies are then stored electronically rather than in hard copy.

The soft-media storage technique permits operations to be performed far more rapidly and more efficiently than was ever possible. To illustrate this point, assume that a 100 page document needs to be updated extensively because of major changes. Further, seventy per cent of the information will not change, yet, seventy per cent information stability does not necessarily translate into 70 pages of unchanged text. In fact, the job is a hundred per cent nonautomated retyping effort. Assuming a typist can type 20 pages a day , forty hours are needed to do the job. Treating the unchanged information as final text, the same job on a word processor can be done in (0.3x40) = 12 hours, but in reality the compression is even greater because of on-the-spect proof reading, far less paper handling etc. A figure of eight hours or less is more realistic. This means that the job can be done five times faster on a word processor.

The advantages of word processing are obvious, corrections become trivial updates and extensive changes can be eliminated. Repetitively used information, like resumes, proposals etc, can be retained permanently on a floppy diskette and can be retrieved as and when required. The format can be altered for each job. However, the advantages of introducing word processing in an office environment depend on the kind and number of documents the office handles. If the office documents we usually revised extensively or form letters with minor internal information changes are often required, word processing is a distinct boon and can yield productivity improvements.

The advantages of word processing are summarised as follows:

1. Increased office efficiency resulting in improved secretarial support for all word originators (including executives)
2. Higher quality output resulting from advanced equipment
3. Improved human resource utilisation with better control and supervision of secretarial personnel through a word processing centre.

In particular, improved productivity is obtained by:

1. Reduced retyping time for error free hard copy
2. Facilitation of document revision and change before committing to paper
3. Faster output speed
4. Reduction in amount of proof reading required
5. Elimination of stationery wastage

All this can be achieved in an office by installing a word processor.

Types of Word Processors

Word processing is available in three forms:

1. Dedicated word processors. These are special purpose computers built to act efficiently as word processors but are generally not suitable for other computing applications. They can be single user, twin user or multiple user (cluster) systems. In the last case, all users share a common disk storage and sometimes share a common processor (shared logic systems).
2. Use of a standard word processing software package on a general purpose microcomputer (where a dedicated system cannot be justified). There is a wide variety of WP packages available which varies in terms of the features offered, the style and the ease of use. Since these packages are usually designed to operate over a wide range of microcomputer types, they cannot always efficiently use the special function keys available on the keyboard. This leads to a combination of keys being used where a single designated key would suffice. Although the system documentation will refer to these key combinations, it is sometimes possible to tailor the system to particular microcomputers.
3. On minicomputers, some manufacturers provide a word processing package which can be used from any terminal in the system. It is generally based on the text editor available to programmers of the system and, while it will not generally constitute a fully blown WP system, it can meet many of the needs in a general office environment. This facility is seldom available on mainframe computers.

A dedicated word processor normally uses a high quality daisy-wheel printer, whereas the printer attached to a microcomputer may be aiming at speed rather than quality.

A typical single-user dedicated word processor has the following facilities:

- document creation, storage and retrieval
- automatic word-wrap, page numbering, centring, underlining, over-typing and reformatting, right justification, proportional spacing
- efficient search
- global search and replace
- forms handling
- spelling check
- file extract and file merge
- sort facility
- column handling
- graphics (usually limited)

- records management
- help facility
- calculation
- column addition
- password security

Components of a Word Processor

A minimum word processor consists of a typewriter-like keyboard, a visual display unit (VDU), storage device, like a floppy diskette and a high quality reasonable speed printer. Basically, the typed-in text is stored on the floppy diskette and can be repetitively used. This ability to hold data in an electronic form, and to manipulate it in many ways before printing it, gives a much larger range of options of transcription, corrections and formatting. For example, with only a few keystrokes, one can rearrange paragraphs, make corrections, include some previously generated standard paragraphs, or alter the form of the final print out; all these at electronic speed.

In-house photo-typesetting is one of the relatively new innovations on word processors. The continuous increase in professional printing and text preparation costs, along with the development of photo-typesetting interfaces for word processor equipment, has encouraged many companies to begin limited in-house photocomposition. Early WP/Photo-typesetting interfaces were based on paper tape, thereby requiring an intermediate step between input and output, to convert the stored information to paper tape for photo-typesetting. Recent photo-typesetters have eliminated this step and are directly word processor compatible, thereby, allowing information stored on removable media to be transmitted directly from the word processor to the photo-typesetters. In this arrangement, the photo-typesetting codes must be entered (along with the original text) by the word processor operator.

Optical Character Readers (OCR), a fairly recent addition to many WP systems, convert typed text into machine readable form for storage on magnetic media. An OCR enables any standard office typewriter equipped with the proper print style and ribbon to function as a WP input terminal. With it one can type the original of a text, thus eliminating a primary typing or transcription step from the text preparation process. After information has been stored on compatible magnetic media, it can easily be printed out on a printer and returned to the author for review or revision. With OCR, one is able to increase the productivity of a WP by eliminating tedious text preparation stages and cutting the time spent on a WP terminal.

Impact of Word Processor on Office Productivity

In our attempts to explain the function of a WP as an aid to greater efficiency and productivity, we define productivity, the means by which it can be increased, the problems that WP faces today and areas of WP application.

1. *Productivity* : $\frac{\text{Output}}{\text{Input}}$

Office Productivity:

Output: i) Quantity of information generated

ii) Quantity and timeliness of information generated

Input: i) Man-hours

ii) Office Stationery

iii) Equipment hours

Productivity of office can be increased by:

i) Reducing cost of information generated

ii) Improving quality and timeliness of information generated

2. *Reducing Cost of Information Generated Typing Productivity:*
   - Normally typing speed 45 wpm-1200 lines per day; in practice 600 lines/day
   - WP raises speed by atleast 100%—achievements in the order of 2000 lines per day have been reported
   - Every typing can be done at draft typing speed
   - Provision to have standard paragraphs with typists providing the link—preparation of standard paragraph numbers and user manual
   - Error correction time reduced—Global search replace
   - Edit efforts reduced

— Formatting improves get-up

— Automatic composing, pre-defined page length, line length and automatic numbering of pages

Reproduction Cost

- Many clear copies at speed of 3000 characters per minute
- Within few minutes type-face can be changed
- Mailing list applications with address select feature
- Saving of stationery due to reduced re-typing

Information Storage and Retrieval

- Electronic filing reduces storage space—5-1/4" floppy diskette stores 360,000 characters or about 250 A4 pages

- Digital devices, amenable to interconnection—crude form of data communication
- Crude form of data based management—query processing systems

3. *Improving Quality and Timeliness of Information*
   - Personalised letters improve image of company
   - Any correction or last minute change/idea facilitated
   - Excellent print quality of documents/letters
   - Sophisticated WP-maintenance of dictionaries to correct spellings
   - Waiting time of clients reduced by fast contract typing

4. *Other Benefits*
   - Job enrichment of typist's job—higher status to secretariat staff and better working condition (air-conditioned atmosphere) leads to less turn-over and high morale
   - In case of emergency, the executive himself can type and gel the documents printed

5. *Problems and Issues*
   - Difficult to get across traditional executives secretary relationship
   - Deciding standard paragraphs that need to be programmed demands good analytical skill and is also a laborious process
   - Minimum volume of standard typing work essential
   - VDU terminal-radiation emission should be at nonharmful levels—visua strain, headache, dissiness are caused sometimes
   - Data/text privacy and security
   - Under-utilisation of computing equipment if work is not properly scheduled
   - Inadequately trained employees can be a bigger headache
   - Compatibility with different systems—documents prepared on one system may require modified using a different system; interface between different vendor's models are yet to become a practical reality.

6. *Potential Situations*
   - Departments that prepare large number of reports
   - Offices that have to frequently revise their documents
   - Bureaus that must send large number of originals
   - Situation necessitating telecommunication between word processors located at different plants

- Extensive use of form letters to standardise mailing list
- Situations where electronic filing is an important consideration

Word processors are most valuable where there is:

- a high volume of routine correspondence
- a requirement to send personalised letters to people on the mailing list-staff, customers, suppliers, members etc,
- a need to produce documents which contain large sections of standardised text e.g. legal documents, specifications or proposals
- a lot of drafting, editing and revision

Features of a Word Processor

Basic Features

- Preparing editing, formatting and printing of letters and reports
- Preparation of original letters and memos for a large number of clients
- Automatic form filing
- Filing and searching of large information stocks

Advanced Features

- System with large number of terminals (4 to 19)
- Shared logic systems
- Shared resources systems
- System with i) communication facilities ii) attached photocomposing unit

Applications of Word Processor

The word processor is so powerful that it is difficult to list all its applications. Some selective applications have been outlined here which may then be extrapolated to fit definitive user needs. As we envisage a growing business, we see a parallel growth in the tumultuous paper work which an office generates through letters, memos, proposals, contracts, financial statements and other related materials which an executive has to handle. Thus, to channelise and optimise the executive workload and not let his energies dissipate in sundry tasks like searching for information or waiting for the preparation and delivery of reports and studies, the word processor is the tool in the offing.

The work which an office typing pool or a single typist would be called upon to do are of four types:

1. *A unique report*—often it is produced in manuscripts, typed in a draft form, and then corrected, polished, altered and retyped in final form.

On a word processor we straight away achieve a saving of fifty per cent of the work *viz.,* the retyping of the big report. Owing to its dynamic editing facility the task of correcting, polishing and altering the report is extremely simple. Apart from assisting a typist with the ease of moving through the text, backwards and forwards, looking for the parts to edit, a word processor enables automatic headings and footings, page numbering, automatic left and right numbering of facing pages and bold printing facilities on page and section headings. Also, if large blocks of the report need shifting these may be accomplished with ease, as the ability to move a column of figures from say the third position to the first on a table.

2. *Repeat work*—this would be a sales or legal document, a quotation, a contract or standard proposal. Some of it is written specifically and the rest is made up of standard sections, perhaps, with a few modifications.

Here the word processor helps the operator to set up a series of files, each one clearly named and containing one of the range of options which may be needed. When a sales or legal document, quotation, contract etc, is named, the word processor is able to copy selected files with the new necessary options pertaining to the document, straight into the document, at the position of the cursor. This feature of creating and retrieving large or small blocks of texts and incorporating them into the document being produced is a very useful time and effect saving feature.

3. *Mailing list*—a letter is produced and this needs to be sent to a few or hundreds of addresses . Their names and other details have to be included, so that each recipient gels an individually typed document.

The idea here is that you want to be able to combine a letter with a file containing names and addresses. At its simplest, this means that you put into the letter, special codes for names, addresses, towns, postal codes and perhaps a salutation. What is a salutation? The name on the letter may be 'Mr. Suresh Kumar,' but if you want to start with 'Dear Suresh.' then 'Dear' will be the salutation. That is the straightforward and obvious use. Most word processors have the additional facility to carry out a dialogue with the operator during the printing. The ability to display on the screen the name of the particular individual whose letter is being printed would enable the operator to keep track of where in the filing list the system has reached. Perhaps, you also need to be able to insert from the key board some particular item for each letter, like an amount of outstanding debt or the delivery time or whatever.

A more powerful word processor system will also be able to print selectively from the list. If you have one large list with codes for sales area or customer interest or some other selection criterion, then the system will allow you to print the letter to all general managers, code 'E5' or all branch managers with sales of, say over Rs. 1,00,000 in the previous month.

4. *Routine correspondence*—letters or memos on a wide range of different topics topics.

The ability to copy a file into your document could be very useful. If you produce estimates, orders, quotations, invoices and the like, you would have a standard copy. You copy the files into the document you are creating and then type in the areas which are specific to the item of correspondence. The idea is almost the same as using pre-printed stationery into the typewriter, but you use plain paper instead. The standard printed part is held on a word processor and you can produce an attractive layout without difficulty for almost all your letters and memos. Also the usual editing and alteration features help and you do not get letters wise alterations on the final version. In addition, it is often useful to reformat a letter after it is typed. Letters with the last couple of lines squeezed to avoid going into the second page can be better produced by simply altering the margin and line per inch until the text fits the single page.

Typical Applications of WP in Various Fields of Work

Insurance and Banking

- — Reports
- — Manuals
- — Directories and listings
- — Policies
- — Benefit books

Manufacturing

- — Catalogues
- — Manuals
- — Reports
- — Brochures
- — Contracts
- — Personalised letters

Architects and Engineers

- — Specifications
- — Impact studies
- — Proposals
- — Biographies

Government Agencies

- — Directories
- — Manuals
- — Reports

— Bulletins
— Memorandums

Legal

— Wills
— Trusts
— Briefs
— Memorandums
— Labour contracts
— Maritime financing
— Commitment letters
— Automated litigation support systems

As one builds more experience and confidence on a word processor, one realises its unique features and appreciates it facilities. Thus, one does not justify the applications which a word processor may perform, but contemplates on the application which the word processor can handle. Word processors are doing to the written word, the same that calculators did for numbers in the past. It is only left to the imagination of an executive how this wonder machine can be productively used to increase office productivity.

Overview of WordStar

WordStar is a screen-oriented, IBM PC-DOS/MS-DOS compatible, integrated word processing system specifically designed for ease of use. Other popular personal computer, based word processing packages are MultiMate, Microsoft Word, Word Perfect, etc. WordStar 5.0 runs on IBM PC, PC/XT, PC/AT or compatibles, though it is advisable to have a hard disk as in the case of most recent software packages. It requires 512 KB of RAM for its full operation and is available from MicroPro International Corporation, USA.

WordStar package includes the following prominent features:

— Easy-to-remember mnemonic commands
— Onscreen tutor for easy learning
— Built-in format sheets for easy documents
— "Undo' to easily restore text
— Built-in telecommunications
— Spelling corrector
— Mail list manager
— Windows onscreen
— Built-in math functions
— Alphabetic and numeric sorting within document

— 'Macros' for recalling often used command sequences
— Supports over 100 printers
— Experience with over 1.5 million owners.

1. Video editing (screen): Rapid display of text on the video screen with no perceptible delay under most conditions. A portion of the document being entered or corrected is always shown on the screen; additions and corrections are immediately displayed. Text and command functions are fully prompted.

2. Automatic disk buffering: Text is moved between disk and CPU memory without user intervention. Thus, file size is limited only by disk capacity.

3. Help menus: Four help levels provide the learning operator with comprehensive prompting instructions without the need to refer to a manual. Help levels may be changed at any time to allow full screen utilisation.

4. Directory display: The IBM MS-DOS file directory is displayable at any time from within WordStar.

5. File management: "copy", "rename" and "erase" are also WordStar functions.

6. Program execution: allows a program (or an operating system utility such as CHKDSK) to be executed, with automatic return to WordStar. This eliminates the need to exit to IBM MS-DOS.

7. Powerful editing commands: include delete character, word, line or block; set/ clear variable tab stop; block move, copy, delete and output to disk; find; find and replace; write/ read to/from other files; set/return to place markers; insert mode and many more.

8. Find and replace: the capacity to search and find a particular word or phrase throughout a document and if necessary replace this wherever it occurs with a desired alternative (global search and replace). In lengthy documents, this helps locate material quickly if corrections need to be made.

9. On-screen printer-image text formatting: the effect of margin settings (either right-justified or ragged-right) is displayed on the screen just as the text will appear on paper. The text is automatically formed to the current setting as it is entered. Either setting can be later changed, and the result 'reviewed.' Both settings can be mixed within a document. Selective margination permits 'cutting' around an illustration.

(Note: This paragraph has a ragged-right margin.)

10. Word-wrap: eliminates the need to enter a carriage return at the end of each line. A word too long to fit at the end of a line is automatically moved to the next line. 'RETURN' is used only to indicate the end of a paragraph or to create a line space. This eliminates many keystrokes and increases the rate of text entry.

11. Block and column operations: the ability to move, copy and delete blocks of text is a powerful tool for use in almost any application. You can also perform all block operations on a column of text. Thus, a column of figures can be adjusted horizontally without adding or removing spaces one line at a time; full width text can be reformed to 1/2 or 1/3 page margin widths, and the result manipulated to produce a multiple-column product.

12. Horizontal-scrolling: you control a 'window' which moves horizontally as well as vertically. This is particularly useful when preparing reports that exceed the width of an 8-1/2" wide page.

13. Split-screen: using a triple-split screen, WordStar allows help menu, IBM MS-DOS file directory and scrolling text to appear independently on the screen.

14. Dynamic page break display: a horizontal dotted line, not part of the text, is shown on the screen where a printer page break would occur. The page break line is dynamically repositioned when text entry or deletion affects page size. Visualisation of a print image allows even an inexperienced operator to perform sophisticated text composition.

15. Automatic-centering: with a two-stroke command, text is automatically centered on a line.

16. Hyphen-help: a user-controlled option that alerts the operator when the last word on a line is too long to fit. The location of a hyphen is suggested. The operator can choose between hyphenation at the suggested location, earlier in the word, or moving the whole word to the next line.

17. Decimal Tab: allows columns of numbers (including dollar signs [$] and commas) to be typed as easily as operating an adding machine. WordStar will line up the decimals automatically. The European format for decimals and commas is supported.

18. Paragraph indent: temporarily sets the left margin to a tab stop so that documents with continuous indentations (such as outlines) can be typed easily.

19. Pagination and formatting: the user has control over page length, top and bottom margins, heading/footing/page number locations, and conditional and absolute pagination directives. The user can easily define the way he wants the margins, tabulation and line space arrangements to work at the beginning of each new document.

20. Headings and footings: flexible headings and/or footings, with or without page numbers, are easily implemented.

21. Printer support: a wide range of letter quality, dot matrix and line printers are supported including Diablo, CITOH, NEC, and Qume, as well as IBM printers. WordStar fully utilises bidirectional printing capability.

22. Print enhancements: boldface, double strike, underline and strikeout, variable line height, variable and alternate character pitch, alternate character set, and alternate ribbon color.

23. Scripting: both $_{\text{sub}}$scripts and ^{super}scripts are fully supported. Print enhancements may be used in all combinations. For example, underlined and boldfaced ^{super}scripts are possible.

* Microspace justification: when printing justified text on a daisy wheel printer, the white space in each line is evenly distributed.

24. Variable line height: is user defined and easily changed (by using dot commands).

25. Variable character pitch: of printed copy is determined by the user (pica, elite, or choice of number of characters per inch). With a combination of print wheels and print commands, a wide variety of print characteristics can be obtained (by using dot commands).

26. Concurrent print function (background printing): printing and editing simultaneously, thus improving operator productivity.

27. Selective page printing: permits you to specify both the first and last page to be printed. In this way, a portion of a document may be printed.

Mail Merge Features

MailMerge is a powerful, easy to use file merging tool. It is an optional module, and can be purchased at any time.

1. Mulliple copy printing: allows the same file to be printed more than once without constant operator attention.

2. Chained printing: a series of files may be printed automatically by calling up the various files from within a document, either while editing or as it is printed. This reduces the time needed to create documents. Disk storage requirements are significantly reduced by eliminating file content duplication on the same disk.

3. Nested printing: files printed using the chained printing feature can themselves contain references to other files.

4. Automatic variable insertion: mailmerge can take a data file and combine it with a text file, inserting the data where variables are specified. The operator can also enter additional data at print time.

5. Print time formatting: paragraph reforming is automatic at print lime. When variables appear mid-sentence, there arc no 'telltale spaces' printed as there are with most other word-processing programs.

6. Mail Merge: can selectively print data in virtually any format. Each field in a data file need not necessarily be used. Thus, the same data file used to print letters can be used to print a customer list (account numbers, comments, etc.) and also their mailing labels.

3. SPREADSHEETS

Introduction

While most microcomputer applications packages are designed for a specific application, such as stock control, payroll or sales and purchase ledger, occasionally a package is developed around a single concept which has applications in many areas. The 'electronic worksheet is the best example of such a package. Again, although most microcomputer applications software packages are specific to a particular make of microcomputer, sometimes a package is so successful that its authors find it commercially sensible to make it available on a wide range of machines. One package to come under this category and available on most of the popular types of microcomputers is Lotus 1-2-3.

Lotus 1-2-3 is one of the most popular spreadsheet package. It is written in C language and developed by Lotus Development Corporation, USA. To run its latest 3.0 version, this package requires IBM AT, PS/2 or compatible running DOS 3.0 or later (for OS/2 1.0 or 1.1); 1 MB of RAM (3 MB for OS/2); hard disk; graphics display to preview graphics. Facilities of this package includes multipage spreadsheets and multiple active worksheets. It supports OS/2, displays graphs and data simultaneously, can use extended memory, background printing, and can work with external database file.

Lotus 1-2-3 is a microcomputer productivity software, which has been developed for use by persons with no special knowledge about computers and programming languages, but with a thorough grasp of their specialised problems. It provides the user a menu-driven user-friendly approach. When this software is loaded in the computer, it displays a menu on the screen. Once the problem solver selects a particular option from the menu, Lotus displays further prompts on the screen asking the user to describe his problem more specifically. Thus by a series of prompts, Lotus elicits the required processing steps for solving the problem from the user himself and finally presents the solution in the desired format.

The electronic spreadsheet is extremely useful applications program for both the business and the home user. Here, we introduce the concepts of an electronic spreadsheet, some of its many applications, and capabilities and details of Lotus I-2-3 package.

What Can Lotus 1-2-3 Do?

On its own, nothing. But with your data input and instructions, you have at your fingertips a powerful, integrated programme that combines three programs in one: a spreadsheet (or worksheet) program, a graphics program, and a data-base management program. A closer look at each component best illustrates how you can conveniently put several capabilities to work without having to use a new program or a new set of instructions.

The first and most sophisticated of the three, the spreadsheet, electronically duplicates an accountant's or bookkeeper's tools: a ledger pad, a pencil, an eraser, and a calculator. With the spreadsheet you enter and correct figures by typing on a keyboard, rather than writing with a pencil, and you view the figures on a computer screen, or monitor, rather than reading a ledger pad.

Once you enter data on the spreadsheet, you can apply a variety of calculation from simple addition, subtraction, multiplication, and division to trigonometric, statistical, and business calculations. With the spreadsheet you can prepare such things as:

1. Budgets
2. Annual reports
3. Portfolio analysis
4. Accounts payable and receivable
5. Production schedules
6. Invoices
7. Income statements
8. Loan analyses
9. Tax statements
10. Developing business plans
11. Graphing trends
12. Maintaining data on employees or clients
13. Managing inventory
14. Performing standard accounting functions

In addition to entering and calculating numbers, the spreadsheet responds to "what if" scenarios. For example, let us assume you own a retail business and you want to know how a holiday sale will affect your profit. You start by entering the current prices of the items you arc selling, the number of items for sale, and the cost of each item. After entering a formula to calculate your projected profit without the sale, you can recalculate to answer the question: If I put several items on sale for 30 per cent less, how will this affect profit? As you enter each new figure, Lotus 1-2-3 automatically recalculates profit and displays the answer on the screen.

But that is only the beginning. By expanding this particular worksheet to include overhead and salaries, you can ask more questions, such as: How will a drop in overhead or an increase in salaries affect profit? And, if you want to discuss the possibilities with others in the office, you can print copies of each version of the worksheet.

The second component, graphics, enables you to create various kinds of graphs, such as a bar or line graph, from the information on the worksheet. Therefore, continuing with the previous example, the retail profits before and after the sale can be viewed on a bar graph where they can be visually compared. The visual impact of the graph makes it an effective communication tool since it is simpler to interpret a graph than it is to interpret columns of numbers. It is also less boring.

Although you may not realise it, you probably have in your possession several examples of data-base management, Lotus 1-2-3's third component. Do you keep an address book in your briefcase? What about a notebook where you tally up your work-related car mileage and bridge tools? Do you keep your paycheck stubs in order? Each is a source of information, as well as a means of managing it. Hence, each is a data base. Other examples include personnel files, inventory lists, customer records, and to do lists. The major difference between managing any of these examples and using database management to do it for you is that Lotus 1-2-3 can instantly retrieve and reorganise all the information without consuming time by turning pages or searching through files.

Another advantage of Lotus 1-2-3's database management is that it can retrieve and organise by using any one piece of the database. For example, consider a traditional phone book as a database. You can find the phone number of a friend only if you know your friend's last name. With Lotus 1-2-3, however, you can find his phone number by entering his address or the first three numbers of his phone number, Lotus 1-2-3 can index every category of information: first name, last name, address, and phone number, plugging in any one piece brings up the entire entry.

In addition to the three main components, Lotus 1-2-3 offers a fourth, more complex feature: keyboard macros, which simplify tasks that you find yourself doing over and over again, such as typing the twelve months of the year across the top of every budget you prepare. Rather than retype the headings each time, you can program your computer to do this for you automatically with two keystrokes. The set of instructions included in the keystrokes is called a macro. Keyboard macros are especially helpful on forms such as invoices that require you to type the same information hundreds or thousands of times. However, macros are considered an advanced use of Lotus 1-2-3. While there are some simple macros that a beginner can quickly put to use, it helps to be familiar with programming procedures.

Now, let us take a closer look at how the four features interact with each other. To do so, assume you are an accountant for a firm that manufactures industrial equipment for fertiliser plants. It is October, and you are conscientiously preparing some figures for your annual report, which you will present at the January board meeting. An early draft should save time, you think to yourself.

You start by finding the Rupee values of your assets and liabilities. Lotus 1-2-3 calculates your total inventory value from a list in the data base, which includes the number of items on hand and their value at cost. From several other worksheets, you transfer more figures, such as cash on hand, accounts payable and receivable, fixed assets, and outstanding loans. Once you have calculated net worth, you want to see what percentage of total assets is represented by inventory. With a few keystrokes, a pie chart represents the unsold inventory as a large part of assets. So far, everything you have done has required only a few keystrokes since you have speeded up this annual task by using macros.

But it is only October. What will happen to net worth if half of the inventory is shipped COD before the end of the year? Lotus 1-2-3 recalculates the figures, and you view the graph again. The results are more positive. But how do the results compare to figures for the past five years ? From previous years' budgets, you transfer the year-end figures for all five years to a line graph, and again the results are impressive. After adding some last minute labels, you print several copies and show them to the sales department managers to see if they agree with your projections.

Some Applications of Electronic Spreadsheets

Many applications of electronic spreadsheets involve collecting numeric information that can be organised in the form of an electronic spreadsheet. Some examples are discussed here.

1. Budgets—Electronic spreadsheets are commonly used to develop and monitor budgets.The budgeted items are usually listed across the rows. The columns indicate various budget periods (weeks, months, years). Certain columns contain summary statistics, such as year to date, quarterly expenditures, and comparison of budgeted amount with actual amount.

2. Inventory Management—Many small businesses use electronic spreadsheets to keep track of inventory. The various inventory items are listed down the rows. The columns give the number of items shipped and the number of items remaining in the inventory at particular times. The electronic spreadsheets may also contain statistics relating to changes in inventory over various time periods.

3. Portfolio Management—Electronic spreadsheets are used to keep track of investment portfolios. Each investment occupies a single line. The columns indicate income from the investments for particular time periods. Some columns may give portfolio statistics, such as total portfolio cost, current yield, current investment value, and total income for the year to date.

4. Proposal Costing—To arrive at a final bid for a contract, an executive must consider hundreds of costs that affect the job, including wage rates, the costs of raw materials, permits, taxes, and the desired level of profits. The data related to the bid may be arranged in the form of a spreadsheet. A complex job is generally broken down into a series of smaller tasks and the costs for each task are computed separately. The cost of the entire task is obtained by adding the costs of the smaller tasks. The electronic spreadsheet can be used to determine the effect on the bid if various costs change.

5. Management Decision Support—Electronic spreadsheets are commonly used to make projections of business conditions. They, are used in analysing the effects of changes in various conditions. (How will shipments be affected if the supply of railroad cars decreases by 30 per cent? What will happen to profits if the cost of sugar increases by 15 per cent and wages increase by 8 per cent?)

Working with an Electronic Spreadsheet

1. Moving Around an Electronic Spreadsheet—Users move the cursor around the electronic spreadsheet, changing the current cell. Most spreadsheets allow many more rows and columns than can be displayed at one time on the screen. If the user moves the cursor off the screen, the program will reveal columns or rows that were previously kept in memory but not displayed on the screen.

2. Entering Data on an Electronic Spreadsheet—To enter data into a cell, the user moves the cursor to the cell and types in the data. If the data consists of a formula, the formula appears only at the top of the screen and not in the cell itself. The electronic spreadsheet automatically calculates the value of the formula and inserts ' the value into the cell. At the same time, the values of all other cells that depend on the value of the current cell are recalculated.

3. Changing the Content of a Cell—To change the content of a cell, the user moves the cursor to the cell and enters the new content. The old content of the cell is lost, and the new cell value is inserted (or computed, if the new cell value is determined by a formula). Any cell values that depend on the value of the changed cell are recalculated. This ability to change the content of a cell easily and to see the effects of the change on the other numbers on the spreadsheet immediately is what makes electronic spreadsheets so useful

4. Editing the Electronic Spreadsheet Electronic spreadsheet programs contain features that make them more useful. They allow the user to save the current contents of the spreadsheet on a disk and to recall the spreadsheet at a later time. They also include a number of editing features that make it simpler to create and change spreadsheets.

The editing features let the user erase the content of a single cell or of an entire rectangular block of cells. They let the user add or remove rows or columns, and they automatically adjust the formulas from one cell to another. The editing features even allow users to merge spreadsheets and to add and subtract spreadsheets on a cell-by-cell basis. They also make it simple to enter or alter the data in the cells.

Spreadsheets are too large to appear completely on the screen. A number of editing features compensate for this limitation. One feature freezes titles on the screen so that when the user brings a remote section of the spreadsheet onto the screen, the horizontal or vertical titles remain on the screen. Some programs allow users to view two or more sections of the spreadsheet at the same time. This is accomplished through the use of separate view windows that display the different sections.

Spreadsheet Details

Worksheet is a grid made up of horizontal rows and vertical columns. The worksheet contains 8192 rows and 256 columns. Each intersection of a row and a column forms a cell, in which you can store data (see Fig. 1).

Row number identifies a horizontal row in the worksheet. It appears on the left border of the worksheet.

Column letter identifies a vertical column in the worksheet. It appears on the top border of the worksheet. Columns are lettered A-Z, then AA-ZZ, then BA-BZ, and so on to IV.

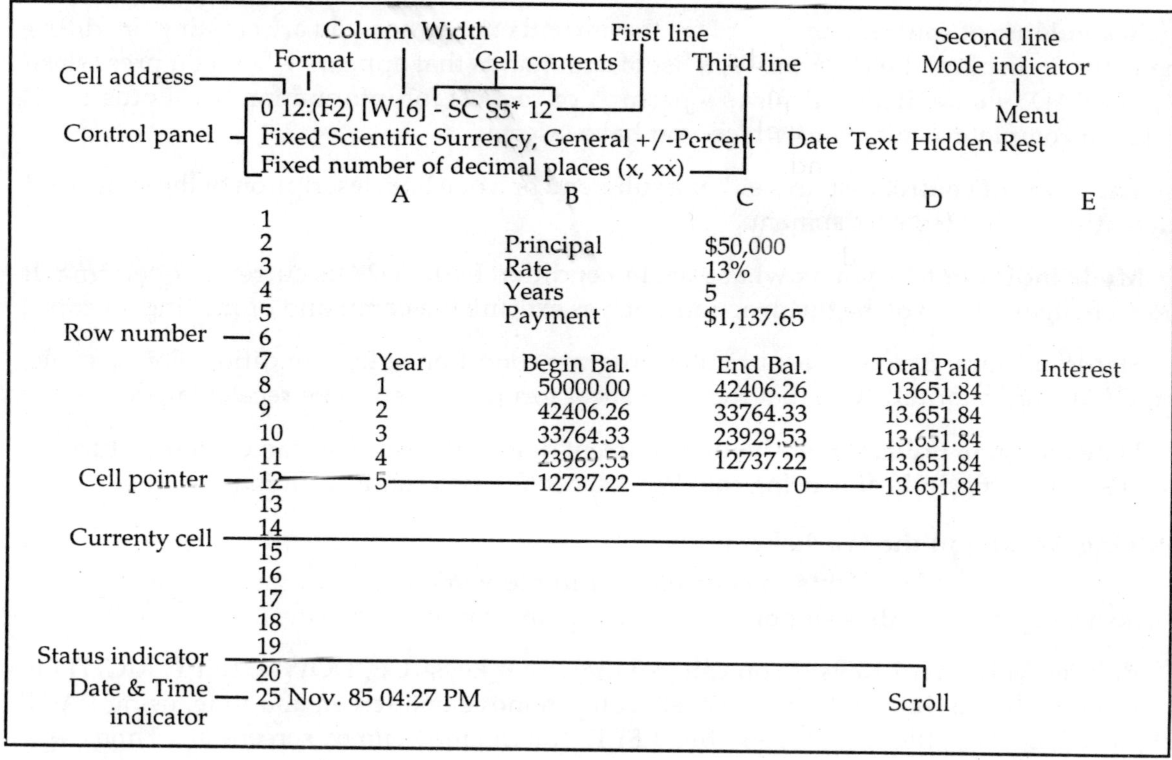

Fig. 1.

Cell is a unit of the worksheet that can store data. Each cell has a unique address that consists of its column letter and row number. For example, B14 identifies the cell in column B, row 14.

Cell pointer is a rectangular highlight that appears on one cell in the worksheet and identifies it as the current cell. You can move the cell pointer to any cell in the worksheet.

Current cell contains the cell pointer, which indicates that your next entry or procedure affects this cell. For example, typing an entry or executing certain commands affects the current cell.

Control panel is located above the worksheet. It contains three lines of information about the current cell, the mode or current state of Lotus 1-2-3 and the commands (actions you tell Lotus 1-2-3 to perform).

First line of control panel contains information about the current cell, including the cell address, cell contents, column width, format and protection status. It also contains the mode indicator. The cell address and contents always appear on the control panel; the other settings appear only when you establish them. The format setting determines the way in which an entry appears in the cell. The protection status tells you if you can currently change the cell contents.

Second line of control panel displays the current entry when you are creating or editing the entry. It displays the main menu, a list of commands that appears when you press slash (/) in READY mode. It also displays a prompt, or request for information thai Lotus 1 -2-3 needs to complete a command which you have selected.

Third line of control displays either a submenu or a one line description of the command currently highlighted on the menu.

Mode indicator tells you in what state or condition Lotus 1-2-3 is currently operating. If often changes when you begin an action, such as executing a command or making an entry.

Status indicator describes a particular program condition or key condition. For example, the CALC indicator tells you that the worksheet formulas need to be recalculated.

Date and time indicator tells you the current date and time. You can change or turn off the display of this indicator using the/Worksheet Global Default command.

Moving Around in the Worksheet

The cell pointer highlights the current cell in the worksheet. You move around in the worksheet by moving the cell pointer with the pointer-movement keys.

Pointer-Movement Keys—You can use the arrow keys (UP, DOWN, LEFT, RIGHT) to move one cell at a time in the worksheet. You can move one screen at a time, using PAGE UP, PAGE DOWN, BIG RIGHT, and BIG LEFT. You can move many screens at a Time using GOTO, HOME or using END in combination with other pointer-movement keys. Many of the pointer-movement keys move the menu pointer among menu commands, in addition to moving the cell pointer in the worksheet.

Data Entry and Editing

You can enter any kind of data in a cell by typing. You can edit an entry as you type it, or return to a completed entry and revise it.

Typing Entries—The simplest method of entering data in a cell is typing. Move the cell pointer to a cell, type the entry, and press RETURN. The entry appears in the cell after you press RETURN. Each character that you type appears on the second line of the control panel. A cursor, or underscore character, indicates where the next character you type will appear. To complete an entry, you can press RETURN or one of the pointer-movement keys. When you press a pointer-movement key, Lotus 1-2-3 completes the entry and moves the cell pointer to another cell in the direction of the pointer-movement key.

When you press RETURN or a pointer-movement key to complete an entry, several things happen (see Fig. 2):

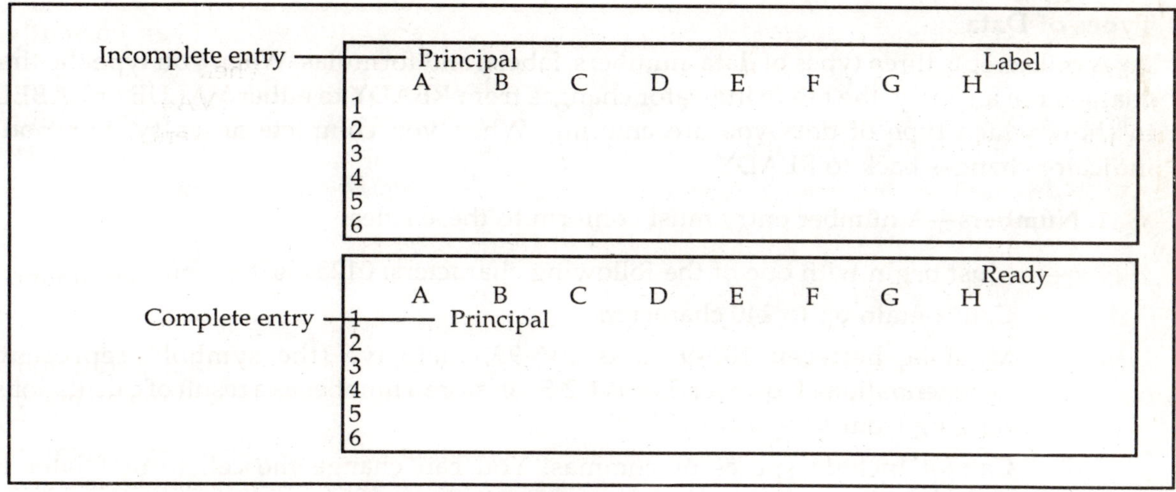

Fig. 2.

1. Lotus 1-2-3 checks for errors in the entry. If it finds an error, Lotus 1-2-3 beeps, places the cursor at the problem location, and switches to EDIT mode.
2. If Lotus 1-2-3 finds no error, it stores the entry in the current cell. The previous entry, if any, disappears from the cell. There is no way to recover the old entry once you complete the new entry.
3. The entry disappears from the second line of the control panel. After you press RETURN, the entry appears on the first line of the control panel. After you press a pointer-movement key, the entry disappears entirely from the control panel.
4. If the recalculation setting is automatic, Lotus 1-2-3 recalculates every formula in the worksheet.
5. Lotus 1-2-3 returns to READY mode.

Editing Entries—You can edit a cell entry as you type it, or you can edit a completed entry. To edit an entry, you must be in the EDIT mode. Lotus 1-2-3 changes to EDIT mode automatically if you try to complete an entry that contains an error. Follow these steps to edit an entry:

1. To edit a complete entry, move the cell pointer to the cell that contains the entry you want to revise. To edit an entry you are currently typing, start with step 2.
2. Press EDIT. The mode indicator in the right corner of the screen changes to EDIT. Use the pointer-movement keys to move the cursor around in the entry.
3. Insert or delete characters at the cursor location.
4. Press RETURN to complete the entry. The cursor can be anywhere in the entry when you press RETURN; it does not have to be at the end.

There is a difference between editing and erasing an entry. To erase an entry, use the / Range Erase command.

Types of Data

A cell accepts three types of data: numbers, labels, and formulas. When you type the first character of an entry, the mode indicator changes from READY to either VALUE or LABEL, to show which type of data you are entering. When you complete an entry, the mode indicator changes back to READY.

1. Numbers—A number entry must conform to these rules:

- Must begin with one of the following characters: 0123456789.+-$(
- Can contain up to 240 characters.
- Must be between 10^-99 and 10^-99, inclusive (the symbol^ represents exponentiation). However, Lotus 1-2-3 can store a number as a result of calculations, ranging from 10^-308 to 10^-08.
- Cannot include spaces or commas. You can change the cell format later to include commas.
- Can have no more than one decimal point.
- Can begin with a currency symbol($), or other nonalphabetic currency character.
- Can end with % to indicate a percentage.
- Can be entered in scientific format, as shown below:

Plus sign Integer between-99 and 99

** **

6.02E+05 = 602.000

— — — **

"c"or"E"

**

**

Positive or negative number

When you enter the first character of a number, the mode indicator on the top right of the screen changes from READY to VALUE. When you complete the number entry, the mode indicator changes back to READY.

Alignment of a Number—A number aligns on the right edge of a cell. You cannot change the alignment of a number entry.

Format of a Number—You can change the format, or appearance, of a number entry in a cell without changing the way Lotus 1-2-3 stores the entry. For example, you can format the entry 65.3 so that it appears as $65.30, 65.3%, or 65. Here are some examples of number entries in different formats:

Number entry	*Format*
- 73	General
$850.32	Currency, 2 decimal places
7254.895	Fixed, 3 decimal places
55.2%	Per cent, 1 decimal place

Long Numbers—A number may have too many characters to fit in a cell. If the format of the cell is General, Lotus 1 -2-3 displays the number in scientific notation. If the format of the cell that contains the number is not General, Lotus 1-2-3 displays asterisks (*****) jn the cell instead of the entry. This docs not affect the way Lotus 1-2-3 stores the entry. When you make the column wide enough, the entire number appears in the worksheet.

Decimal Places—Lotus 1-2-3 can store a number with up to 15 decimal places. The control panel, however, displays a maximum of 9 decimal places. If you enter a number with 12 decimal places, for example, Lotus 1-2-3 calculates the entry using 12 decimal places, although you can see only 9 decimal placc numbers on the control panel.

2. Labels—Any entry that Lotus 1-2-3 determines is not a number or a formula, is a label. Often, label entries are descriptive text such as MAY SALES or Principal. A label can consist of any characters in the Lotus International Character Set (LICS).

A label must conform to these rules:

— Must begin with either a label-prefix character or any character that does not indicate the start of a number or formula.
— Can contain up to 240 characters.
— Can contain number characters, as long as the first character is a label-prefix character.

When you enter the first character of a label, the mode indicator changes from READY TO LABEL. When you complete a label entry, the mode indicator changes back to READY.

Label-Prefix Characters—Beginning an entry with a label-prefix character determines how the entry is aligned in the cell. There are three choices for labels: right-aligned, centered, or left-aligned. If you do not enter a label-prefix character, Lotus 1-2-3 automatically aligns the label entry according to the default worksheet alignment. Unless you change it, the default label alignment is left. A label-prefix character does not appear in the worksheet cell; it appears on the first line of the control panel when the cell pointer is on the cell.

You can also type a backslash(®) as the first character of a label entry. Characters you type after the backslash repeat across the worksheet cell. For example, ®* creates a cell filled with asterisks.

Entering Numbers as Labels—To enter a label that starts with a digit or another character that Lotus 1-2-3 recognises as a number character, use a label-prefix character. A label-prefix character identifies the entry as a label, no matter what characters the entry contains. For example, use a label-prefix character at the beginning of an entry such as 96 Lake Street. If you omit the label-prefix character in such an entry , Lotus 1 -2-3 beeps and changes to EDIT mode so that you can correct thc entry.

Long Labels—If you enter a label entry that is loo long to appear in one cell, the entry extends into the blank cells to the right. If the cells to the right are filled, Lotus 1 -2-3 cuts off the entry at the right edge of the cell. Lotus 1-2-3 stores the whole entry even if it cannot display the whole entry in the worksheet cell. To make the complete entry appear in the worksheet cell, erase the cell entries to the right, or widen the column that contains the entry.

3. Formulas—A formula is an instruction to calculate with numbers or text. It can contain values, such as 8, operators, such as + , and cell address, such as A7. When you enter a cell address in the formula, Lotus 1-2-3 calculates with the value contained in that cell. A formula can also contain @ functions, which are discussed later. A formula results in a value.

A formula must conform to these rules:

— Must begin with one of the following characters: 0 1 2 3 4 5 6 7 8 9. + (@ # $
— Can contain between 1 and 240 characters.
— Cannot contain spaces, except within a range name or a text string.
— Must begin with a plus sign (+) if the first part of the formula is a cell address.

When you enter the first character of a formula, the mode indicator on the top right of the screen changes from READY to VALUE. When you complete the formula, the mode indicator changes back to READY.

Viewing a Formula—When you complete a formula entry, its value, or result, appears in the worksheet cell. For example, after you enter the formula 25+75, the value 100 appears in the cell. To see the formula itself, move the cell pointer to the cell that contains the formula and look at the first line of the control panel. You can change the format of the formula cell so that the formula, rather than its value, appears in the cell.

Ranges

A range is a rectangular block of cells. It can be a single cell, a row, a column, or several rows and columns (see Fig. 3). Lotus 1-2-3 prompts, or requests, you to enter a range during many commands. For example, Lotus 1 -2-3 prompts you to enter a range when you use the/Move command to move a group of cells to another part of the worksheet. You can also enter a range in an @ function, (see Entering Formulas).

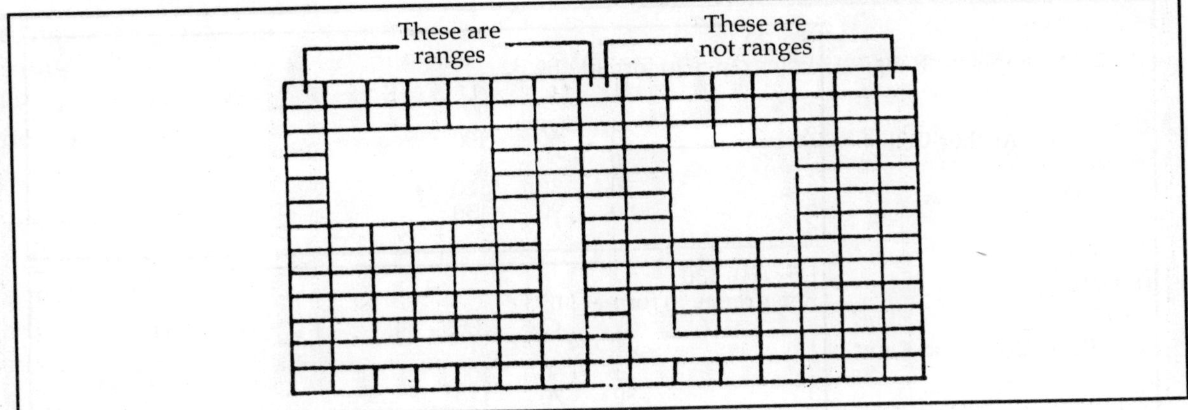

Fig. 3.

Entering Ranges Ranges can be entered in three ways:

1. Typing cell addresses
2. Highlighting the range by expanding the cell pointer
3. Using a range name that you create with the /Range Name Create command.

1. Typing Cell Addresses—You enter a range address by typing the addresses of any two diagonally opposite comers of the range, separated by one or two periods. For example, G5..H29 specifies the range whose corner cells are G5 and H29. Do not use spaces in a range address. When you are entering a range during a command, press RETURN to complete the range address. For example:

Enter range to format: Al2..H 19 RETURN

Lotus 1-2-3 displays range addresses with the upper left and lower right comer cells, separated by two periods.

2. Highlighting a Range—To highlight a range during a command, move the cell pointer to a cell that is in one corner of the intended range and press PERIOD. This cell is now the anchor cell. The cell that the pointer is currently on is the free cell, indicated by the cursor. The range address appears on the control panel: the anchor cell address and the free cell address, separated by two periods.

Use the pointer-movement keys to expand the range by moving the free cell to another cell in the worksheet. Lotus 1-2-3 highlights the entire area between the anchor cell and the free cell. To complete specifying the range address, press RETURN (see Fig. 4).

Some commands, such as /Range Format, automatically make the current cell the anchor cell. If you want to make another cell the anchor cell, press ESCAPE, move the pointer to the desired cell, and press PERIOD.

1-2-3 Prompts for Ranges — B2 : 20 Enter range to format : B2.B2 — Point

Anchor Cell — B2

	A	B	C	D	E	F	G	H
1								
2		20	60	100				
3		30	70	110				
4		40	80	120				
5		50	90	130				
6								

Press Down and Right — D5 : (F0) 130 Enter range to format : B2.D5 — Point

	A	B	C	D	E	F	G	H
1								
2		20	60	100				
3		30	70	110				
4		40	80	120				
5		50	90	130				
6								

Press Return to Complete Range — D2 : (C2) 20 Enter range to format : B2.D5 — Ready

	A	B	C	D	E	F	G	H
1								
2		$20.00	$60.00	$100.00				
3		$30.00	$70.00	$110.00				
4		$40.00	$80.00	$120.00				
5		$50.00	$90.00	$130.00				
6								

Fig. 4.

3. Naming a Range—To make a range easier to refer to, you can name it. For example, you can give the range A54..B98 the name SALES. After you name a range, you can use the range name instead of typing the range address or highlighting the range in a command or formula. A range name is often easier to remember than a range address, because the name can describe the contents of a range.

Defined Ranges—With most commands, Lotus 1-2-3 remembers the most recent range you indicated. This range is called a defined range. The next time you select the same command, Lotus 1-2-3 highlights the defined range and displays the upper left and lower right comer cell addresses on the control panel. You have three choices:

1. Accept the current definition. Press RETURN to leave the range definition unchanged.
2. Change the definition. Use the pointer-movement keys to change the highlighted range, and then press RETURN; or you can press BACKSPACE or ESCAPE and highlight a new range.
3. Enter a new definition. Type a range address, type an existing range name, or press NAME and choose a range name from the menu.

Entering Formulas

Lotus 1-2-3 allows you to enter three types of formulas:

1. Arithmetic formulas, which calculate with numeric values using arithmetic operators. For example, +H 16/12 divides the number in cell HI 6 by 12. (see Table 1).
2. Text formulas, which calculate with labels using the text operator, the ampersand (&) character. For example +B4& "Revenues" combines the label in B4 with the word Revenues.
3. Logical formulas, which compare values in two or more cells using the logical operators. A logical formula is a statement that produces a value that is either 0 (meaning FALSE) or 1 (meaning TRUE). For example, +BALANCE>=500 RETURNS THE VALUE 1 (TRUE) if the value in a cell named BALANCE is greater than or equal to 500. Otherwise, it returns the value 0 (FALSE).

Values You can enter the following values in a formula:

— Numbers (450, -92. 7.1 El 2)
— Text strings enclosed in double quotation marks ("Suresh K Basandra", "Total")
— Cell addresses of cells that contain numbers or labels (A12, FF23)
— Range names (JAN SALES)
— @functions [@SUM(A4..A8)]

Order or Operations—Table 1 shows the operators you can use in formulas and their precedence numbers. These numbers represent the order in which Lotus 1-2-3 performs
Table 1

Precedence of Operations

Operator	*Operation*	*Precedence Number*
^	Exponentiation	7
-	Negative, Positive	6
*/	Multiplication, Division	5
+ -	Addition, Subtraction	4
= < >	Equal, Not Equal	3
< >	Less Than Greater Than	3
< =	Less than or equal	3
> =	Greater than or equal	3
#NOT#	Logical NOT	2
#AND#	Logical AND	1
#OR#	Logical OR	1
&	String combination	1

operations in a formula. Lotus 1-2-3 performs an operation with a higher precedence number be fore an operation with a lower precedence number. Operations with the same precedence number are performed sequentially from left to right.

Overriding Precedence Numbers—You can override precedence numbers by putting parentheses around an operation. Lotus 1-2-3 performs operations in parentheses first. Within each set of parentheses, precedence number apply. You can include up to 32 sets.of parentheses within parentheses in a formula. Example below shows how Lotus 1 -2-3 performs the operation in a formula according to precedence number:

450 + ((5000 + A20) *.145) / 12 — J30

4th 1st 2nd 3rd 5th

Lotus 1-2-3 will perform the operations in the above order.

Relative, Absolute and Mixed Cell Addresses—Cell addresses in formulas can be relative, absolute or mixed. The difference between relative, absolute and mixed cell addresses is important when you copy formulas.

1. Use a relative address to refer to the position of a cell in relation to the cell that contains the formula. A relative address is not a permanent reference to a particular cell. For example:

Cell address	*Meaning in a formula in HII*
G5	the cell one column left and six rows above this one

2. Use an absolute address to refer to the same cell, no matter where you copy the formula to. An absolute address is a permanent reference to a particular cell. For example:

Cell address	*Meaning in a formula in HII*
G5	Cell G5.

3. Use a mixed address to make a cell reference that is part relative and part absolute either the column letter or the row number remains constant. For example:

Cell address	*Meaning in a formula in HII*
$G5	the cell in column G, 6 rows above this one
G$5	the cell one column left of this one. in row 5

Cell addresses are relative by default.

Indicating Absolute, Relative, and Mixed Ranges—When typing a cell or range address, specify an absolute or mixed address by typing the $ in front of the appropriate row number or column letter. You can also indicate absolute, mixed and relative addresses when pointing. After you point to a cell or range and before you type the next character, press ABS repeatedly. The range address on the control panel cycles through absolute, mixed and relative:

Range address	*Action*
@sum(C50..C65	press ABS
@sum(C50..C65	press ABS
@sum(C$50..C$65	press ABS
@sum($C50..$C65	press ABS
@sum(C60..C65	press ABS

You can edit an existing cell or range address. Move the cell pointer to the cell that contains the formula and press EDIT. Move the cursor to the address you want to change, and press ABS repeatedly to cycle the address through relative, absolute and mixed. You can also type the $ in front of the appropriate letter or number to make the address absolute or mixed. Delete all the dollar signs ($) to make the address relative.

Entering Addresses in Formulas—You can enter a cell or range address in a formula by typing it or by pointing to it. With the pointing method, you use the pointer-movement keys to move the cell pointer to the cell or range whose address you want to enter.

Pointing to a Cell—To point to a cell in a formula, first type an operator (see Table 1). Then move the cell pointer to thc cell whose address you want to include. The cell address appears on the control panel . Type the next operator, or press RETURN to complete the formula. The pointer returns to the cell in which you are entering the formula, (see Fig. 5).

Pointing to a Range—The only kind of formula that contains a range is an @function. To point to a range in an @function, first type the @function name and a left parenthesis. Then move the cell pointer to a cell, or one corner of the intended range and press PERIOD. This cell is now the anchor cell. The cell that the cell pointer is currently on is the free cell, indicated by the cursor. The range address appears on the control panel — the anchor cell and the free cell, separated by two periods. Until you press a pointer-movement key, the anchor cell and the free cell are the same.

Use the pointer-movement keys to expand the range by moving the free cell to another cell in the worksheet. Lotus 1-2-3 highlights the entire area between the anchor cell and the free cell. Complete the range address by typing the next character in the @function.

Changing the Entry—When you point to a cell or range in a formula, two keys let you change the cell or range you have selected: ESCAPE and BACKSPACE. The effects of these keys are described below:

Key	*Single Cell*	*Range*
ESCAPE	Erases address; returns cell pointer to formula cell; made indicator returns to VALUE	Erases free cell address; returns pointer to anchor cell, unanchored, mode indicator remains POINT
BACKSPACE	Returns cell pointer to formula cell; mode indicator remains POINT	Returns pointer to formula cell, unanchored mode indicator remains POINT

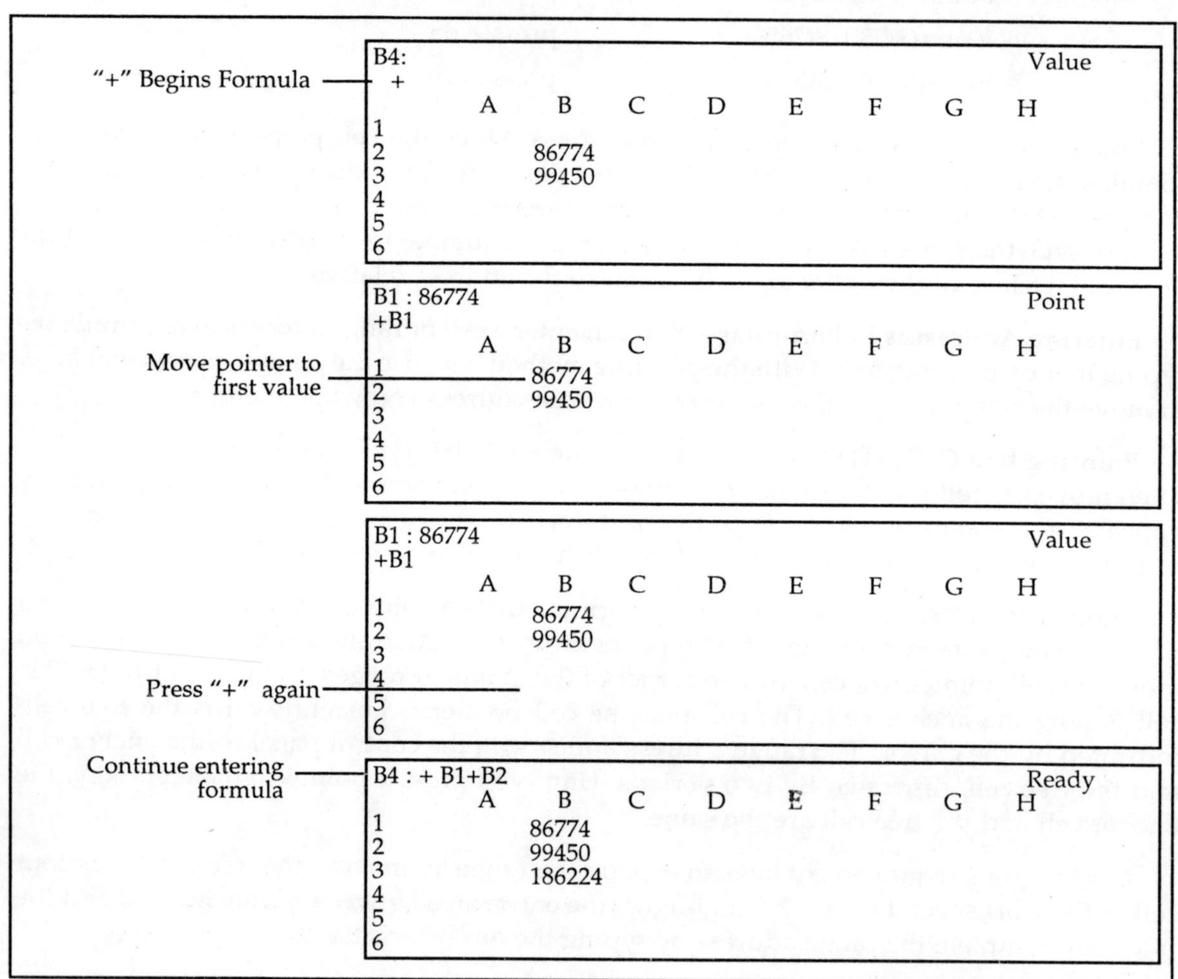

Fig. 5.

@Functions—Lotus 1-2-3 has a special set of built-in formulas called ©functions. ©functions are different from regular formulas because you supply the values, but not the operators.

Format of a Function—An @function contains specific elements: The @function name and the values, which are enclosed in parentheses. Values in @functions are called arguments. An @function can have no arguments, one argument, or several arguments.

```
Name of @function          Close parenthesis
!                          !
@NAME(argl. arg2...)
```

Many @functions allow you to perform common calculations more easily than standard formulas. For example, the @function @SUM(B4..B10) performs the same task as the formula +B4+B5+B6+B7+B8+B9+B10, but the @function is easier to enter. Other @functions perform complex calculations efficiently. For example, the @function @PV calculates the present value of an annuity, which would otherwise require a complicated formula.

Indicators

An indicator is a highlighted word that appears in the upper right corner of the control panel or at the bottom of the screen. Lotus 1 -2-3 has three kinds of indicators: mode status, and date and time.

1. Mode Indicators—During a Lotus 1-2-3 session, a mode indicator is always visible on the upper right corner of the control panel. This indicator tells you in what state or condition Lotus 1-2-3 is currently operating. Often the mode indicator, changes when you begin action, such as executing a command or making an entry. For example, when you begin to enter a label entry, the mode indicator changes to LABEL.

Mode Indicator	*Meaning*
EDIT	An entry is being edited or needs to be edited
ERROR	An error has occurred; press ESCAPE or RETURN to clear
FILES	A menu of files is being displayed
	A /Data Query Find operation is in progress
HELP	The Help facility has been invoked
LABEL	You arc entering a label
MENU	A command menu is being displayed
POINT	The cell pointer is pointing to a cell or range
READY	Lotus 1-2-3 is ready for the next entry or command
VALUE	You are entering a number or formula
WAIT	A command or process is being executed

2. Status Indicators—Status indicators, which appear on the bottom right corner of the screen, indicate a particular program condition or key condition. For example the CALC indicator tells you that the worksheet's formulas need to be recalculated, and the NUM indicator tells you that the number key has been pressed.

Status Indicator	*Meaning*
CALC	The worksheet's formulas need to be recalculated; press the CALC key
CAPS	The CAPS LOCK key is on
CIRC	The worksheet contains a formula that refers to itself (occurs only when the recalculation order is Natural)
CMD	Lotus 1-2-3 is pausing during a macro
END	The END Key is on
NUM	The NUM LOCK key is on
OVR	The INSERT key is on
SCROLL	The SCROLL LOCK key is on
STEP	Single-step mode has been turned on; once invoked, macros will be processed one step at a time
SST	A macro is currently being executed one step at a time

3. Date and Time Indicator—Lotus 1-2-3 displays the date and time in the lower left corner of the screen. You can change or turn off the display of this indicator using the / Worksheet Global Default command.

Lotus 1-2-3 Keys

The following table contains a brief description of the standard Lotus 1-2-3 keys. To determine which keys on your computer's keyboard are equivalent to these keys, see the keyboard guide available with Lotus 1-2-3 package.

KEY	**DESCRIPTION**
ABS	Cycles a cell address through relative, absolute and mixed in POINT and EDIT modes
BACKSPACE	Erases character to left of cursor; if a range is selected, erases current range
BACKTAB	Moves cell pointer on screen to the left in READY mode; moves cursor five characters to the left in EDIT mode
BREAK	Cancels current procedure
CALC	Recalculates all worksheet formulas in READY mode; converts a formula into its current value in VALUE mode and EDIT mode
CAPS LOCK	Makes letter keys produce only upper-case letters; number and punctuation keys are not affected
COMPOSE	When used in combination with certain keys, makes international characters

CONTROL	When used in combination with cetain keys, changes the function of those keys.
DELETE	Erases current character in EDIT mode
EDIT	Places highlighted entry on the control panel for editing
ESCAPE	Cancels current entry or range, or returns to previous command step
GOTO	Moves cell pointer to the cell you specify
GRAPH	Displays the graph most recently specified
HELP	Invokes the Help facility
INSERT	Switches between inserting the text by moving existing text to the right and replacing existing text.
MACRO	Invokes a macro when used in combination with a macro name
NAME	Produces a menu of the current range names in POINT mode
PERIOD	When entering a range, anchors pointer if unanchored, or cycles anchor cell and free cell in range
QUERY	Repeats the last /Data Query command
RETURN	Completes an entry, a command, or part of a command
SCROLL LOCK	Switches arrow keys between moving the pointer and moving the window
SHIFT	When used in combination with another key on the typewriter section of the keyboard, produces the upper symbol on the key
SPACE	Inserts a space
STEP	Invokes single-step mode for macros: Macros are processed one step at a time
TAB	In READY mode, moves pointer one screen to the right; in EDIT mode, moves cursor five characters to the right
TABLE	Repeals the last /Data Table command specified
WINDOW	Switches pointer between the two windows when there is a split screen

Help Facility

At any time while you are using Lotus 1 -2-3, you can press HELP to invoke the Help facility. Lotus 1-2-3 temporarily suspends the session and displays information about the operation currently in progress. The HELP indicator appears in the upper right corner of the control panel. Each Help screen includes a menu of additional Help topics. Use the pointer-movement keys to select a topic, and press RETURN. Press BACKSPACE to view the previous Help screen. To return to the worksheet, press ESCAPE.

GRAPHICS

Introduction

Graphics are a quick and efficient visual way of communicating statistical data. Often, a single graph can provide a welcome shortcut to a busy executive by presenting the information contained in page after page of numeric data. Until recently, computer-generated graphics were very expensive to create. They could be created only through the use of expensive graphics workstations and associated graphics software. In recent years, the cost of the hardware has plummeted, and general purpose graphics software packages has become widely available. Today's graphics software can be used in a broad range of applications. Moreover, unlike most older graphics software, most current programs do not require expensive, specialised graphics terminals. The result has been a boom in the use of business graphics.

What is Computer Graphics?

Computer graphics is a pictorial or graphic representation displayed or produced by a computer. There are two essential parts to the original definition; first, creating the graph or picture, and second, the role of the computer. Computer-produced graphics may be displayed on a CRT (Cathode Ray Tube), formed by deposits of ink on paper on transparency film, recorded on photographic film, or printed on a line printer. Graphics may be in black and white or in colour. As for the role of the computer, it may create a picture by convening numeric information into graphic format, modify graphic information or merely produce the picture from previously stored plot commands.

Computer graphics can be subdivided into several classifications. Graphic plotters or plotter/printers produce hard copy you can hold in your hand. The term "hardcopy graphics" usually means graphics on paper but is sometimes extended to include other non-volatile output of computer pictures (i.e. output that will not be destroyed when the power is turned off). Thus, we could stretch the definition to include copies of pictures saved on tape or disk and also photographs or slides. There are CRT graphic devices which create volatile or "soft" graphics. When you turn the power off, no picture remains. Depending on the application, you may use either or both types of graphic output.

Another term you hear increasingly often is "interactive computer graphics," The word interactive is subject to many interpretations, but it always means there is some communication between the user and the computer in "real time" while the program that creates graphics is running. Most interactive applications involve the use of a graphics display (CRT), but this is not a requirement. Digitisers can be used to input data and plotters to output it in an interactive manner, as can an alphanumeric keyboard, without the presence of a CRT. In some interactive applications, the user selects from a menu or list which picture is to be drawn, or perhaps its size or colour.

In other applications, when the user sees the picture or plot, he chooses a suitable program branch or course of action. For example, in process control, he may turn a machine off or close a valve depending on what he sees. In a third type of application data may be entered while the program is running, using an input device such as light pen or digitiser.

Graphics Generation Methods

Current computer graphic output devices are of two main types, vector and raster. Both soft and hard copy devices can be classified in this way.

A vector device creates graphics by drawing continuous lines from one defined point to another. In general, vector devices provide high quality output with high resolution. On a vector display, lines are drawn on the CRT by an electron beam moving directly from one endpoint of a line to the other. The beam excites phosphors on the face of the CRT so the lines become visible. A vector display is sometimes called a stroke writer; vector devices are also called calligraphic devices. A vector display has a limit to the total length of lines that can be drawn without flicker becoming a problem. Unless all lines can be redrawn within the refresh cycle (normally 1/60 of a second), the plotted data will appear to flicker on the screen. Stroke writers are found in the most expensive turnkey systems. On a vector plotter lines are drawn with a pen just like when you write with a pen. Pen speed on a vector plotter is sacrificed somewhat for line quality.

A raster device, on the other hand, creates graphics in an entirely different manner. To understand this you need to know what constitutes a raster. A raster device has a fixed number of dots or locations, arranged in a fixed number of rows and columns. You can think of raster as being a two-dimensional matrix or as an area divided into smaller areas, like a sheet of postage stamps. A raster is sometimes described by the number of rows and columns. Thus, a sheet of 100 postage stamps is a 10 x 10 raster. The resolution of a raster device depends on, and increases with, the number of rows and columns per unit area. Imagine a giant sheet of postage stamps spread over a section of a college football stadium. This sheet of postage stamps has greater resolution than the card cheering section located in the same area (where each student sitting in the section holds a large "card" over his head to produce a picture) because there are more stamps than cards per unit area. On a device which creates graphics, each location in the raster or matrix corresponds to a location in the computer's memory. Raster devices are growing in popularity and resolution as computer memory decreases in price and increases in availability.

A raster device creates graphics by selectively turning dots on or off. Again a raster device can be a CRT or a hard copy device. On a raster graphics printer, dots which are "on" are printed on paper; dots which are "off result in blank paper. Raster plotters or printers can be either impact (like a typewriter), or thermal (where heat creates print on special paper) or electrostatic (where an electric charge on the paper attracts toner). On a raster display, dots correspond to screen locations which are either on or off (illuminated or not illuminated). To determine if a dot is on, a raster device "scans" or examines an area of computer memory many times each second. A raster is usually scanned from top to bottom, one row at a time, left to right in each row. The larger the print or display area, the greater the resolution; the more colours that can be displayed, the more computer memory is required. Because a location in computer memory can change value instantaneously, raster graphics on the CRT can be updated in real time. In fact, the image could change every refresh cycle. Raster devices can create filled areas quickly; there is no limit to the amount of a screen's area that can be illuminated. Flicker is not a problem. Raster printers can generally plot complex graphs more quickly than vector plotters, but with less resolution.

Colour Graphics At A Glance—Colour, graphics is a microcosm of the larger world of graphics. The same generation methods, vector and raster, exist in the colour world. The same trends toward increased quality and resolution are evident. Vector plotters have progressed from one pen models to models with multi-colour automatic pen selection. Some stroke writing displays the use of a beam penetration technique to excite phosphors of different colours deposited in distinct layers on the face of the CRT. In the raster world, more colours are possible, and, each year, new systems with better colour, both CRT and hardcopy devices, appear on the market. Skeptics say you do not need colour for graphics, but most people involved in graphics will secretly admit that colour is the name of the game. The development of colour graphics will parallel the development of colour TV; the thrust is toward reduced cost and improved quality.

Improvements in the quality of colour raster displays imply some advances in technology. To be able to specify colour implies additional memory, for along with the position you must specify the colour of a point or line. In a raster device, using three primary colours to create eight colours takes three times as much memory for storage of the raster image. If you want colours displayed in various shades and intensities, say hot pink or deep purple, you need to add 3 to 16 times more memory depending on how many colours you have and how you specify them. Considering these colour improvements together with the trend toward increased raster resolution, it is obvious that a large increase in memory is required for even a small increase in resolution when colour is included.

To achieve higher resolution requires more complex circuitry to drive the CRT. Colour systems already in production have video circuitry six times as fast as that in your colour TV set. Higher resolution CRTs will require further advances in this area. Colour systems also require more powerful microprocessors to handle the more complex algorithms necessary to display colour graphics. Improvements in colour will require the development of both microprocessors and algorithms. Finally, development of colour hard copy to accurately and inexpensively reproduce raster CRT images lags behind CRT development. There are those who believe colour graphics will not really take off until good solutions to the problem of raster hard copy exist.

Uses of Computer Graphics

According to one study, the field of computer graphics is growing al the rate of 25% per year. This growth can also be seen in the increasing number and kinds of graphics systems available, the number of installations using graphics and the variety of applications which have developed. Applications of computer graphics are sometimes broken down into two classifications. One is data display or data presentation graphics; the other is design and image graphics.

Data display graphics provide symbolic representation of numerical data. This data can be from scientific investigation, industrial monitoring and testing, or management statistics. Mostly graphics are used for data display applications. The common forms of display graphics are bar charts, line graphs and pie charts. Such graphics are designed for human appeal and clarity.

Design graphics, on the other hand, represent actual physical or geographical data. The form of the graphics depends entirely on the application. Generally speaking, design graphics require higher resolution devices than do data display graphics and have a high degree of interactiveness. Design graphics include computer-aided design (CAD), computer-aided manufacturing (CAM), image processing and mapping. Historically, the first computer graphics users fell under the design category and used graphics in military and computer-aided design applications. CAD has now spread well beyond the automotive and aircraft industries where it had its beginnings. Design graphics play an important part in the manufacture of printed circuit boards and in electronic design. Other design applications include apparel graphics (pattern and fabric cutting), structural engineering (finite element analysis), and mechanical drafting. Turnkey systems and large plotters are frequently used in design graphics applications.

Another group of design graphics applications can be classified as image processing. Image processing started with the analysis of satellite resource photos. Computer-aided tomography (CAT) for medical analysis of X-rays is an addition to the list of image processing applications. Closely related to image processing is mapping. Mapping includes construction of maps from census data, maps for business planning (store locations and demographics), surveying and civil engineering maps, and maps to monitor utilities and natural resources. As you can see, the uses of computer graphics arc varied and widespread.

Good Graphic Form(s)

In the previous section we divided computer graphics into two types, design graphics which are used interactively to create pictures, and data display graphics which usually produce graphs from stored data. In this section we will discuss the three common types of graphs used in data display graphics: line graphs, bar charts and pie charts. The objective is to give some insight into the variety of graphs that can be created to convey numerical information, and to teach you some principles of good graphic form. Please do not be concerned, at this point in time, that you do not know enough about graphic programming to write the program to actually draw the graph. Just try to understand each form so that you can judge which one is best suited to a particular application and what makes the form effective.

What is good graphics form? There is no easy answer. To measure the success of a graphic presentation, you would need to test whether the information was correctly conveyed in less time than could have been done verbally or in a text form. From graphics, the viewer should gain some information about mathematical or numerical relationships between data.

In designing a graph, you need to consider the nature of the data, the medium of presentation (CRT, slides, paper, in colour or black and white), the purpose of the chart, the audience (size and type) and the time available for preparation and presentation. Some of these concerns are more important than others.

1. Line Graphs

Let us first consider the line graph, sometimes called a rectilinear coordinate chart. Line graphs are used in both business and scientific applications. The points in a data set are connected, in order, by a single line, sometimes straight. More than one set of data points can be represented on a single graph, with each line differentiated by colour or line type (dotted, dashed or solid). While line graphs usually have linearly scaled perpendicular axes, one or both axes may be scaled logarithmically. These graphs are called semi-log and log-log graphs respectively. Logarithmic scaling is used where data extends over a wide range of values and appears most frequently in scientific, as opposed to business, applications. A line chart is frequently used to plot some variable versus time; the X-axis usually denotes time. Other uses of line charts include frequency distributions and any charts where data is

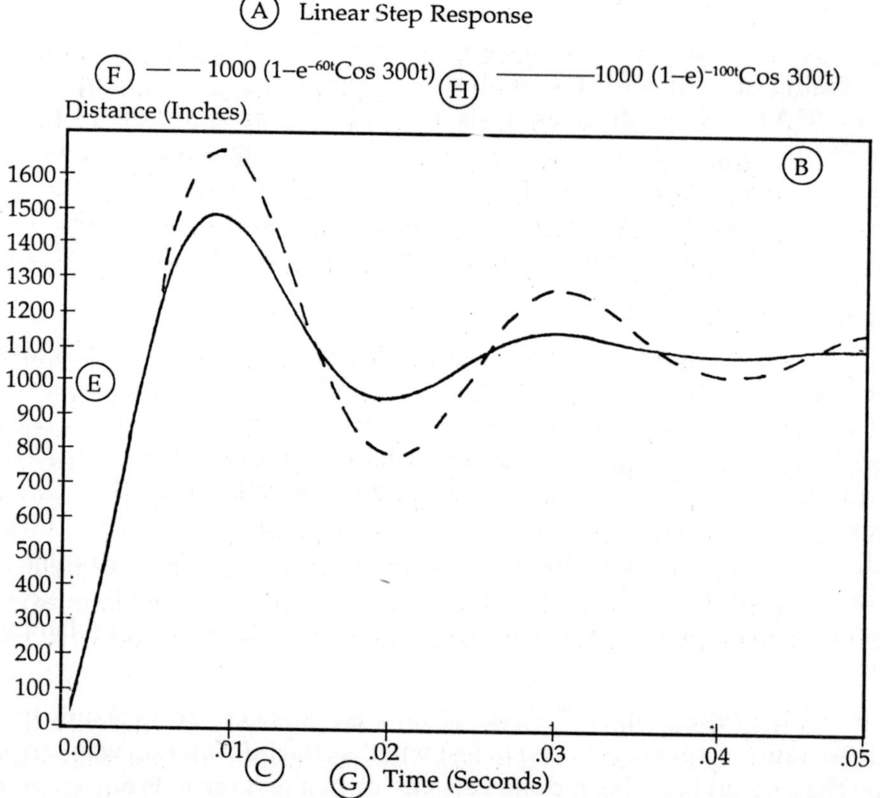

Fig. 6. A Linear Line Chart Showing Step Response Overtime.

a function of two variables. Examples of a linear and a semi-log line graphs are given in Figures 6 and 7 respectively.

Line graph shown in Figure 6 is used to illustrate the essential parts of almost all graphs. Every graph should have a title (A) which states what, where and how. The title is best placed above the picture. The area covered by the graph is usually framed (outlined) (B) and that area is scaled to fit the data. The axes are marked with this scale (C), (D) and tick marks (small lines at regular intervals) (E), or grid lines (which extend across the plotting area) are drawn along the axes. Axes are labeled and tilled, (F), (G) usually with horizontal labels placed below the X-axis and-above the Y-axis so as not to detract from the data presented. It is common practice to leave superfluous zeros off axis labels and indicate the multiplier in the title. When there are multiple lines on a graph, each line should be identified with either a horizontal label near the line or a legend placed away from all lines (H). The legend is often placed to the left of the Y-axis labels or below the title. The most important point to remember when annotating a graph is that nothing should detract from the plotted data.

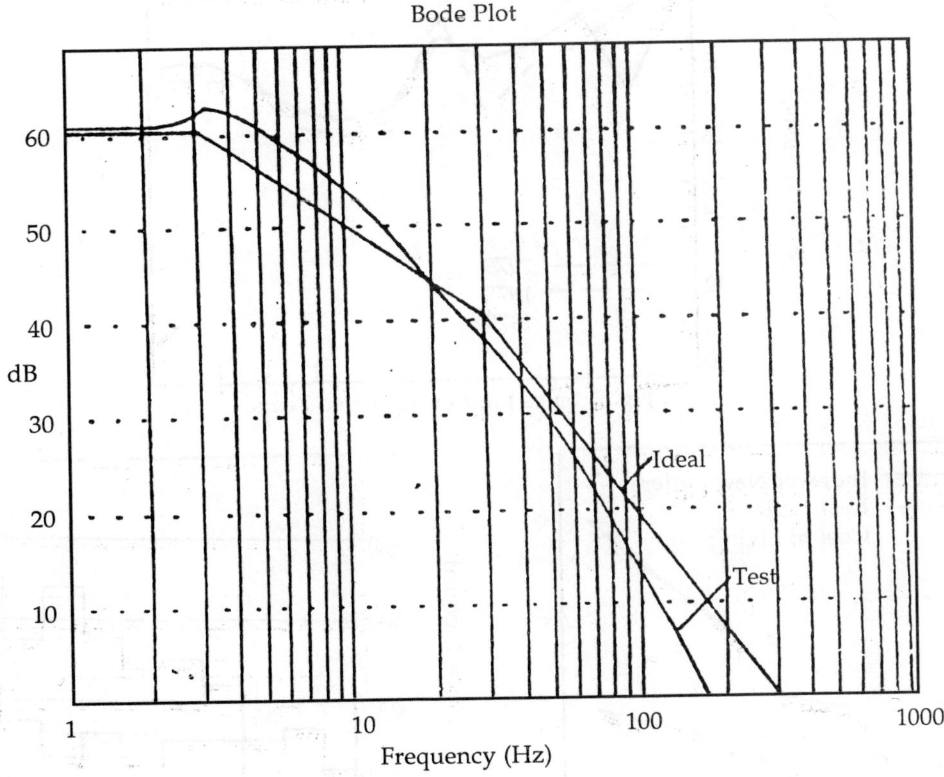

Fig. 7. A Sami-log Plot Where the X-axis is Logarithmic and the Y-axis Linear.

Now for some common variations of a line graph. One variation is to have two separate scales in the X or Y direction, one for each of the two lines of a graph. Care must be taken to

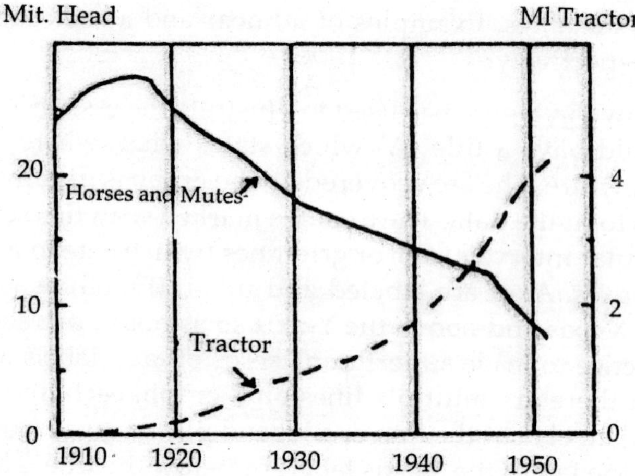

Fig. 8. Horses and Mules, and Tractors on Famrs Jan. 1

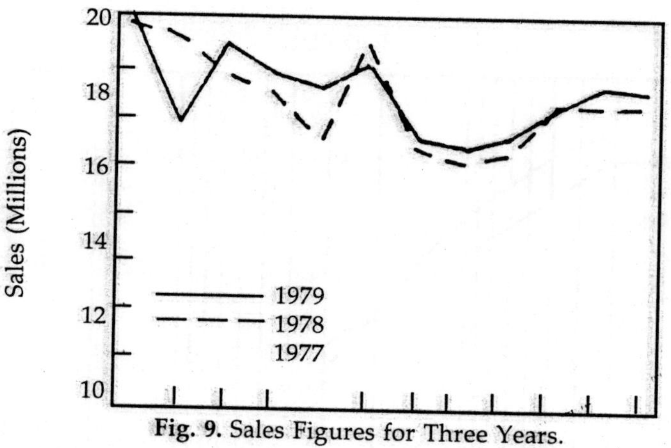

Fig. 9. Sales Figures for Three Years.

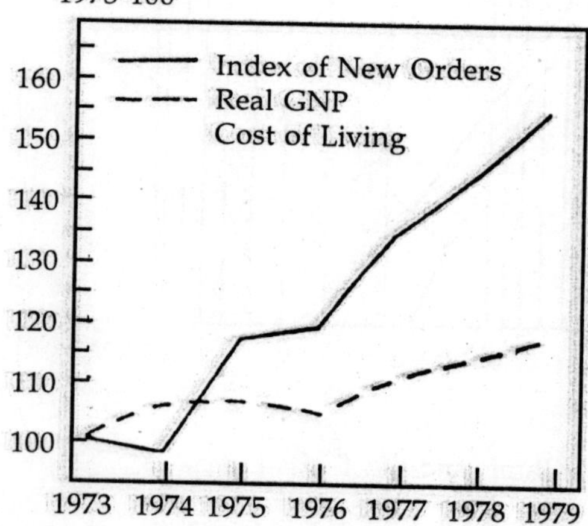

Fig. 10. Economic indicators for Camelot

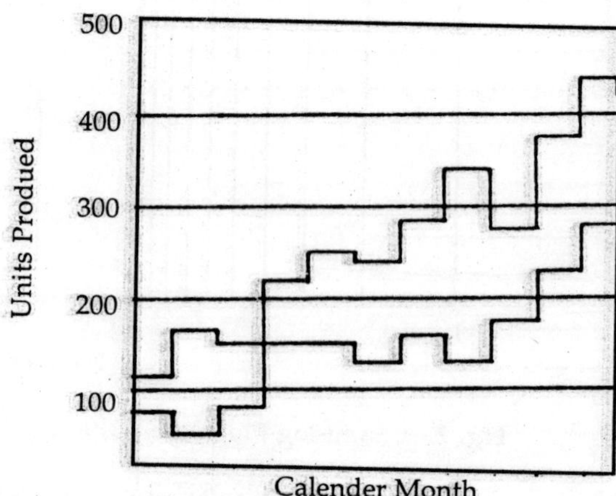

Fig. 11. A Surface Step Chart

interpret data on the proper scale. Look at the graph shown in Figure 8 and determine when the number of tractors equalled the number of horses or mules. If you did not examine the scaling on both sides, you probably said 1945, but on closer examination you will see that in 1945 there were approximately 2.2 million tractors and 12 million horses or mules. The two values are never equal on this graph.

Another simple variation is the plotting of more than one time period on the same axis. Figure 9 shows sales figures for three years. It is much easier to compare January figures in successive years on this graph than if it were spaced out over 36 months in the X-axis. In a third variation an extra reference line is plotted; for instance the cost of living line might be plotted on a graph designed to show the index of new orders and real GNP as in Figure 10

The final variation we will illustrate is a surface chart. Here the areas between lines are shaded. Surface charts are not well suited to vector graphics because of the length of time required to do area fill. They are, however, well suited to raster graphics. A surface step chart is shown in Figure 11. On a step chart, a horizontal line is drawn at the proper Y value. This line extends over one whole lime interval. The line then steps to the next value.

2. *Bar Charts*

The bar chart is a popular chart especially appropriate for comparing size or parts of a total. The length of each bar is proportional to the quantity or amount of each category represented. We will make no distinction between bars that are horizontal and bars that are vertical. However, some people call graphs with vertical bars column graphs. There are many variations of the simple bar graph. Illustrated here are six variations of the bar graph.

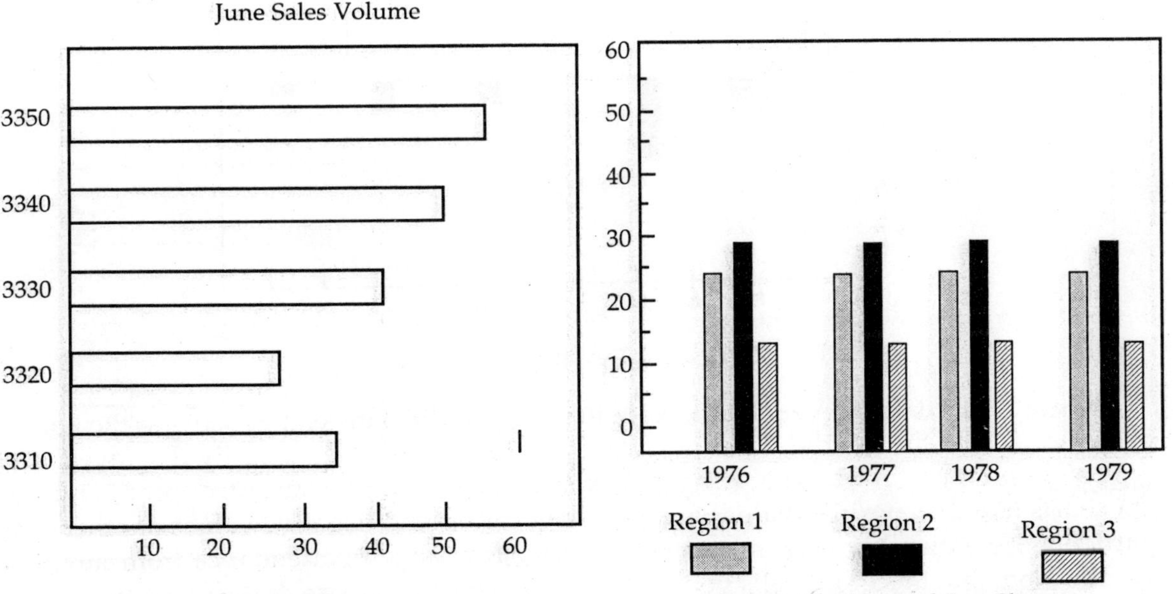

Fig. 12. A Simple Bar Chart

Fig. 13. A Clustered Bar Chart

Figure 12 is a simple bar chart consisting of five bars representing sales volume for each of five items. Five is sometimes cited as the upper limit for the number of items represented on one chart. This however depends on the data; for instance, there is no reason why ten years of sales data showing a trend could not be represented on a graph of total sales. Five is probably a valid limit if the sales graph shows a year's sales by region and is to be used to compare regions with one another.

Figure 13 shows sales by region for three divisions over a four year period. When more than one bar refers to the same X-axis value and the bars for that value are close together or touching, we call the graph a clustered or comparative bar chart. Again, there is an upper limit to the number of bars that can be "clustered" and still be an effective graph. Each bar of the cluster is usually a different colour or hatched using a distinct pattern. This means a four colour plotter can produce a graph with four shaded bars per cluster. A monochromatic graph can also have four, one solid bar, two with hatching (narrow and wide), and one clear area. The solid shading should be in the smallest segment because it is easiest to interpret the value of a shaded area. For easy pattern recognition, a large hatch pattern should be reserved for large areas. You seldom put a large patterned floral wallpaper in a 9 x 10 foot room!

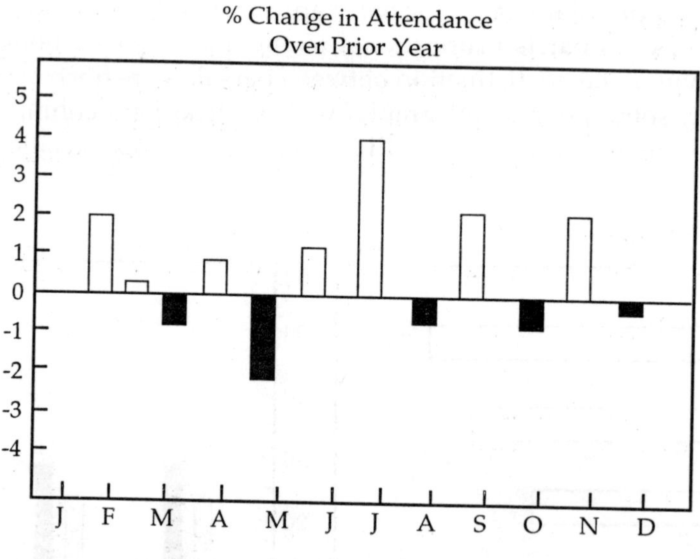

Fig. 14. A Deviation Bar Chart

Figure 14 is a deviation bar chart. Note that the zero line, instead of being at the bottom of the scale, is in the middle. Thus positive and negative values are easily displayed. This type of graph is useful when showing an increase or decrease in quantity, or profit and loss. On charts like this, positive values are often one colour and negative values another. This particular deviation bar chart shows the percentage change in attendance from month to month. Note that this graph tells you nothing about the % increase or decrease for the year as a whole, except that, because you see more bars above the line, you might assume attendance increased. Total attendance figures might be added to this chart using a second Y-axis scale, or the data plotted in line graph form, if the main interest was in the total attendance. The graphic form you use will depend somewhat on the ideas you wish to convey.

A segmented or stacked bar graph. Figure 15, consists of one bar for each X-axis value, with portions of each bar coloured or patterned to represent the Y-value for one component. In this example, which uses the same data used in Figure 13, the whole bar represents the total sales in a given year. Each pattern identifies that part of the total attributed to one region. The most important segment is usually placed on the bottom of the "stack." Each bar could be represented as a separate pie chart (see next section).

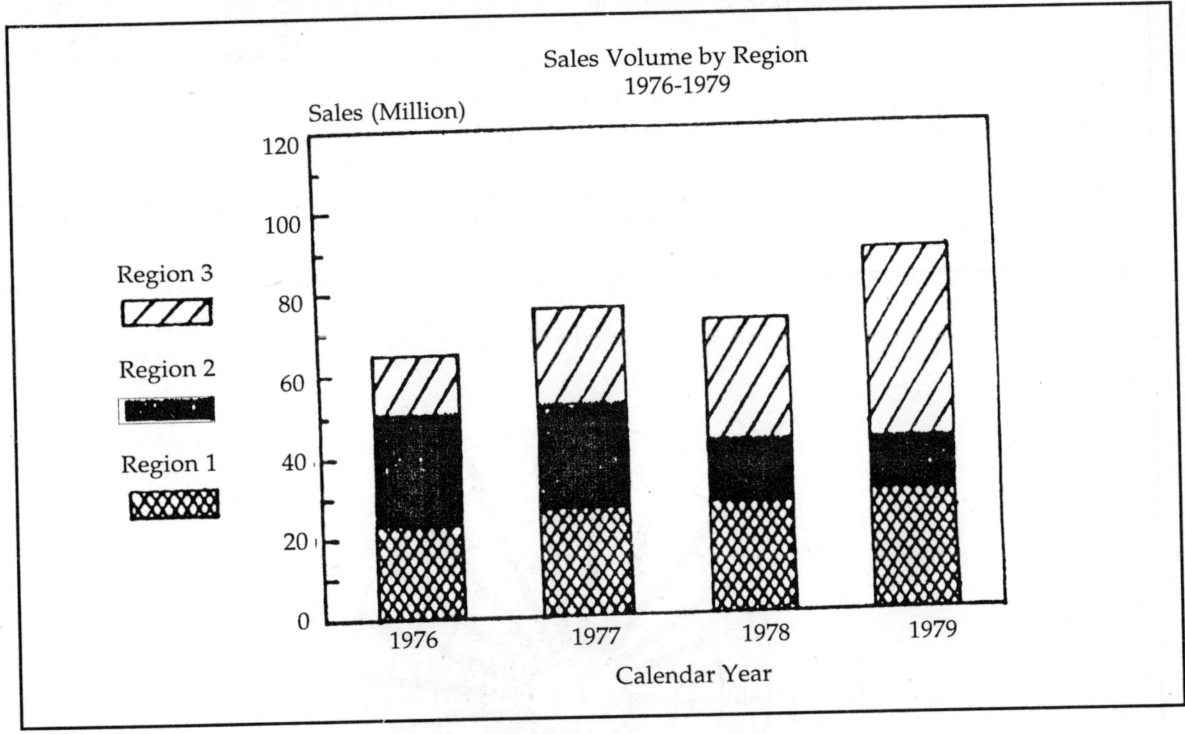

Fig. 15. A Segmented Bar Chart

Figures 16 and 17 are less frequently used forms. Figure 16 is a sliding bur chart where the length of the bar is significant and shows the range of values of one variable over one unit of time. This form is frequently used to chart stock movement as shown by this plot of the Dow Jones Industrial average. Figure 17 is a non-standard bar graph where the second axis is circular and concentric circles determine the Value of the bars, while the direction of the bars parallel the positions on a 24 hour clock and thus relates to hours. Other non-standard bar graphs might place bars on map locations or on a variety of symbols.

Dow Jones Industries
High →
Close →
Low →
920
900
880
860
840
820
800
23 30 7 17 21 28 4 11 18 25 1 8 15 22 29
Nov.
Dec.
Jan.
Feb.

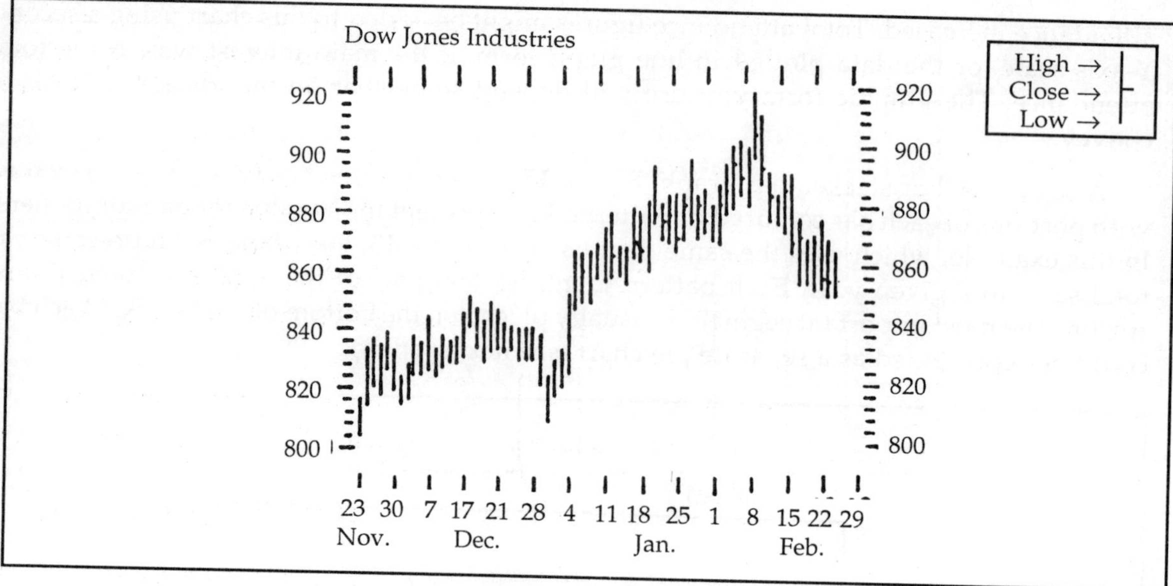

Fig. 16. A Sliding Bar Chart

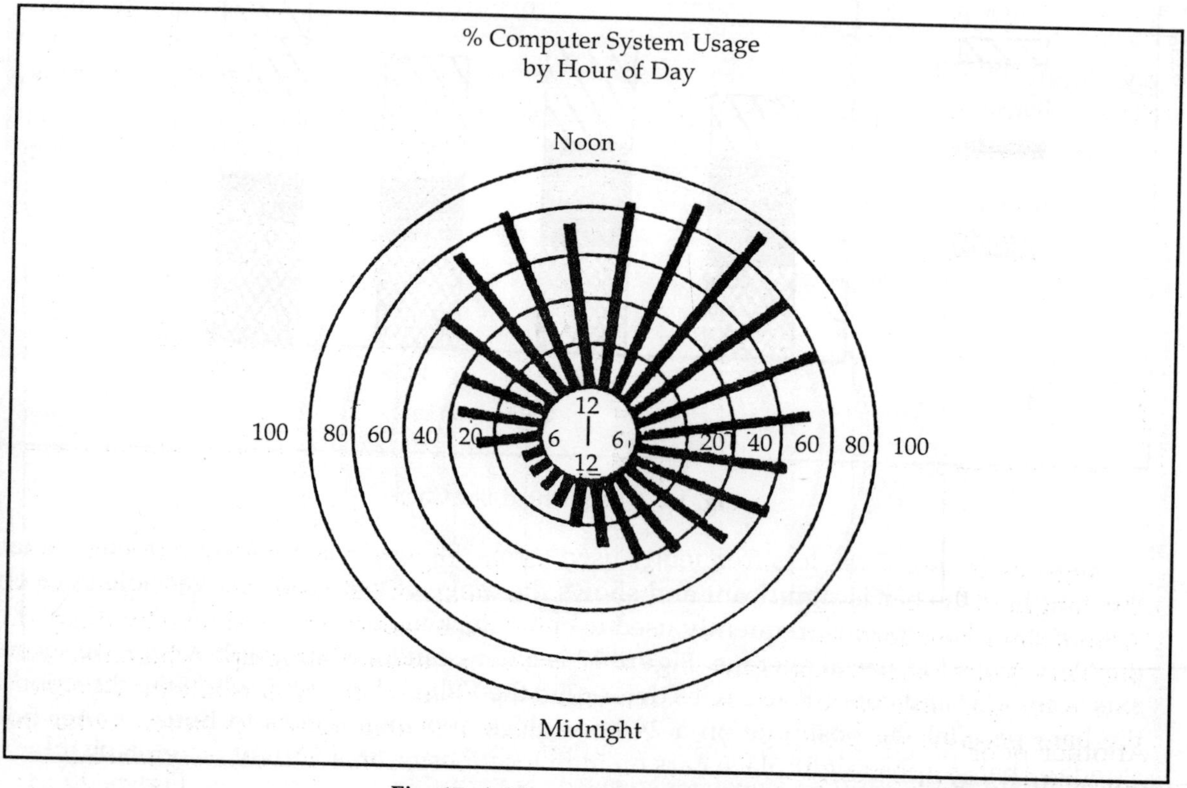

% Computer System Usage
by Hour of Day
Noon
12
6
6
12
100 80 60 40 20
20 40 60 80 100
Midnight

Fig. 17. A Non-standard Bar Chart

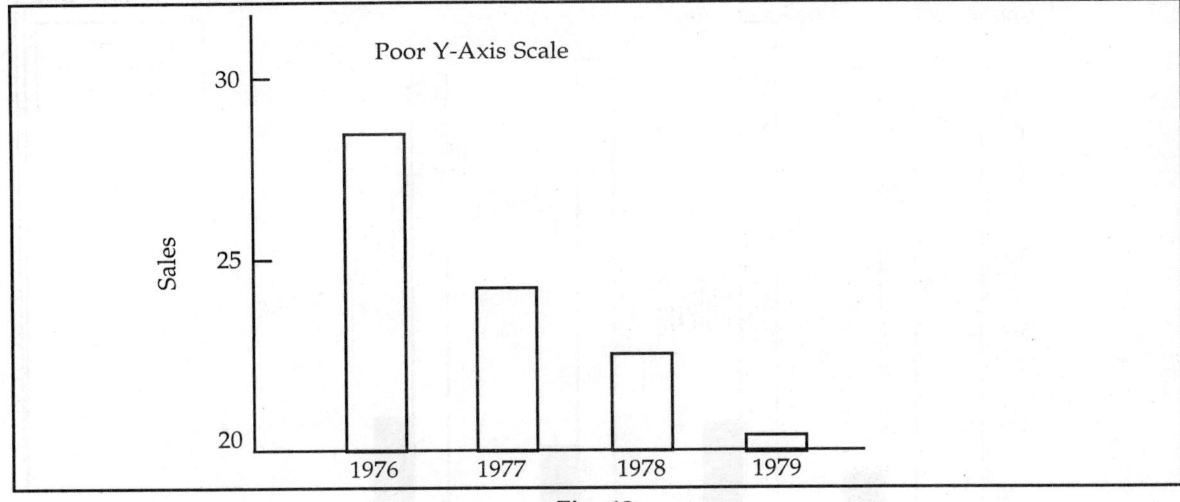

Fig. 18.

Certain practices should be followed while creating bar charts. The bars should be of uniform width with evenly spaced bars. Minimum spacing is half the width of the bars and maximum spacing should still enable the eye to move from one bar or cluster to the next. The scale should always include the zero value. If you look at Figures 18 and 19, you are apt to say, Figure 18 indicates a much greater rate of decrease in sales. Actually the two graphs portray the same data, but the Y scales start at different values.

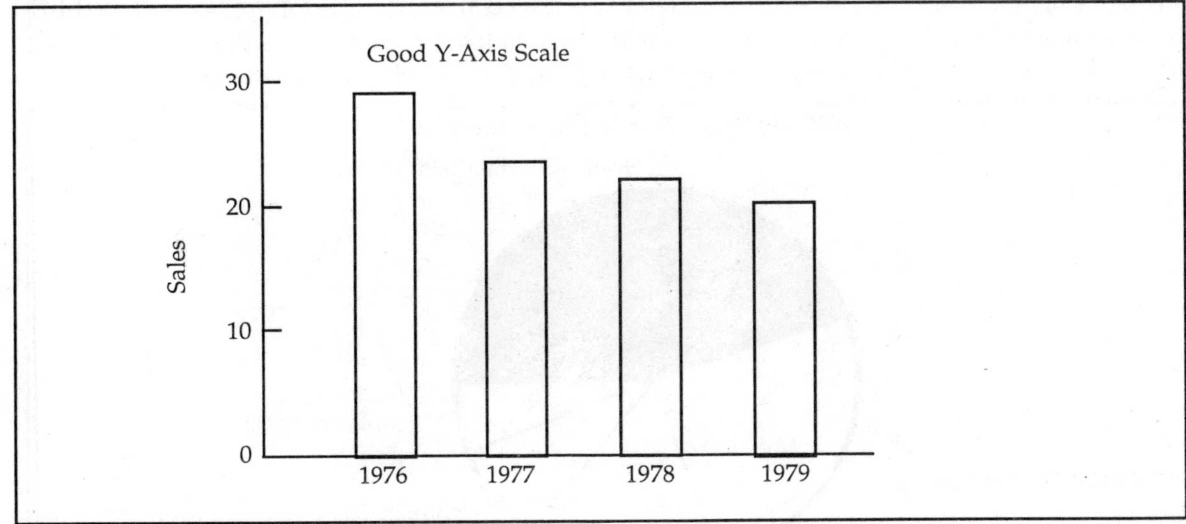

Fig. 19.

Another poor practice is to cluster values that are widely different. The eye probably cannot evaluate both columns in one glance. Try it with the chart shown in Figure 20 as opposed to Figure 13. Are you a believer now?

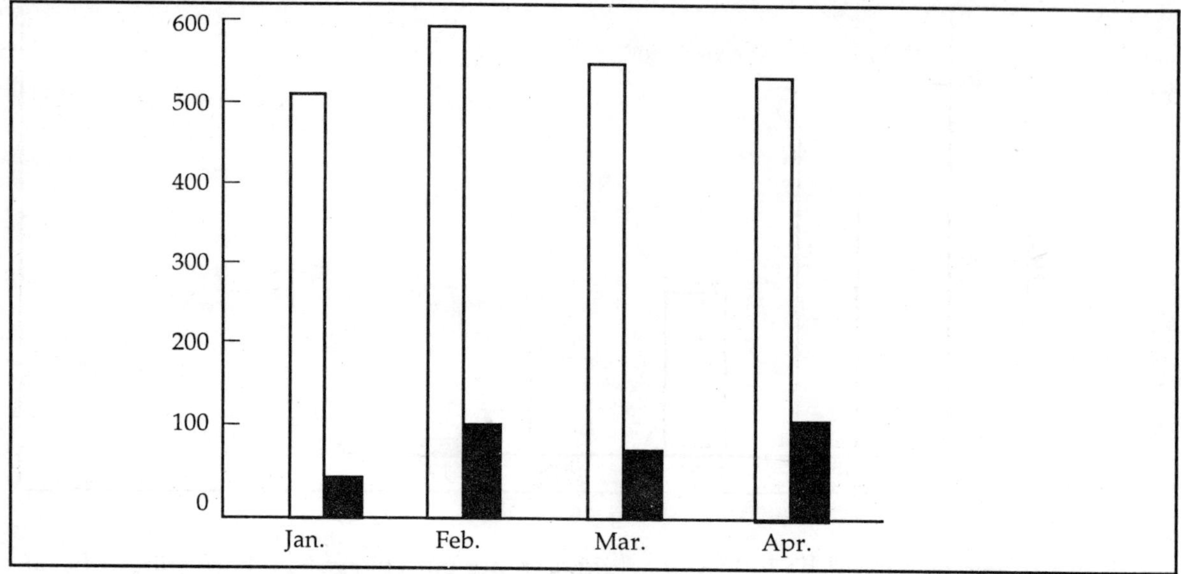

Fig. 20

3. *Pie Charts*

Pie charts show parts of a whole entity. The slices of the pie are the component parts. There are two variations on the pie chart. First, one or more slices may be "exploded", that is offset slightly from the center as if partialy removed from the pie plate. Second, a third dimension can be added to the pie so that it resemebles a coin or disc. Figures 21and 22 depicts the examples of a standard pie chart and an 'exploded' pie chart respectively.

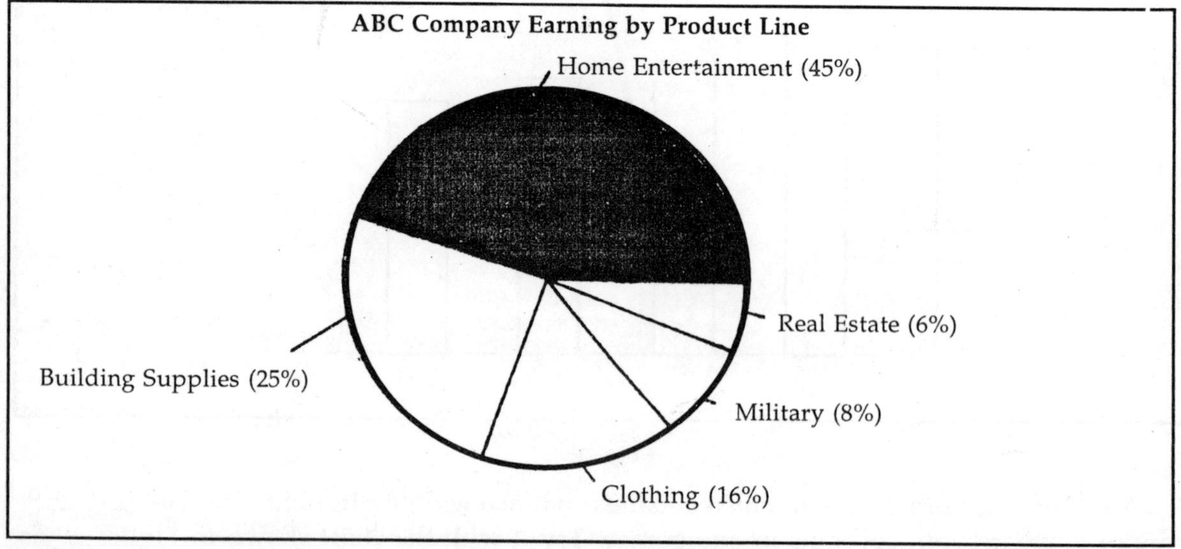

Fig. 21 A Standard Pie Chart

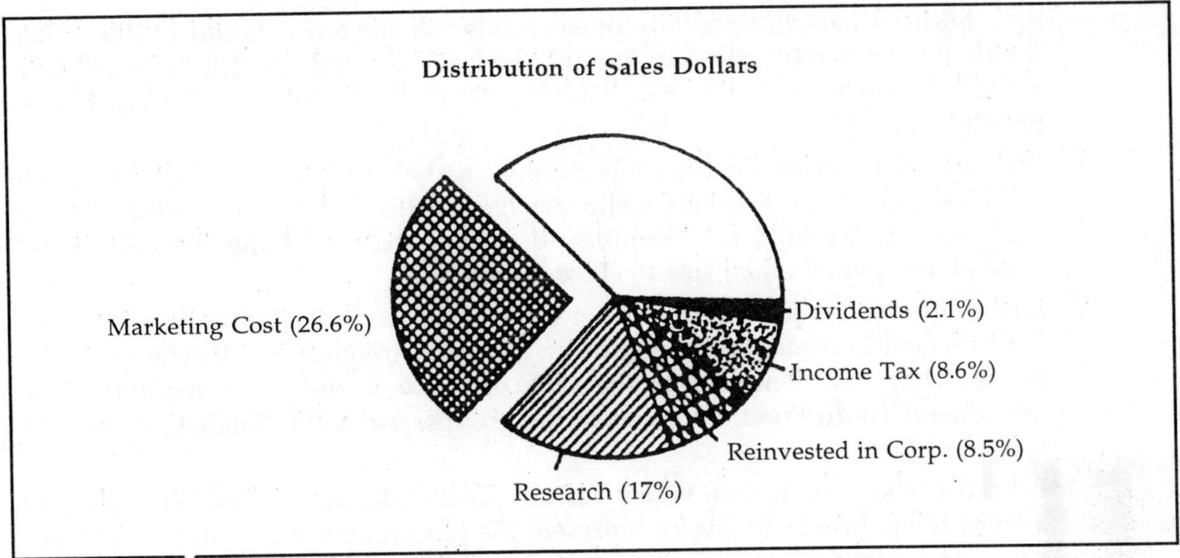

Fig. 22. A "Exploded" Pie Chart

To construct a pie chart, the data is computed as a percentage of the total and each data value (per cent) is converted to its appropriate segment of a full 360 degree circle. Sections are usually arranged according to size and differentiated by colour or hatching. Each segment is labeled; the labels are best placed outside the pie; labels placed inside tend to distort the information. Percentage values are sometimes included with the labels and may be placed inside the pie.

The pie chart is not well suited to graphs with many segments (more than 6) or with several segments of small size (3 degrees or less). It is often advisable to group these small segments as "other" and if necessary show a breakdown of "other" in a separate segmented bar or in the accompanying text. Pie charts have great appeal with non-technical audiences, perhaps because they are frequently found in the general press and there is no necessity for the viewer to calculate the coordinate position of a point or bar.

Choosing Graphics

A beautifully designed graphics presentation can help you make your point with punch and make a good impression at the same time. But you should also beware: Poorly designed graphics can be downright embarrassing. These tips will help you steer clear of graphics gaffes and make your presentation effective.

1. Choices of Chart Types

1. An area graph is a line graph in which the area under the horizontal line represents a quality. You can use this type of graph to show elapsed time and the area under the curve to represent cumulative value.
2. Bar graphs show relationships or comparisons between variables. While you

may position bars horizontally or vertically, all the bars should be the same width. If used in pairs, the bars should touch and the spacing between each pair should be equal. To distinguish the bars, use different colors, tonal variations, hatching, or dots.

3. Pictographs are used for the same purpose as bar graphs, except that you use symbols from your software's clip art library instead of bars. Each symbol represents a size unit, for example, 10. Rather than doubling the size of the symbol, use two of equal size to show a unit of 20.
4. Line graphs show the differences between variables. You can use them to show percentage differences between groups, as well as frequency or distribution of a group. They can demonstrate the rank of an item and show magnitude or movement. To differentiate between the groups, use solid, hatched, dotted, or coloured lines.
5. Pie charts show the way in which various parts make up a whole. The whole is always 100 per cent; the pieces represent the percentages made up the different parts. You might use the, of example, to show the various sources of your profit The most effective way to arrange the pieces of the pie is to place the largest wedge at the top, the other pieces clockwise according to size. The largest slice should have the lightest tone, with each smaller piece becoming progressively darker. The wedges may be named and numbered. For emphasis, separate one slice from the remaining portions.
6. Organisational charts demonstrate positions or rank within an organisation. Center each name within a rectangle, with lines connecting each related position. Rank order is indicated from top to bottom or left to right, with equal ranks being on the same level.
7. Sociograms or nets show how groups interact. You show relationships by using lines. Arrows indicate the direction of interactions. If you wish, you can place numbers above the lines to indicate frequency of interactions.

2. *Graphics Layout Pointers*

1. Make sure that your data is completely correct. (You'd be surprised how many times all the percentages don't add up to 100.)
2. Use as few words as possible.
3. Position words so that they read from left to right.
4. To emphasise a point, use capital letters, bold typeface, italics, underlining, increasing size, colour, or texture.
5. Use headings to clarify the topic you are addressing with your graphic and make sure that headings are consistent throughout the presentation.
6. To make sure your charts are legible, use a simple, clean type style such as Helvetica. Do not crowd the information together or put too much data into one

graphic. Instead, break apart the information into concepts that can be quickly and easily grasped, using a different graphic if necessary. Leave lots of white space around text and graphics.

7. Consider the distance from which your audience will view the presentation. Do a test run to see whether the size of the material is legible at that distance.
8. Text can be centered, or left or right justified. Margins should be consistent throughout the presentation, wherever possible.
9. Border frame the presentation. You may use solid, heavy black, or coloured lines, two or more parallel lines, and tones or textures to fill them in. But remember, when you make borders be sure you use them consistently.
10. Colours should be chosen with the document and audience in mind. What might be nice for a neighbourhood newsletter would not necessarily work for the chief executive officer (CEO) of a corporation. Keep the number of colours limited on the graphic, and remember that some colours (blue and green, for example) appear heavier than others (such as yellow and orange). If possible, arrange heavier colours below lighter ones.
11. Composition is what makes a page look good. Good composition involves leaving adequate margins around the artwork. Remember that if the page is bound on the left side, you will need to allow extra space to make the left and right margins visually equal. Generally, bottom margins should be larger than top ones, especially if you are making a border around the design. You should also take care to ensure that the visual weight of the text and graphics looks balanced, with each relating to the other and enhancing the other. If all else fails, look at attractive layouts professionally prepared and model your composition after them.

While these points won't make you a graphics expert, they will get you going. But before you go, remember the last and golden rule of graphics: "When in doubt, leave it out."

REVIEW & REMEMBER

Software plays a critical role in computer-based information systems because our hardware would be useless without it. Software comprises the instructions that tell the hardware what to do. If possible you should first select the software that meets your information needs, then choose compatible hardware.

Software can be divided into two major categories—systems software and applications software. Applications software is a collection of related programs designed to perform a specific task to solve a particular problem for the user. Systems software starts up (boots) the computer and function as the principal coordinator of all the hardware components and applications software programs.

Many off-the-shelf applications software packages are available to the user, and reviews of these packages can be found in several types of publications, including popular computer magazines. The six major categories of applications software are general business management, industry-specific, special disciplines, education, personal/home management, and general-purpose for the user.In the category of general purpose software, the main types of software you will encounter in an average business are: Word processing, electronic spreadsheet, database management systems, graphics, integrated software, desktop managers, desktop publishing software and computer-aided design-programs.